21/09

AQA Geography B

GCSE

David Payne
Phil Lamb
John Rutter

Consultant editor
David Payne

 Nelson Thornes

Published in 2009 by:
Nelson Thornes Ltd
Delta Place
27 Bath Road
CHELTENHAM
GL53 7TH
United Kingdom

09 10 11 12 13 / 10 9 8 7 6 5 4 3 2 1

A catalogue record for this book is available from the British Library

ISBN 978 1 4085 0331 7

Cover photograph by iStockphoto/caracterdesign

Illustrations include artwork drawn by Peters & Zabransky, Angela
Knowles and Barking Dog Art

Page make-up by GreenGate Publishing, Tonbridge, Kent

Printed and bound in Spain by GraphyCems

Contents

Nelson Thornes and AQA

Nelson Thornes has worked in partnership with AQA to ensure this book and the accompanying online resources offer you the best support for your GCSE course.

All resources have been approved by senior AQA examiners so you can feel assured that they closely match the specification for this subject and provide you with everything you need to prepare successfully for your exams.

These print and online resources together **unlock blended learning**; this means that the links between the activities in the book and the activities online blend together to maximise your understanding of a topic and help you achieve your potential.

These online resources are available on kerboodle! which can be accessed via the internet at **www.kerboodle.com/live**, anytime, anywhere. If your school or college subscribes to kerboodle! you will be provided with your own personal login details. Once logged in, access your course and locate the required activity.

For more information and help on how to use kerboodle! visit **www.kerboodle.com**.

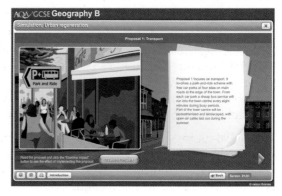

How to use this book

In this section you will learn:

Look for the list of **Learning Objectives** based on the requirements of this course so you can ensure you are covering everything you need to know for the exam.

AQA Examiner's tip

Don't forget to read the **AQA Examiner's Tips** throughout the book as well as practise answering **Examination-style Questions**.

Visit **www.nelsonthornes.com/aqagcse** for more information.

AQA examination-style questions are reproduced by permission of the Assessment and Qualifications Alliance.

The content of this book is divided into eight chapters which cover the topics of study within the GCSE Geography B course. Here is a short introduction to each chapter.

■ Unit 1: Managing places in the 21st century

Chapter 1 The coastal environment

With over four billion people worldwide living in coastal areas and numbers growing rapidly, the need to understand the physical and human processes that shape coastal areas is crucial.

Coastal areas are one of the fastest changing global environments and are being constantly reshaped by natural processes and the demands of economic development. They have both economic and environmental value and are consequently areas where conflicting demands create the need for careful management. The increasing threat of rising sea levels will make the planning and management of coastal areas even more important in the future.

Chapter 2 The urban environment

The world is becoming increasingly urban. In 2008 the proportion of people living in urban areas rose to over 50% and this number is expected to increase to 70% by 2025. Rapid economic development in many parts of the world is resulting in millions of people moving to urban, industrial areas in the hope of improving their quality of life.

Urban change creates both challenges and opportunities. In developing countries urban growth can be a stimulus for economic development, but at the same time creates social and environmental challenges. In developed countries the need for urban regeneration is providing opportunities to modernise and reimage declining urban areas.

The global future will be increasingly urban. This will create a growing need for sustainable management in existing towns and cities. It will also provide the opportunity to plan new urban areas that operate with both people and the environment in mind.

■ Unit 2: Hostile world

Chapter 3 Living with natural hazards

Many people now live in hostile areas of the world. Areas close to plate boundaries are at risk from earthquakes and volcanic eruptions. In some parts of the world, tropical storms or wildfires pose dangers for people. In order to reduce the threat from natural hazards, people have to be able to understand their causes and effects in order to prepare for and respond to them and reduce the damage that they might cause.

Chapter 4 The challenge of extreme environments

Due to increasing population pressure and demand for resources, more and more people are living in extreme environments. These areas are under increased threat from economic activities that exploit raw materials such as oil and gas. Increased tourism in some extreme environments could also damage these sensitive areas. People have to face the challenge of adapting to and managing these inhospitable yet beautiful and fragile areas. Hot deserts and their margins, tropical rain forests and cold environments all have to be managed in a sustainable way in order to protect these environments for future generations.

■ Unit 3: Investigating the shrinking world

Chapter 5 The globalisation of industry

The world is becoming more connected. Technology such as the internet and mobile phones and developing transport links has made this possible.

Industry has taken advantage of technological change and is becoming increasingly globalised, with companies organising and locating all over the world. These changes have brought about huge impacts on both people and the environment and need to be carefully managed to ensure future sustainability.

There are many opportunities presented by these changes for both more developed and less developed countries. Not all the trade resulting from the growth in industry is fair, however. While increasing globalisation has helped many countries become richer, in some cases, it is also responsible for widening the gap between rich and poor.

The challenge of the 21st century is to manage economic globalisation in a way that benefits everyone today without harming the opportunities for future generations.

Chapter 6 Global tourism

In recent years increased opportunities to travel have turned many people into global consumers of tourism. The growth of global tourism has brought wealth to far-flung corners of the world but can have negative impacts on people and the environment. Consequently there is a need for careful management to ensure future sustainability.

There are many reasons for the increase in global tourism. Many people have more money and an increasing amount of free time. Technological advances mean it is possible to fly halfway around the world in just 24 hours. Catering for leisure time is now big business and specialist companies have developed to serve all kinds of interests. Many less developed countries are using tourism to try and improve their living conditions. In some cases, bringing in visitors is helping countries become wealthier; in others, tourism is responsible for damaging the environment and widening the gap between rich and poor.

The challenge of the 21st century is to manage the growing tourism industry in a way that benefits people today without harming the opportunities for future generations.

■ Unit 4: Local investigation including fieldwork and geographical issue investigation

Chapter 7 Energy in the 21st century

The demand for energy will continue to increase in the 21st century as many parts of the world go through a period of rapid industrialisation. In the short term, increases in energy demand will be met by burning fossil fuels, adding further to the threat of global warming.

As fossil fuels become scarcer and more expensive there will be an increasing need to use renewable methods of electricity generation and alternative methods to power motor vehicles.

The energy challenge for the 21st century is to generate more energy in a sustainable way and use the energy that is generated as efficiently as possible.

Chapter 8 Water: a precious resource

Water is vital for life and is the world's most recycled resource. The natural water cycle is often adapted to provide water for drinking, farming, energy production, industry and a number of other uses. These different demands can put pressure on the natural water cycle and increase the threat of environmental problems. The international nature of many river basins means that the risk of political conflict over water issues may become increasingly common.

Clean water and access to sanitation systems is seen as a fundamental human right and yet in many parts of the world people do not have access to water and adequate sanitation, resulting in high rates of water-related disease and death.

The challenge of the 21st century is to ensure that everyone has access to clean water and proper sanitation systems. Sustainable methods of water management will be needed to guarantee water security for future generations.

Controlled Assessment

Some activities in this book are related to the Controlled Assessment and are designed to help you prepare for the tasks your teacher will give you. The tasks in this book are not designed to test you formally and you cannot use them as your own Controlled Assessment tasks for AQA. Your teacher will not be able to give you as much help with your tasks for AQA as we have given with the tasks in this book.

1 The coastal environment

1.1 The coast: a multi-use area

Why does the coast attract increasing numbers of people?

Coastal areas provide economic, environmental and recreational opportunities, which is why increasing numbers of people wish to live on or near the coast.

Business development in coastal areas creates job opportunities and the physical environment provides an attractive place to live.

The growing interest in outdoor recreational activities makes coastal areas increasingly appealing. In many parts of the world there is also increasing demand for housing in coastal areas as people are able to afford second homes or retire to the coast.

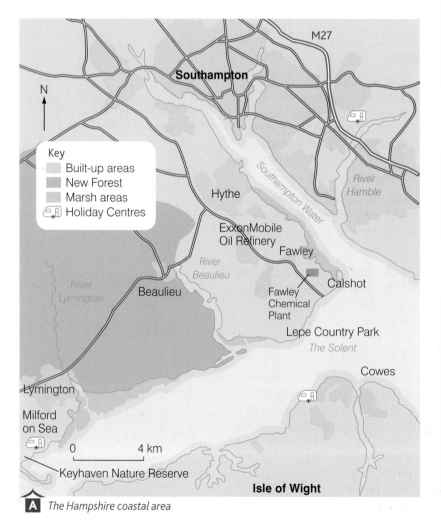

Key
- Built-up areas
- New Forest
- Marsh areas
- Holiday Centres

M27

Southampton

N

Southampton Water

River Hamble

Hythe

ExxonMobile Oil Refinery

Fawley

River Beaulieu

River Lymington

Beaulieu

Fawley Chemical Plant

Calshot

Lepe Country Park

The Solent

Cowes

Lymington

Milford on Sea

0   4 km

Keyhaven Nature Reserve

Isle of Wight

A *The Hampshire coastal area*

B *A marina on the River Hamble*

The Hampshire coastal area around Southampton is one of the busiest ports in the UK (see Map **A**). A range of human activities can be found here, including:

ExxonMobil oil refinery

This is the largest oil refinery in the UK, covering over 2,000 hectares. It handles over 2,000 ships a year carrying 25 million tonnes of oil. The deep-water frontage allows some of the world's largest tankers to dock, and more than 3,000 people work in the refinery.

Fawley chemical plant

This is one of the largest chemical plants in Europe, producing paints, adhesives and rubber. The large, flat site with deep-water frontage is ideal for the storage and movement of raw materials and finished products.

Lymington and Cowes

These are world-famous sailing resorts with large marinas and sailing clubs. The areas have many hotels, nearby camping and caravan sites.

Keyhaven Nature Reserve

With over 800 hectares of mudflats and salt marsh, Keyhaven is an internationally important area for migrating birds. It is run by Hampshire Wildlife Trust and the area provides the opportunity for a wide range of recreational and educational activities.

Southampton

Southampton is the largest city in the south of England, with a population of over 250,000. It is a regional shopping centre and a major container port. The city is also a recreational sailing area and a centre for marine research, education and technology.

Calshot Activity Centre

One of the largest outdoor activity centres in the UK, offering a range of water-based activities.

The port of Southampton

The port of Southampton developed because of the sheltered deep-water harbour offered by Southampton Water. It is ideally located for shipping routes to the Middle East, the Far East and the USA, and has good rail links to the rest of the UK. The port has a number of facilities including:

- the second largest container facility in the UK, with a harbour frontage of over 1 km next to a rail freight terminal
- a vehicle shipment terminal that handles 750,000 vehicles a year
- a bulk terminal that handles agricultural imports and raw materials; it is also linked to a fertilizer processing plant and a glass recycling facility
- three cruise terminals that handle over 200 ships a year.

The River Hamble

The River Hamble is used by local and international sailors and contains a number of marinas and boat-building/repair businesses. It is a nature conservation area and attracts walkers and bird-watchers.

Lepe Country Park

This is a popular recreational area with beach, cliffs and historic D-Day remains of World War Two. It is used for a range of activities including swimming, wind- and kite-surfing and fishing.

∞links

Find out more about Keyhaven at **www.rspb.org.uk**

Learn more about the port of Southampton at **www.abports. co.uk** and **www.cunard.co.uk**

Find out more about the River Hamble and Lepe at **www.hants.gov.uk**

Did you know ??????

7% of the whole of UK trade goes through Southampton.
50% of all trade with the Middle East and Far East goes through Southampton.

Activities

1   Explain why the population of many coastal areas is increasing.

2   The Hampshire coast around Southampton is called a 'multi-use coastal area'. Why is this?

3   Why is Southampton Water a good location for industry and shipping?

4   Can you think of any other activities not mentioned on these two pages that coastal areas may be used for?

extension   Use the internet to investigate another coastal area that has a wide range of uses. A good example is Florida (USA).

1.2 Coastal areas and economic development

How are coastal areas a valuable economic resource?

In many parts of the world coastal areas have become economic **growth poles**. The development of industry, trade links and tourism has created a wide range of opportunities that have encouraged increasing numbers of people to move to these areas. This can be seen clearly in more developed parts of the world, in places such as Florida and the Californian coast in the USA, and on the Mediterranean coast in Europe. More recently, developing countries have realised that the coast is an important resource that can be used to generate business and wealth. The following examples look at two parts of the world where coastal areas play an important part in the development process.

Dubai – the world's largest area of coastal development

The largest and most expensive coastal development project in the world is currently taking place on the coast of Dubai in the United Arab Emirates (UAE) (Map **A** and Photo **B**).

The centrepiece of the coastal development project is the construction of three palm-shaped islands, along with another 300 islands in the shape of the Earth's continents and the solar system (Photo **D**). The first of the palms to be completed, The Palm Jumeirah, has an international hotel, a shopping mall with 200 shops and a yachting marina. The 'fronds' of the palm contain more than 1,000 beachside villas and apartments. When all the palms and islands are completed, the length of the Dubai coastline will have increased by 400 km. The UAE government sees the Dubai coast as an excellent location for the development of a range of business opportunities. It has spent millions of pounds improving the local **infrastructure** and developing new port facilities and an international airport. The current developments will cost over £500 billion, making this the biggest programme of building the world has ever seen.

Recent developments in Dubai

- Duty-free shopping centre for international travellers
- 11 km coastal strip of international hotels, resorts and marinas
- Dubailand – 24 theme parks and shopping malls
- Resort airport with golf courses, swimming pools and private beach
- Largest indoor ski dome in the world
- Port terminal for international cruise ships
- Exhibition and conference centres
- Port complex used for trade throughout the Middle and Far East
- Industrial estates producing high-tech products for export
- International financial centre for the Middle East

In this section you will learn:

- how the coast is an important resource for economic development
- about some places where coastal development is taking place.

∞ links

Learn more about development in the UAE at **www.nakheel.com**

A The Middle East

B Part of the Dubai coastline

AQA **Examiner's tip**

Remember a case study of one coastal area that has been developed as an economic resource.

C	Visitors to Dubai (approx. numbers)
1990	970,000
1995	2,200,000
2000	3,900,000
2005	6,200,000
2010	8,400,000 (est.)

D Satellite photo of the coastal development project in Dubai

Bahia, north-east Brazil – using tourism to improve living conditions

Bahia is one of the poorest states in Brazil, with low incomes and few job opportunities. As part of a 15-year development programme to create economic opportunities and improve living conditions for local people, US$2 billion is being put into tourist development in the region. In one area, 75 km north of the city of Salvador, a US$400 million investment has helped to create a number of large hotels and holiday resorts along a coast of white sand and coconut palms. A newly built international airport brings tourists directly to the area from Europe and North America. Two of the major areas of development are at Costa do Sauípe and Praia do Forte.

Costa do Sauípe

This area was developed as a holiday resort for package holidays and second home owners (Advertisement **E**). The development aims to work with the environment and has strict conservation rules. It also includes a programme to develop projects that will improve living conditions for local people (the Berimbau programme).

Praia do Forte

This has been called Brazil's first 'eco-resort' because it is being developed with the protection of nature in mind. The motto of the area is 'enjoy without destroying'.

Activities

1. Explain why the coast offers opportunities for business development.

2. a. Describe the different types of business development taking place in Dubai.

   b. Draw a line graph to show the increase in visitor numbers to Dubai.

   c. Why are increasing numbers of tourists visiting Dubai?

   d. Why is the resident population of Dubai increasing so rapidly?

3. Explain how the development of tourism can improve economic and social conditions for local people.

extension Use holiday brochures and newspaper travel sections to:

- find out more about tourism in Dubai and north-east Brazil

- identify other coastal areas in developing countries where tourism is being developed.

Sauípe

A high-quality leisure resort set on a beautiful stretch of coastline, in the state of Bahia. Benefits include 300 days of sunshine a year and an 18-hole championship-designed golf course.

- Villas, bungalows; 2 and 3 bedroom apartments, with 24-hour security and 5-year construction warranty

- Unspoilt beach and lagoon, riding centre and two spas

E An advertisement for Sauípe

links

Learn more about these two tourist resorts in north-east Brazil at www.costadosauipe.com.br and www.praiadoforte.org.br

The coastline is being constantly reshaped by wind, waves and the effects of the weather. Where coastlines are made of more resistant rock or are sheltered from the **prevailing wind**, changes to the coastline occur more slowly. Where coastlines are made of weaker rock or are open to storm waves and heavy rainfall, whole areas can change in minutes as a result of coastal landslides and rock falls (Photo **A**).

What happens when waves reach the coast?

As waves reach the coast the base of the wave is in frictional contact with the seabed. The **crest** of the wave breaks because it is moving faster than its base. The energy of the breaking wave pushes it up the beach as **swash**. When all of the energy has been used, the wave has reached its highest point up the beach. It then runs back down the beach as **backwash**.

Constructive and destructive waves

Waves are the most significant force in reshaping coastlines. There are two main types of wave: constructive waves which help to build beaches (Diagram **B**), and destructive waves which are able to erode cliffs rapidly and remove beach material (Diagram **C**).

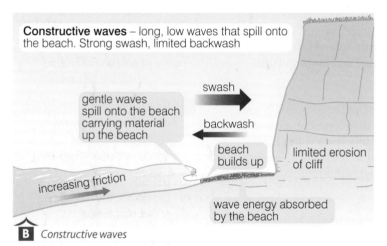

Constructive waves – long, low waves that spill onto the beach. Strong swash, limited backwash

swash

gentle waves spill onto the beach carrying material up the beach

backwash

beach builds up

limited erosion of cliff

increasing friction

wave energy absorbed by the beach

B Constructive waves

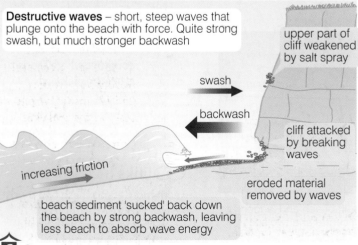

Destructive waves – short, steep waves that plunge onto the beach with force. Quite strong swash, but much stronger backwash

upper part of cliff weakened by salt spray

swash

backwash

cliff attacked by breaking waves

increasing friction

eroded material removed by waves

beach sediment 'sucked' back down the beach by strong backwash, leaving less beach to absorb wave energy

C Destructive waves

A The changing coastline

How do erosion and weathering affect coastal environments?

The coastal system acts like a conveyer belt. Material is worn away from some places and moved by waves and then deposited in other places. Erosion and weathering are the first part of this process.

D *The coastal system*

Marine erosion

There are three main types of **marine erosion**: abrasion, attrition and hydraulic action.

Abrasion (corrasion)

During storm conditions waves pick up sand and pebbles. As waves break, this material is hurled at the cliff face. This 'sandblasting' effect is the most powerful source of coastal erosion in the UK.

Attrition

Sand and pebbles are constantly colliding with each other as they are moved by waves breaking on a beach. This action wears away the beach material, making it increasingly smaller and more rounded.

Hydraulic action

The sheer force of waves breaking against a cliff causes parts of the cliff to break away. Also, as waves hit a cliff face, air is compressed into cracks, blasting away fragments of rock.

E *The hydraulic action of the waves*

Weathering

In coastal areas there are two significant types of **weathering**.

Corrosion (solution)

Sea water is very corrosive and can slowly dissolve chalk and limestone, increasing the size of cracks and joints so that the forces of erosion are more effective. Salt spray can get in cracks and when it evaporates salt crystals are formed. As the crystals grow in size they can force rocks apart.

Wetting/drying

Softer rocks such as clay expand when they are wet and contract when they dry out. This continued expansion and contraction can weaken rocks and make them more easily eroded.

⚭links

Find out more about coastline processes and landforms at **www.swgfl.org.uk/jurassic** and **www.jurassiccoast.com**

Did you know ??????

During storms, breaking waves can exert a force of up to 50 tonnes per square metre on a cliff face.

Activities

1 Use annotated diagrams to explain:
   a   constructive waves
   b   destructive waves.

2 Explain what is meant by 'the coastal system'.

3 a   What is meant by:
      i   marine processes
      ii subaerial processes?
   b   Explain how erosion and weathering help to reshape the coastline.

4 Suggest how rock type may affect the rate of erosion.

extension   Explain how human activity may leave coastal areas more vulnerable to weathering and erosion.

What landforms are associated with 'hard' coastlines?

Wave energy is only one factor that explains the rate of erosion and resulting **landforms** in coastal areas. The characteristics of the rocks found at the coastline also play a significant part in the resulting features created by erosion and weathering. Coastal areas that are made up of well-structured rocks with few lines of weakness often result in spectacular cliff coastlines. This is particularly the case with igneous rocks, but also with sedimentary rocks such as chalk and limestone. These rocks are more resistant to wave energy, so rates of erosion are slow and distinctive landforms are created (Photo **B**). This can be seen clearly on chalk **headlands** where wave action produces a number of particular landforms (Diagram **A**).

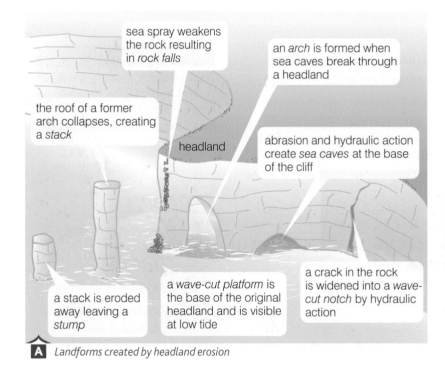

sea spray weakens the rock resulting in *rock falls*

an *arch* is formed when sea caves break through a headland

the roof of a former arch collapses, creating a *stack*

headland

abrasion and hydraulic action create *sea caves* at the base of the cliff

a stack is eroded away leaving a *stump*

a *wave-cut platform* is the base of the original headland and is visible at low tide

a crack in the rock is widened into a *wave-cut notch* by hydraulic action

A   *Landforms created by headland erosion*

Why are 'soft' coastlines vulnerable to rapid erosion?

Many parts of the UK have soft coastlines that are affected by a combination of erosion and weathering. Rocks such as clay and gravel do not have a strong structure and become unstable when wet. A combination of heavy rainfall soaking through the rock, and wave attack at the base of the cliff, may trigger cliff slumping and landslides (Diagram **C**).

One of the most spectacular landslides in the UK happened in Scarborough in 1993. The Holbeck Hall Hotel slid into the sea after a period of heavy rainfall (Photo **D**). The article on the following page describes the event.

AQA   *Examiner's tip*

When describing the formation of coastal landforms such as stacks or spits, process terms and the correct sequence of formation are required to achieve the highest marks.

B   *A headland and bay*

∞ links

Find out more about the erosion of headlands at **www.swgfl.org.uk/jurassic**

Key terms

Landform: a physical feature that has been shaped by erosion/ weathering.

Headland: where land juts out into the sea.

Slipping plane: line of weakness, often where a previous landslide has occurred.

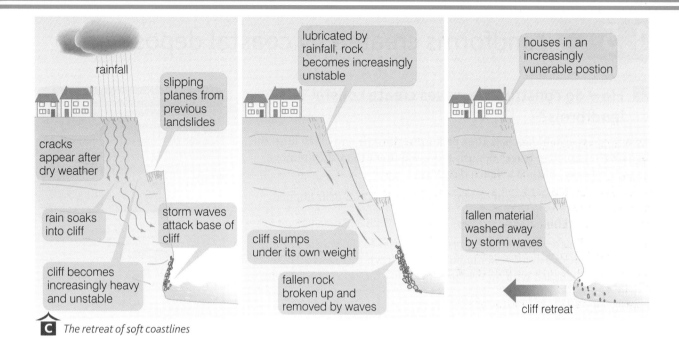

C *The retreat of soft coastlines*

Landslide Moves Hotel Nearer to the Sea!

On Friday morning guests at the Holbeck Hall Hotel woke to find cracks in their bedroom walls and parts of the hotel garden missing. Guests were quickly evacuated when it was feared that a landslide was about to destroy the hotel. Throughout the remainder of Friday thousands of tonnes of rock dropped 60 metres into the sea and by late afternoon the hotel was teetering dangerously on the edge of the cliff. The hotel began to slip more quickly as the high tide washed away debris at the bottom of the cliff. The landslide followed a period of heavy rainfall which seeped down into the **slipping plane**. A local coastal engineer said 'After a long dry period there were a number of deep cracks in the clay. Heavy rainfall then penetrated the cracks, lubricating the clay and increasing the weight of the whole cliff. Gravity did the rest!'

Scarborough is on a 60 km stretch of Europe's fastest eroding coastline – in places the soft cliffs are being swept away at over 10 metres a year.

D *The Holbeck Hall Hotel landslide*

Activities

1. a What is meant by:
   i a hard coastline,
   ii a soft coastline?
   b How does rock type affect rates of coastal erosion?

2. a Draw a sketch of a headland.
   b On your sketch name five features caused by wave action.

   c Explain the formation of:
   i a wave-cut notch, ii an arch,
   iii a stack.

3. Explain how the Holbeck Hall Hotel landslide was a result of rock type and weather conditions.

extension Find out more about processes and features associated with hard and soft coastlines. Take a virtual journey along the Holderness coast at www.hull.ac.uk/coastalobs

How do constructive waves create coastal landforms?

As waves approach the coast they pick up **sediment** and carry it up the **beach**. Constructive waves deposit more sediment than they remove, so over a period of time a beach develops.

There are two main types of beach: swash aligned and drift aligned.

Swash aligned beaches

These are formed when waves approach parallel to the coastline, and swash and backwash move sediment up and down the beach. This creates a wide beach with an even profile along the shoreline. During storm conditions ridges of sediment (berms) can form along the beach (Photo **A**).

Drift aligned beaches

These are formed when waves approach at an angle to the coastline. The swash moves sediment up the beach at the same angle, while the backwash moves it back down the beach under the force of gravity. In this way sediment is moved along the beach by a process known as longshore drift (Diagram **B**). This creates a beach with an uneven profile. On some coastlines longshore drift is slowed down by building **groynes**. These trap sediment on the updrift side and help to preserve the beach.

In this section you will learn:

how waves move beach sediment

how the deposition of beach sediments creates coastal landforms.

A *A swash aligned beach with berms*

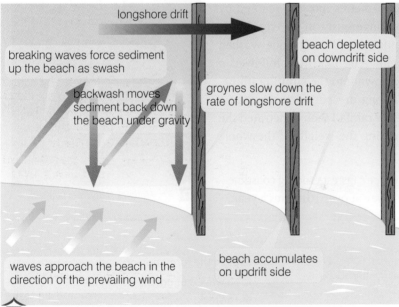

- longshore drift
- breaking waves force sediment up the beach as swash
- backwash moves sediment back down the beach under gravity
- beach depleted on downdrift side
- groynes slow down the rate of longshore drift
- waves approach the beach in the direction of the prevailing wind
- beach accumulates on updrift side

B *Longshore drift*

The formation of spits and bars

Spits and bars are ridges of sand or shingle that have been transported by longshore drift and then deposited as the coastline changes direction or wave energy is reduced as the sea becomes shallower. Where the coastline changes direction, sediment is deposited in the same direction as the original coastline.

AQA Examiner's tip

The process of longshore drift can be easily explained with a simple, labelled diagram. Practise drawing this as it can be used to help answer several types of questions.

Did you know ??????

Millions of tonnes of sand and shingle are dredged each year from the seabed for the construction industry.

Key terms

Sediment: material that is eroded and deposited by the action of water or the wind.

Beach: an accumulation of sand and shingle.

Groyne: wooden or concrete barrier built across a beach.

A spit is joined to the land at one end and the seaward end is usually curved by wave action and ocean currents. A bar is formed when a spit extends across an opening and connects two areas of coastline. Where a spit is extended until it joins an island, the resulting feature is called a tombola. An example of this can be seen at Chesil Beach which connects the Dorset coastline to the Isle of Portland.

∞links

Find out more at www.nfdc.gov.uk
→ Key Haven Nature Reserve →
Hurst Castle spit

Case study

Hurst Castle spit, Hampshire

Hurst Castle spit is a shingle spit which developed as a result of longshore drift along the Hampshire coast. The sudden change of the shape of the coastline at Milford on Sea resulted in the development of a spit that reaches over 2 km into the Solent. The main features of Hurst Castle spit can be seen in Photo **D**.

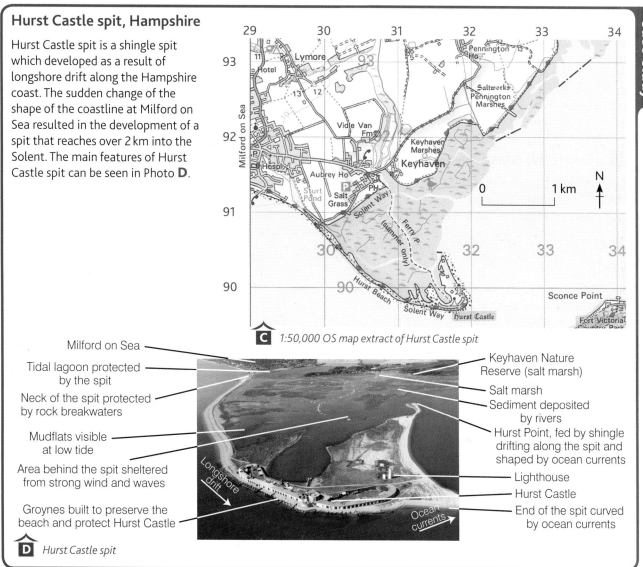

C *1:50,000 OS map extract of Hurst Castle spit*

Milford on Sea

Tidal lagoon protected by the spit

Neck of the spit protected by rock breakwaters

Mudflats visible at low tide

Area behind the spit sheltered from strong wind and waves

Groynes built to preserve the beach and protect Hurst Castle

Longshore drift

Ocean currents

Keyhaven Nature Reserve (salt marsh)

Salt marsh

Sediment deposited by rivers

Hurst Point, fed by shingle drifting along the spit and shaped by ocean currents

Lighthouse

Hurst Castle

End of the spit curved by ocean currents

D *Hurst Castle spit*

Activities

1 Use an annotated diagram to explain longshore drift.

2 Describe and explain the use of groynes.

3 Using Map **C**:
  a Identify evidence that suggests that the area is low-lying.
  b Explain the formation of the mudflats and marshes shown on the map.

4 **a** Draw an outline sketch of Hurst Castle spit.
  b Annotate your sketch to describe and explain the main features of the spit.

extension The sheltered areas of salt marsh and mudflats found behind spits provide an ideal habitat for rare plants and birds. Investigate Blakeney Point, a sand/shingle spit in Norfolk, which is a designated nature reserve www.english-nature.org.uk / www.nationaltrust.org.uk

Protecting coastal areas from natural processes

Why is there a need to protect coastal areas?

The boundary between land and sea is one of the most fragile environments on Earth and is being constantly reshaped by the forces of nature (Photo **A**). With growing numbers of people living in coastal areas, the need to protect the coast from the threat of flooding and erosion is increasing. With the added threat of increasing sea levels, the challenge is to find ways of protecting coastal areas without damaging what are often sensitive environments.

How is the coastline managed in England and Wales?

In the UK the Department for Environment, Food and Rural Affairs (Defra) is responsible for the protection of the coastline from flooding and erosion. It is not possible to protect every part of the coastline: not only would it be too expensive but it would also change the whole of the coastal environment. Because of this Defra, along with local authorities, has to decide:

- which parts of the coastline should be protected
- which methods should be used to protect different areas.

In order to make these decisions more manageable, the coastline of England and Wales has been divided into 11 areas called sediment cells (Diagram **B**). The boundary of each cell is usually a natural barrier such as a headland or a river **estuary**. Each cell is further divided into sub-cells to create smaller units for planning. A shoreline management plan (SMP) is developed for each sub-cell. This is a document that sets out plans for the management of a length of coast, taking into account coastal processes and human and environmental needs.

How does a shoreline management plan work?

A shoreline management plan (SMP) recommends how each coastal sub-cell should be managed, using the following Defra criteria.

Defra – coastal management criteria

hold the line – maintain the existing coastline by building defences

advance the line – build new defences seaward of the existing defences

managed realignment – allow the land to flood and construct a new line of defence inland

no intervention – allow natural processes to shape the land.

A *The frontier between land and sea*

Key terms

Estuary: the tidal part of a river

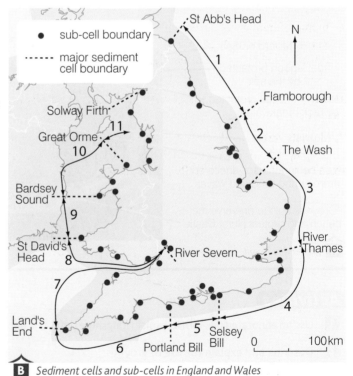

Key:
- sub-cell boundary
- major sediment cell boundary

St Abb's Head · Flamborough · The Wash · River Thames · River Severn · Selsey Bill · Portland Bill · Land's End · St David's Head · Bardsey Sound · Great Orme · Solway Firth

0   100 km

B *Sediment cells and sub-cells in England and Wales*

∞**links**

Learn more about coastal management at
www.dorsetforyou.com

Diagram **C** shows part of sub-cell 3b in Norfolk with the recommendations from the shoreline management plan.

What methods can be used to protect coastal areas?

Different methods are used to protect coastal areas from the effects of flooding and erosion. These methods are usually divided into what are known as 'hard engineering' and 'soft engineering'.

Hard engineering

This controls the power of the sea by building barriers between the sea and the land, often in the form of sea walls. Concrete or wooden groynes are also used to reduce beach loss.

Soft engineering

This attempts to work with the natural environment. There are two main methods of soft engineering:

- beach replenishment and recycling, which helps to preserve a wide, gently sloping beach that can absorb energy from storm waves

- managed realignment, which allows the sea to flood inland until it reaches a natural barrier of higher land.

In many coastal areas, a mix of both hard and soft engineering methods is used (Map **D**).

Hard engineering methods are used where there is a need to protect built-up areas, while soft engineering methods are used in less built-up areas or more environmentally sensitive areas.

Did you know ??????

Globally, nearly 5 billion people live within 50 km of the coast.

AQA **Examiner's tip**

Know the Defra criteria for a shoreline management plan.

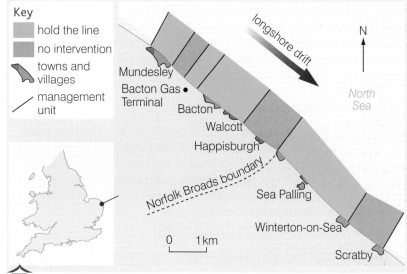

C   Shoreline management plan for part of sub-cell 3b in Norfolk

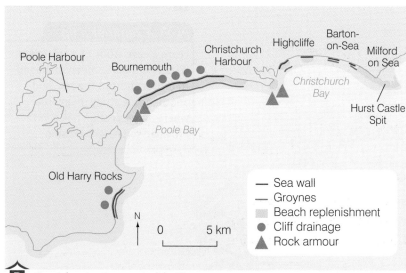

D   Coastal protection – part of the Wessex coast

Activities

1   Explain why the coastline is called 'the frontier between land and sea'.

2   a   What is meant by a shoreline management plan?

    b   Explain how a shoreline management plan is used.

3   Suggest why some parts of the Norfolk coast (Diagram **C**) are protected whereas others are not.

4   Describe the different types of coastal engineering in the part of the Wessex coastline shown in Map **D**.

extension   Explain why different types of coastal engineering may be suitable for different locations.

A tale of two villages – north-east Norfolk

■ How can coastal protection decisions cause conflict?

It is not possible to protect every area from the effects of coastal processes. Consequently, decisions have to be made about which areas to protect. These pages look at the examples of Happisburgh and Sea Palling in north-east Norfolk. The shoreline management plan (SMP) for this part of the coast recommended that Sea Palling should have a 'beach management strategy' and be protected by using heavy engineering techniques. At Happisburgh the SMP recommended that no protection should be put in place, leaving the village under threat of rapid erosion (see Map **C** on page 21).

Coastal management at Sea Palling

In 1953 a sea wall was built at Sea Palling (Photo **A**). Together with the wide sandy beach, this was seen as a good way to protect inland areas from flooding. By the 1990s most of the beach had been washed away and the sea wall was being directly attacked during storms. In order to build up the beach and protect the area from wave attack, the following measures have been implemented:

- 100,000 tonnes of boulders were placed in front of the sea wall
- 1 million cubic metres of sand brought in to replenish the beach
- four offshore reefs built parallel to the coast. These reefs break the waves before they reach the beach and absorb storm energy. Sediment is trapped behind them, creating a wide beach. A second set of reefs was later added to the south of Sea Palling.

In this section you will learn:

- ~~that difficult decisions have to be made about which coastal areas to protect~~
- about the issues and conflicts associated with the need to make difficult decisions.

Did you know ???????

North-east Norfolk has a coastline of approximately 68 km. About half of the coastline is made up of soft sand and clay cliffs that are easily eroded by strong North Sea waves. In some places the coastline has retreated by as much as 30 m a year and many buildings have been lost.

The coastline and beach provides an important economic and environmental resource for the area.

A *Coastal defences at Sea Palling*

AQA *Examiner's tip*

Learn a case study of a stretch of coastline that has been managed to protect it from the sea, and another case study of an area where no protection has been provided to prevent erosion.

B *1:50,000 OS map extract of the north-east Norfolk coast*

Coastal management at Happisburgh

The soft clay coast at Happisburgh has been under constant attack in recent years as waves batter the coastline and erode the rain-weakened cliffs. The original defences – **timber revetments** built in the 1950s – have been destroyed by the waves over the years and by 2000 there was little defence against North Sea storm waves (Photo **C**). During the winter storms thousands of tonnes of cliff material can be washed away, making this area one of the most rapidly retreating coastlines in the UK along with Scarborough (see pages 16–17). It is estimated that the cliffs at Happisburgh are retreating by an average of 10–15 metres a year and already over 30 buildings have been lost (Photo **D**). In 2002, as an emergency measure, 4,000 tonnes of boulders were used to create a **rock bund** in front of the cliff (Photo **C**). This was seen as a temporary measure to slow down the erosion while a more permanent solution was found.

Local residents' hopes for a more permanent coastal defence scheme were dashed in 2006 when the SMP stated that the area should be allowed to retreat. Since then local people have launched the 'buy a rock for Happisburgh' appeal, which is raising money to extend the existing rock bund.

⊙⊙links

Learn more about coastal management of the north-east Norfolk coast at
www.happisburgh.org.uk and
www.buyarockforhappisburgh.com

Key terms

Timber revetments: open structures of planks which act as breakwaters but allow sand through the gaps so that a beach develops.

Rock bund: mound of rocks built in front of cliffs for protection.

C   *Coast at Happisburgh showing the rock bund and the remains of the 1950s timber revetments*

D   *Cliff erosion at Happisburgh*

Views of local people in north-east Norfolk

Sea Palling has to be protected – otherwise the Norfolk Broads, a conservation area, would flood.

It doesn't seem fair to spend millions of pounds at Sea Palling while Happisburgh is left to fall into the sea.

Our house in Happisburgh is now worthless. The cliff edge is only 40 metres away – our neighbours have already abandoned their house and moved inland.

With rising sea levels, either more money will need to be spent defending soft coastlines or they will have to be left to erode.

Not every place can be protected – at Sea Palling there are caravan parks, local shops and other amenities. At Happisburgh, the loss of a few houses is not enough to justify millions of pounds being spent on coastal defences.

Happisburgh is a thriving village which attracts lots of visitors in the summer.

Happisburgh is an important environment and heritage centre – this will be lost if it is not protected.

Activities

1 Using evidence from Map **B**:

   a show how the area is used by tourists

   b explain why the area is at risk from flooding

   c describe what would be lost if the coastline retreated 250 metres.

2 Describe the methods being used to protect Sea Palling from coastal processes.

3 Use Photos **C** and **D** to describe the effects of coastal erosion at Happisburgh.

4 a Explain the conflict created by the decision to protect Sea Palling and not Happisburgh.

   b Do you think that Happisburgh should have a coastal protection scheme? Explain your answer.

extension   Explain how protecting a coast in one area may create problems further along the coastline.

Using hard engineering to protect the coast

What is hard coastal engineering?

Coastal areas are often protected against erosion and flooding by using hard engineering methods. Hard engineering reduces the energy of breaking waves by building large structures between the sea and the land, or by building breakwaters that force waves to break before they reach the beach (Photo **A** and Diagram **B**).

Examples of hard engineering methods

Sea walls

Reinforced concrete structures that create a rigid barrier between the sea and the land.

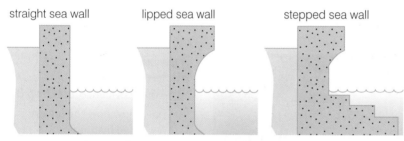

straight sea wall   lipped sea wall   stepped sea wall

A Hard coastal engineering

Rock armour (rip-rap)

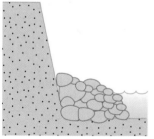

Large rocks placed at the foot of the cliffs or in front of sea walls to reduce erosion.

Revetments

Open structures made of wood or concrete that absorb the energy of the waves before they reach the cliff face.

Gabions

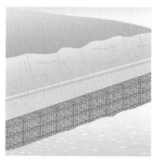

Steel cages filled with rocks and stacked in front of cliffs to reduce erosion and cliff falls.

Offshore breakwater

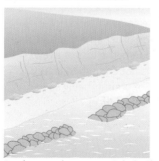

Rocks or other materials built up into offshore bars to make waves break before they reach the beach.

Groynes

Wooden or concrete structures designed to break waves and preserve the beach.

 B Some examples of hard engineering

Hard engineering at Ventnor, Isle of Wight

The coastline to the east of Ventnor on the Isle of Wight is particularly vulnerable to wave attack because:

■ the beach is very narrow and provides limited protection against storm waves

■ the south-westerly direction of the wind creates powerful storm waves in the winter that can be over 1m higher than normal levels

■ storm waves are able to pick up shingle from the seabed and attack the coast by the action of abrasion.

Coastal protection was required at Ventnor to protect millions of pounds' worth of property which is close to the top of the cliffs.

Hard engineering was seen as the only option for protecting the coast because of a lack of a wide beach and the weakness of the cliffs.

The main type of hard engineering is the sea wall. It has a promenade along the top which is used as an amenity by both local people and visitors. Other examples of hard engineering at Ventnor can be seen in Photos **D–F**.

C   *The Isle of Wight, off the south coast of England*

D   *Tetra pods at Ventnor*

F   *Sea wall at Ventnor*

E   *Rock amour (rip rap) at Ventnor*

links

Learn more about coastal management on the Isle of Wight at **www.coastalwight.gov.uk**

Activities

1 a   Write a definition of hard engineering.

   b   Use annotated sketches to explain how any three hard engineering methods protect coastlines.

2 a   Explain why coastal protection is needed at Ventnor.

   b   Describe the range of methods used on the Ventnor coastline.

3   Using the photos on these pages, explain why some people think that hard engineering methods are not very environmentally friendly.

extension   Investigate the West Bay coastal defence scheme, a hard engineering scheme in Dorset, at **www.dorsetforyou.com** → Environment and Planning → Planning → Coastline-protection

AQA *Examiner's tip*

Be able to describe a range of hard engineering methods used to manage and protect areas of coastline.

1.9 Protecting the coastline: beach replenishment

What is beach replenishment?

Beach replenishment is a way of protecting and preserving the beach so that it acts as a natural defence against the sea. A wide and gently sloping beach is one of the most effective defences against storm waves because the beach is able to absorb the energy of the breaking waves. Having a wide beach can reduce the rate of cliff erosion and also help to protect coastal areas from the threat of flooding.

Why is beach replenishment called 'soft engineering'?

Beach replenishment is an example of 'soft engineering' because it provides a natural defence against the sea without damaging the environment. It does not involve building sea walls or using rock or concrete structures and is consequently seen as being more environmentally friendly.

The following example shows how beach replenishment and the use of technology are being used to protect Pevensey Bay in East Sussex from the threat of flooding.

In this section you will learn:

what is meant by 'soft engineering'

how a beach replenishment scheme works.

AQA **Examiner's tip**

Beach replenishment is an example of soft engineering. Ensure that you can describe how this form of coastal management works.

Find out ... 🔍

Use the internet to find out more about the Pevensey Levels.

Case study

Pevensey Bay beach replenishment scheme

Pevensey Bay is a low-lying coastal area in East Sussex that will be increasingly threatened by coastal flooding as sea levels rise (Map **A**).

A 1:50,000 OS map extract of Pevensey Bay

Immediately inland from the sea are over 10,000 properties, a number of caravan parks and the main coastal road and rail links. Also found here are the Pevensey **Levels**, an environmentally protected area. Because of the environmentally sensitive nature of the area, hard engineering methods would not be appropriate. Consequently a beach replenishment management scheme is being used to protect the area from the threat of flooding.

How does the Pevensey Bay coastal defence scheme work?

Three main techniques are being used at Pevensey Bay.

1 Beach replenishment

Longshore drift moves beach material along the coast from west to east. This means that the beach at Pevensey Bay is losing up to 25,000 cubic metres of beach material each year. In order to maintain beach levels, 5,000 cubic metres of sand and gravel is transferred by lorry from further west and another 20,000 cubic metres is taken from the sea bed and sprayed back onto the beach using a specially adapted ship.

2 Beach recycling

As beach sediment drifts from west to east, some parts of the beach lose sediment and other parts gain beach sediment. To try to even out this natural movement, material is moved from areas where it has built up and is put back in its original position. Beach recycling is often carried out after winter storms when the largest natural movement of material has taken place.

3 Beach reprofiling

During winter storms, beach material is carried down the beach by strong backwash. This can leave upper beach levels low and vulnerable to wave attack. Bulldozers are used to push the material back up the beach to create a gently sloping **beach profile**.

Using new techniques

The scheme provided the opportunity to use a number of new beach management techniques, including:

- Global Positioning Systems (GPS) to track the movement of beach material and identify where replenishment is required
- using plastic materials for groyne construction instead of tropical hardwood
- using tyre bales – over 40,000 compressed car tyres were buried to provide a stable base for the replenishment of the beach. If this proves successful in the long term, it will be a useful way of reducing the volume of beach replenishment material required – it is also a good way of recycling old tyres!

B   *A ship spraying sand onto the beach at Pevensey Bay*

C   *A bulldozer moving material on the beach*

D   *A beach after replenishment and recycling*

Activities

1   Explain why a beach is a good defence against storm waves.

2   How would the inland area at Pevensey Bay be affected if the sea broke through the coastal defences?

3   Explain what is meant by:
  a   beach replenishment   b   beach recycling   c   beach reprofiling.

4   Why would hard engineering not be appropriate for Pevensey Bay?

extension   How successful has the Pevensey Bay coastal defence scheme been?

links

Find out more about the coastal defence scheme at Pevensey Bay at **www.pevensey-bay.co.uk**

Key terms

Levels: areas of flat land, often with many rivers/streams.

Beach profile: the shape of the beach.

▇ Why are some coastal environments under threat?

Coastal development, pollution and climate change are having a significant impact on coastal environments. A study carried out in 2008 suggested that a number of fragile coastal **ecosystems** have already been seriously damaged. It was estimated that 50 per cent of the world's coral **reefs** had been affected by human activity and could be dead within 40 years if nothing is done to protect them (Diagram **A**).

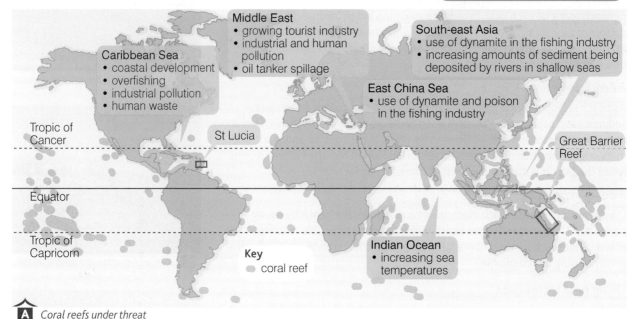

Middle East
- growing tourist industry
- industrial and human pollution
- oil tanker spillage

South-east Asia
- use of dynamite in the fishing industry
- increasing amounts of sediment being deposited by rivers in shallow seas

Caribbean Sea
- coastal development
- overfishing
- industrial pollution
- human waste

East China Sea
- use of dynamite and poison in the fishing industry

Tropic of Cancer

St Lucia

Great Barrier Reef

Equator

Tropic of Capricorn

Key
coral reef

Indian Ocean
- increasing sea temperatures

A Coral reefs under threat

What are coral reefs?

Coral reefs are formed by colonies of tiny animals (polyps). When the polyps die they leave behind a skeleton made up of calcium carbonate. This accumulates and forms coral reefs with living coral on the top surface.

Coral reefs develop in warm, shallow seas and are often referred to as the 'gardens of the sea' because of the extensive range of plant and animal life they contain (Photo **B**).

Why are coral reefs important?

- ▪ They contain rare species of plants and animals.
- ▪ They form a barrier which protects coasts from storm waves.
- ▪ They provide nutrients for fish stocks, which helps local fishing industries.
- ▪ They are a major tourist attraction, with over 250 million visitors a year.

B Coral reefs are important, but fragile

Why are coral reefs fragile?

Coral reefs are fragile because they develop slowly in clean, clear water. They are easily damaged by pollution and **sedimentation** and may die if touched by divers. In tourist areas the illegal collection of coral for souvenirs is a major threat.

The Soufrière Marine Management Area, St Lucia

Many Caribbean coastal areas are under increasing pressure from competing human activities such as tourism and fishing. This creates particular management challenges, especially in environmentally sensitive areas. The Soufrière Marine Management Area (SMMA) was set up to protect one of the most productive coral reefs on the west coast of St Lucia. The SMMA divided the coast on either side of the main town of Soufrière into five distinct zones. Within each zone only particular activities are allowed. The regulations are strictly enforced by wardens. Water quality and coral conditions are regularly monitored.

The aim of the SMMA is to cater for the needs of the local economy whilst protecting the fragile coral reef. Recent surveys have shown that the level of damage to the reef has declined while the commercial fishing and tourism industries have not been adversely affected.

∞ links

Learn more about the SMMA at **www.smma.org.lc**

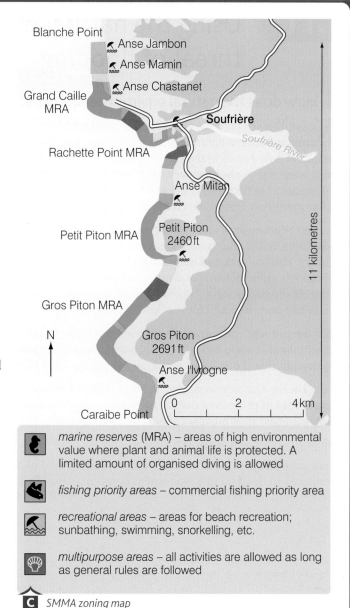

marine reserves (MRA) – areas of high environmental value where plant and animal life is protected. A limited amount of organised diving is allowed

fishing priority areas – commercial fishing priority area

recreational areas – areas for beach recreation; sunbathing, swimming, snorkelling, etc.

multipurpose areas – all activities are allowed as long as general rules are followed

C SMMA zoning map

Activities

1. Explain why areas of coral reef are under threat.

2. Why are coral reefs important environments?

3. Describe and explain the methods being used to protect the coastal environment in St Lucia.

extension Find out about the Great Barrier Reef, Australia – the largest collection of reefs in the world – at **www.gbrmpa.gov.au**

Think about the pressures faced by the area and how the pressures are managed.

Key terms

Ecosystems: communities of plants and animals within a particular physical environment.

Reefs: ridges of rock near the surface of the sea.

Sedimentation: deposition of fine sand.

Using the natural environment to reduce the threat of flooding

■ How does the natural environment protect the coast?

The natural environment has always protected coastal lowlands from storm waves and provided a natural barrier against flooding. Two hundred years ago many coastal areas in the UK and Europe had extensive salt marshes which were able to absorb wave energy during storms and protect inland settlements from flooding. In tropical areas mangrove swamps provided similar protection against the effects of tropical storm surges.

In recent years areas of salt marsh have been drained and mangrove forests removed so that coastal areas can be developed for farming or industry. This has removed a natural barrier and made coastal areas increasingly vulnerable to flooding. It has been suggested that the effects of the 2004 Asian tsunami (Photo **A**) were made worse because mangrove forests had been removed for the development of tourist resorts.

Since the tsunami, mangrove forests have been replanted and hotels rebuilt further inland in some areas, as part of new coastal protection programmes. It is thought that this will also guard against the threat of rising sea levels.

In the UK the restoration of salt marshes is increasingly seen as a natural way of protecting coastal areas from the threat of flooding. It is being achieved by a process called 'managed retreat'.

A *A coastal resort being inundated with floodwaters during the Asian tsunami*

What is managed retreat?

Managed retreat, or managed realignment, is a method of allowing low-lying areas to flood up to a new line of defence inland. Salt marshes will then develop on the newly flooded areas (Diagrams **B** and **C**).

Key terms

Earth bund: constructed mound of earth.

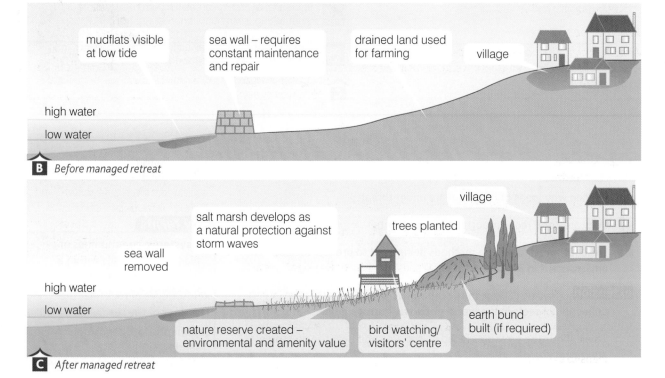

mudflats visible at low tide

sea wall – requires constant maintenance and repair

drained land used for farming

village

high water

low water

B *Before managed retreat*

village

salt marsh develops as a natural protection against storm waves

trees planted

sea wall removed

high water

low water

nature reserve created – environmental and amenity value

bird watching/ visitors' centre

earth bund built (if required)

C *After managed retreat*

Managed retreat – Wallasea Wetlands Creation Scheme, Essex

Wallasea Island (Map **D**) lies on the Essex coastline, between the Crouch and the Roach estuaries. The area had been protected by a sea wall for many years and the land behind the sea wall used for farming. By 2004, the existing sea wall was in a poor state of repair and close to collapse in some places. Rebuilding the wall in its current position was not seen as worthwhile, because with rising sea levels it would put other areas at risk as water was funnelled upstream. Consequently, managed retreat (realignment) was seen as the best option in this area.

Why was managed retreat (realignment) seen as a good option at Wallasea?

- It created 115 hectares of new mudflats and salt marshes on the northern part of Wallasea Island, a natural habitat for wildlife.
- Salt marshes provide a natural defence against flood tides and will be increasingly important as sea levels rise.
- It allows floodwater to spread out and reduces the risk of flooding further inland.
- The existing farmland is of poor quality.
- It improved fish nurseries in the area.
- There were few buildings in the area.

How was the scheme carried out?

1 A new sea wall was built inland of the existing coastline.

2 An **earth bund** was built to separate fresh water from salt water, creating two separate environments.

3 A number of artificial islands were created to provide nesting places for birds.

4 700,000 tonnes of mud was pumped onto the area to create the new salt marsh.

5 In June 2006 the final landscaping took place and the old sea walls were breached, allowing the sea to flood the newly created landscape.

Has it been successful?

A monitoring programme is being carried out to assess the effects of the scheme. Photo **E** shows what the area looks like today.

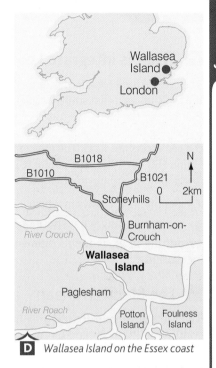

D *Wallasea Island on the Essex coast*

E *The realigned landscape at Wallasea today*

Activities

1 a Describe the impact of the tsunami wave shown in Photo **A**.

  b How might replanting mangrove forests help to protect tropical coastal areas?

2 Use an annotated diagram to explain 'managed retreat'.

3 a Why was Wallasea Island a suitable area for a managed retreat scheme?

  b Describe the advantages of the Wallasea Wetlands Creation Scheme.

extension The Royal Society for the Protection of Birds (RSPB) has proposed a scheme to return the remainder of Wallasea Island to salt marsh. The Wallasea Island Wild Coast Project will create nearly 800 hectares of salt marsh. Find out about the project on the RSPB website at **www.rspb.org.uk**

Did you know ???????

Five hundred years ago there were 30,000 hectares of salt marsh around the Essex coast. Today there are just 2,500 hectares left.

∞ links

Find out more about the Wallasea Wetlands Creation Scheme at **www.defra.gov.uk** and **www.abpmer.net/wallasea**

1.12 Managing the coastal zone

What is integrated coastal zone management?

The coastal area (or zone) is more than just the shoreline – it also includes the built-up area that stretches inland and the shallow seas and marshes that border the land. Integrated coastal zone management (ICZM) is about managing the whole of the coastal area and not just the narrow strip where the sea meets the land. The idea of ICZM was introduced by the European Union (EU) in 1996. The aim of ICZM is to protect coastal areas from over-development and environmental damage. This is done by:

- identifying the ways in which a coastal area is being put under pressure
- recommending what should be done to reduce pressures on the area
- putting in place the recommendations and checking that they are working.

The Mediterranean – a coastal area under pressure

The Mediterranean coastal area includes over 20 countries from 3 continents (Map **A**) and has a resident population of over 300 million. This number doubles during the summer months with the influx of tourists. The coastline is 45,000 km long and along the coast there are 600 cities, more than 1,000 ports and marinas and hundreds of industrial areas and power stations. In many areas tourism is the major industry, often concentrated on the narrow strip of land along the shoreline. Tourist numbers are expected to continue increasing over the next 20 years (Table **B**).

Pressures on the Mediterranean coastal area

- Increasing levels of sea pollution as industrial waste and untreated sewage are pumped into the sea (Map **A**).
- Increased urbanisation of coastal areas as population increases.
- Damage to environments by the development of hotels and holiday resorts (Photo **C**).
- Growing threat of desertification as increasing amounts of underground water are used.
- Growing levels of air pollution from industry and transport.
- Increased risk of accidents as the number of ships in the Mediterranean Sea increases.
- Water shortages because of increases in demand and climate change.

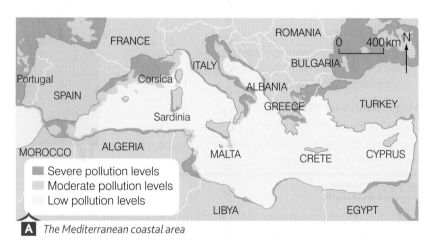

A The Mediterranean coastal area

B Growing tourist numbers (millions)	
2000	175
2005	200
2010	230 (est.)
2015	255 (est.)
2020	290 (est.)
2025	315 (est.)
2030	350 (est.)

Managing the Mediterranean coastal area

In 2006 the United Nations Environment Programme (UNEP) produced a report that described the current state of the Mediterranean area and suggested a course of action that would stop its continuing destruction. The report, called 'The Blue Plan – a sustainable future for the Mediterranean', made a number of recommendations, the aim of which is to 'clean up the Mediterranean by 2020'. Included in the recommendations are the following:

- Make 10 per cent of all coastal areas protected environments (nature reserves).
- Reduce building development along the coast and introduce protected 'green areas' between areas of development.
- Develop inland tourism to relieve pressure on the coast.
- Issue guidelines to ensure that tourist developments fits in with the environment.
- Treat all waste water before it is pumped into the sea.
- Encourage the increasing use of water conservation methods.
- Encourage energy-saving measures and the development of renewable energy.
- Introduce stricter rules to reduce pollution.

C *A Mediterranean tourist resort*

Activities

1 a Which three continents border the Mediterranean Sea?

  b Suggest why the Mediterranean coast is a popular holiday destination.

2 Explain how the growth of tourism can bring both advantages and disadvantages to local areas.

3 Look at the information in Table **D**.

D *Facts about the Mediterranean Sea*

	1970	1980	1990	2000	2010 (est.)	2020 (est.)
Urban population (millions)	150	190	225	260	310	350
Water demand km²/year	190	220	260	290	310	320
Energy demand million tonnes oil equivalent	380	540	660	810	1,080	1,320

  a Draw line graphs to show each of the data sets.

  b Describe the pattern of each graph.

  c Use your graphs and the information on these pages to describe the pressures on the Mediterranean Sea.

4 Explain how any five of the Blue Plan recommendations may reduce the pressures on the Mediterranean Sea.

extension Explain the difference between integrated coastal zone management and shoreline management.

Key terms

Integrated management: management of the whole of an area/system rather than parts of it.

Sustainable management: management that meets the needs of the present while preserving an area for future generations.

Did you know ???????

The Mediterranean coastal zone is an area of over 2 million km², of which only 98,000 km² remain untouched by development.

⚭ links

Learn more about managing the Mediterranean coasts at **www.planbleu.org** and **www.unep.org** (Mediterranean Sea).

How will climate change affect coastal areas?

It is increasingly clear that the climate is changing. The decade 1999–2008 saw:

- eight of the warmest years since records began
- the highest surface temperature of the North Atlantic Ocean on record.

With the numbers of people living in coastal areas growing, the threat of global warming to these areas will become increasingly significant. Scientists have suggested that climate change could affect European coastal areas in a number of ways:

- Climate change is likely to raise sea levels and bring more rain in winter.
- There may be more winter storms.
- Coastal lowlands will be at increased risk of flooding.
- Rates of coastal erosion are likely to increase.
- There will be increasing numbers of landslides on soft cliff coastlines because of higher rainfall and increased rates of erosion.
- Protecting coastlines from erosion and flooding will become more difficult and more expensive.

Planning for rising sea levels

A new approach to planning for rising sea levels has been developed by coastal experts from a number of European countries. It is called the 'Response project' and is used to identify areas at risk from rising sea levels and to recommend methods that may reduce risks. The Response project works by collecting information about coastal areas and putting it on a series of maps so that it can be easily understood. It is then used to make decisions about future coastal planning and management.

> **In this section you will learn:**
>
> how climate change may affect coastal areas
>
> how information can be used to plan for rising sea levels.

> **Did you know ??????**
>
> - Global warming in Europe is 40 per cent higher than the world's average and it has already caused significant problems: storms in 1999 and 2002 caused £8 billion worth of damage.
> - British insurance companies have estimated that a half-metre rise in sea level could cause up to £30 billion of damage.

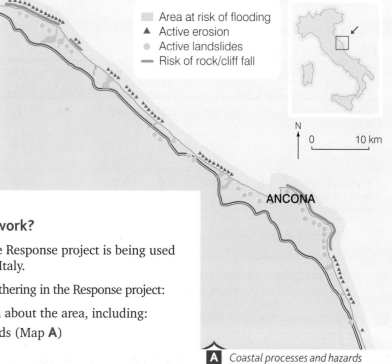

Area at risk of flooding
▲ Active erosion
● Active landslides
— Risk of rock/cliff fall

ANCONA

A *Coastal processes and hazards*

How does the Response project work?

The following example shows how the Response project is being used in the area around Ancona in eastern Italy.

There are three stages of information gathering in the Response project:

1. Collecting background information about the area, including:
   - the coastal processes and hazards (Map **A**)
   - the existing coastal defences
   - the economic and environmental value of the area.

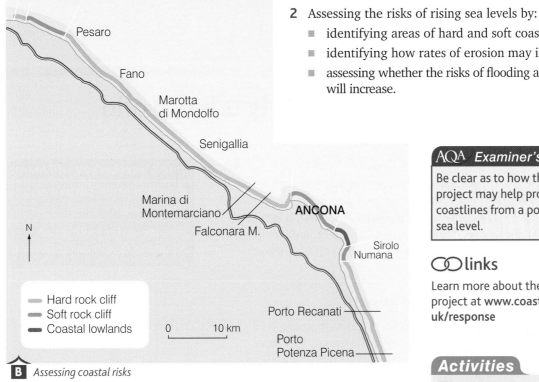

B *Assessing coastal risks*

Hard rock cliff
Soft rock cliff
Coastal lowlands

0   10 km

2   Assessing the risks of rising sea levels by:
   - identifying areas of hard and soft coastline (Map **B**)
   - identifying how rates of erosion may increase
   - assessing whether the risks of flooding and landslides will increase.

> **AQA** *Examiner's tip*
>
> Be clear as to how the Response project may help protect some coastlines from a possible rise in sea level.

∞links

Learn more about the Response project at **www.coastalwight.gov.uk/response**

3   Offering guidance to planners and decision makers by:
   - suggesting the likely impact of sea levels rising (Map **C**)
   - recommending how areas at risk may be protected.

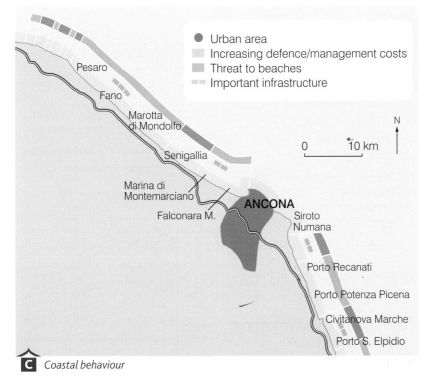

C *Coastal behaviour*

- Urban area
- Increasing defence/management costs
- Threat to beaches
- Important infrastructure

0   10 km

Activities

1   How may climate change affect coastal areas?

2   a   What is the Response project?

   b   How does it help the management of coastal areas?

3   Using the maps of the Ancona region of Italy:

   a   Describe the coastal processes, hazards and risks in the area 10 km either side of the town of Ancona.

   b   Explain how the information in **1**, **2** and **3** may be useful when deciding how to manage the coast around Ancona.

extension

   a   What is meant by the 'economic and environmental value of an area'?

   b   Why is this information important to coastal managers?

Maps **A**, **B** and **C** are of the Marche region on the east coast of central Italy. This region has suffered from considerable coastal erosion in recent years.

2 The urban environment

2.1 Living in an increasingly urban world

In 1950 fewer than one person in three lived in a town or city.

Today half of the world's population live in an urban area and by 2015 the proportion will be 60 per cent.

In 1950 New York was the only global **megacity**; by 2015 it is estimated that there will be 27 megacities, 21 of them in developing countries with the majority in Asia, the continent with the largest number of people living in urban areas.

Rates of urban population growth

Urbanisation is generally linked with economic development. As a country moves from a mainly rural agricultural economy to a more industrial, commercial economy, the population becomes increasingly concentrated in towns and cities. Countries that have reached high levels of economic development usually have an urban population of over 75 per cent of the total population and the rates of urban population growth are low. This can be seen in Europe, North America and Oceania where urban growth rates are less than 1.5 per cent. In developing countries where urban populations are still relatively low, the rate of growth is higher. In 2008 Africa was the least urbanised continent but had the fastest rate of urban growth (Graph **B**).

Urban sprawl

Urban areas do not only grow in terms of numbers of people, they can also grow in physical size. This is known as **urban sprawl**.

As urban areas develop, there is a growing demand for building land. In urban centres the amount of available land is limited, so there is increasing pressure to build on the urban–rural fringe.

In recent years an increasing number of people are moving away from urban centres to live in the suburban fringe areas. These areas are seen as having more space and a better living environment, but are still close enough to the urban centre for work or leisure activities (Photo **D**).

In many developing countries wealthier people are moving from the city centres to more affluent **suburbs**, because they feel it is a safer environment, away from the slums and squatter areas found in many inner city centres.

What are the causes of urbanisation in developing countries?

The major cause of urbanisation in developing countries is rural–urban migration. Poor social and economic conditions in rural areas encourage people to move to urban areas where they may have more opportunities to access basic facilities. See Table **C**.

> **In this section you will learn:**
>
> about the global pattern of urban change
>
> the reasons for rapid urban growth in developing countries.

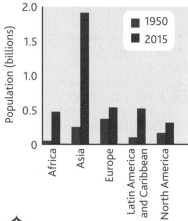

A Urban populations, 1950 and 2015 (projected)   Source: UN

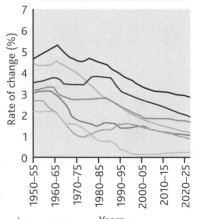

B Urban growth rates   Source: UN

C *Access to services in developing countries*

Country	% of urban/rural population with access to:					
	Safe water		Education		Health care	
	Urban	Rural	Urban	Rural	Urban	Rural
Bolivia (South America)	76	18	78	22	86	38
Mozambique (Africa)	48	16	90	38	98	30
Pakistan (Asia)	96	36	92	44	99	35

The problem of natural disasters and lack of land ownership in rural areas further adds to the pressure to move to urban areas where there may be more employment opportunities and higher incomes.

Many migrants are aged between 15 and 35 years, so urban populations are often youthful, adding to the pressure of urban growth as a result of high birth rates.

Urbanisation in China

With rapid economic growth in recent years, China is experiencing high rates of urban growth as millions of migrants move towards newly developed industrial areas seeking work.

D *A spacious suburban area*

AQA *Examiner's tip*

Make sure that you can explain some of the causes of rural–urban migration in developing countries.

Key terms

Megacity: a city of 10 million people or more.

Urbanisation: the process of urban growth.

Urban sprawl: the outward growth of urban areas.

Suburbs: outlying districts of a town or city, often dominated by housing.

Chinese Cities Grow at an Alarming Rate

Over the last 10 years an average of 8 million Chinese peasant farmers have moved into the cities each year – making it the fastest and largest national scale of urbanisation in history. Chinese towns and cities are growing at an alarming rate – in 2007 China had nearly 100 urban areas of over 1 million people, in Britain there were just 5!

Meanwhile in Shanghai, one of the main business centres in China, the economic boom is creating thousands of jobs and attracting migrants from hundreds of kilometres away. In 1981 Shanghai had only 121 buildings over 8 storeys high. The rate of building is such that in 2009 this figure will have reached over 1,200, with new businesses opening daily.

Activities

1 a Describe the actual and projected rates of urban growth for:
- Africa
- Asia
- Europe

b Suggest why rates of urban growth are predicted to fall in the next 50 years.

2 Explain the link between urbanisation and economic growth.

3 The reasons people move to urban areas in developing countries are often described as:
- 'push factors' which push people away from a place
- 'pull factors' which attract people to a place.

Using examples, explain how push and pull factors encourage rural–urban migration.

4 a Three different websites gave the population of Mexico City as 27, 21 and 18 million in 2008. Suggest reasons for the differences in the figures.

b Why might estimates of future urban populations in developing countries be inaccurate?

extension Use the United Nations website to identify the projected 20 largest cities in 2015.

a Plot and name these cities on a world map.

b Describe and suggest reasons for the pattern shown on your map.

How does urban growth increase environmental pressures?

The development of towns and cities puts pressure on the urban environment in the following ways:

- A growing demand for transport increases vehicle emissions (Photo **A**).
- Increasing demand for energy leads to the building of power stations, which increases air pollution.
- Air pollution is caused by burning firewood and coal in the growing urban slums in developing countries.
- Water courses become increasingly polluted by industrial and human waste.
- Waste is often burnt, creating additional toxic pollution, or it is left in growing waste dumps where it may pollute water systems.
- As urban areas grow the rate of building increases, reducing the amount of green space.

The following article describes how rapid industrial growth is creating a number of environmental problems in the Chinese city of Chongqing.

A   *Smog hanging over the city of Los Angeles*

The Environmental Cost of Economic Growth

The use of cheap, poor-quality coal and a rapid increase in car ownership are causing significant pollution problems in a number of Chinese cities. In 2008 it was estimated that 16 of the planet's 20 dirtiest cities were in China. In Beijing the Chinese government had to remove 3 million cars from the roads and close down factories during the Olympic Games in order to try and reduce dangerously high levels of pollution.

In Chongqing, the fastest growing city in China, the high level of atmospheric pollution is responsible for thousands of premature deaths and cases of **bronchitis**. In 2006 air quality failed to reach the recommended government minimum health standards on an average of 1 day out of every 4 – on some days the **smog** was so dense that that it never appeared to get light!

Chongqing is growing at such a rate that it cannot cope with the volume of human waste – vast garbage tips have grown on the edge of the city. One landfill site only opened in 2003 and already contains more than a million tons of rubbish.

Improving the urban environment

In a recent conference an urban planner said:

> 66 *Without effective environmental management the general quality of urban environments will decline – leading to poorer levels of health for the whole community.* 99

The following example describes how the environment is being improved in the Brazilian city of Curitiba. Curitiba, a city of over 2 million people in southern Brazil, was one of the first cities to put in place a 'sustainable urban master plan'. In spite of facing the challenges of many developing cities such as low incomes and a rapidly growing population, Curitiba has become a model of environmental management that other urban areas are increasingly copying.

What are the main features of Curitiba's environmental management strategy?

- A traffic-free city centre – Curitiba was the first Brazilian city to have pedestrianised streets.
- A fully integrated bus system that is cheap and reliable – individual fuel use is 25 per cent less than that in most urban areas in Brazil.
- The development of green urban space – parks, river walkways and cycle-tracks have been built. Over 1.5 million trees have been planted.
- Recycling of buildings – old buildings are converted into new uses, saving resources and helping to maintain the character of the city.
- A green exchange system – slum dwellers who collect garbage can exchange it for food or bus tickets. Children can exchange bags of collected garbage for toys or school supplies.
- A public housing programme – the urban poor are given the opportunity to build basic homes. This ensures that most people have access to clean water and proper sanitation systems.
- A recycling programme – 70 per cent of rubbish is sorted, recycled and sold, reducing the need for landfill. The money earned is used to improve social facilities in the city.
- Strict environmental laws reduce industrial pollution.
- Environmental education is part of the school curriculum.

Activities

1   What causes air pollution in urban areas?

2   Explain the Flow Diagram **B**.

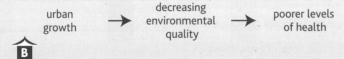

| urban growth | → | decreasing environmental quality | → | poorer levels of health |

B

3   Explain how any five features of Curitiba's environmental management strategy might improve the urban environment.

extension   It has been said that managing transport is the key to improving the urban environment. Do you agree with this statement? Justify your decision.

Did you know ??????

According to the World Health Organization:

- 1.5 billion urban dwellers live in areas where pollution exceeds recommended safe levels
- half a million deaths a year are as a result of sulphur emissions from vehicles and burning waste material.

Key terms

Bronchitis: inflammation of the tubes (bronchioles) leading into the lungs.

Smog: mixture of smoke and fog.

Photochemical smog: where smog combines with sunlight to form ozone, causing serious health problems such as breathing problems, eye irritations, vomiting.

Sustainable: meeting the needs of people without damaging the environment or exploiting resources.

Did you know ??????

In a recent survey:

- 60 per cent of New Yorkers wanted to leave the city
- 70 per cent of people in São Paulo (Brazil) felt it would be better to live elsewhere
- 99 per cent of people in Curitiba (southern Brazil) were happy with their city.

Find out ... O⎯

Use the internet to find out more about environmental management in Curitiba.

AQA Examiner's tip

Be able to describe the environmental pressures some cities face because of rapid urbanisation.

The threat of natural hazards in urban areas

What is a natural hazard?

An event such as a flood, tropical storm, **tsunami** or earthquake only becomes a hazard when it affects people.

Why do people live in hazardous areas?

Millions of people live in urban areas that are threatened by natural hazards. For example, looking at a world map, it is easy to see that:

- over 70 per cent of the world's population live near a river or the coast, which puts millions of people at risk from extreme weather and flooding events
- many of the world's largest cities are built in areas where there is a risk of earthquakes or volcanic eruptions.

Los Angeles – a multi-hazard city

Many urban areas are 'multi-hazard' locations – Los Angeles in the USA is an example of this (Photo **A**).

Los Angeles, with its attractive climate, sandy beaches, subtropical vegetation and snow-capped inland mountains, is a striking environment that has seen rapid population growth in the last 50 years. Yet it is one of the most hazardous cities on Earth! The city sits on the San Andreas Fault and has experienced a number of serious earthquakes, and the coast is in the Pacific tsunami zone. In the winter months heavy rainfall can cause flooding and landslides, and summer droughts provide perfect conditions for wildfires.

In spite of all this, the area is seen as one of the best places to live in the USA. As one resident said:

> 66 It's a great place to live and has a range of highly paid jobs. We are outside on the beach most of the time and don't worry about hazards – they don't happen often. Also we are well prepared and have insurance. 99

In highly developed countries, building practices are stricter and hazard planning is more effective. In developing countries, slum dwellers and people living in poor-quality housing are more vulnerable to natural hazards (Photo **B**).

Managing the threat of flooding in urban areas

Managing the threat of flooding in urban areas has often been about responding to events by building defences after a flood has occurred in order to reduce future risk. This approach is increasingly seen as unsustainable because it lacks proper planning, and putting flood defences in one place may often increase the risk of flood to another.

More recently flood management plans have been developed. These are seen as a way of looking at a whole river system to allow a sustainable flood risk strategy to be developed, which can take account of any future changes.

In this section you will learn:

that many people live in hazardous areas

how the risks of natural hazards in urban areas can be reduced.

A Like Los Angeles, San Francisco lies on the San Andreas Fault

B Balakot in Pakistan after the earthquake in 2005

AQA Examiner's tip

Know a case study of an urban area that has been affected by a natural hazard; think where, why, when and what happened.

Key terms

Tsunami: tidal wave caused by an undersea earthquake.

Floodplain: a low-lying area next to a river that is vulnerable to flooding.

Britain's summer floods 2007

In July 2007 at the end of a two-month period of above-average rainfall, some of the heaviest rainfall ever recorded fell on southern Britain. In parts of Oxfordshire over 100 mm of rain fell in 24 hours – about a sixth of the amount the whole area might expect in a year! With the ground saturated from previous rainstorms and river levels already dangerously high, rivers began to burst their banks and flow across their **floodplain**, flooding towns alongside the Thames, Severn and Avon rivers. The heavy rainfall caused landslips and mudslides in a number of areas, disrupting roads, railways and power supplies (Map **C**).

links

Learn more about the 2007 floods at **www.bbc.co.uk** – search 'Tewkesbury floods 2007'.

Learn more about flood management at **www.environment-agency.gov.uk**

Upton-upon-Severn
- over 1,000 people trapped by rising water
- the army had to deliver food and bottled water

Stratford-Upon-Avon/Warwick
- much of the town centre under water
- 30 nearby towns and villages affected by flooding

Tewkesbury
- much of the town under water
- town centre cut off for days
- 55 people rescued by Royal National Lifeboat Institution (RNLI)

Evesham
- under 1.5 metres of water at the height of the flood

Buckingham
- many roads under water
- 70 homes/businesses flooded

Pangbourne
- main road flooded
- 400 homes affected

Maidenhead
- town centre flooded

London
- parts of SW London flooded
- underground railway disrupted

Gloucester
- people evacuated from dockside area
- thousands of people without water for days
- people evacuated from trains caught in the flood
- electricity supply affected

Reading
- town centre flooded
- main shopping centre closed

Wokingham
- a number of houses flooded

Sutton/East Surrey
- 80,000 people warned to boil drinking water

River Avon

River Severn

River Thames

0   100km

 C *The worst-hit areas during the British floods, summer 2007*

The Thames Region Flood Management Plan

Although the River Thames catchment area covers less than 10 per cent of the area of England and Wales, nearly 25 per cent of the total population live and work within it, making it one of the most urbanised areas of the country. In order to reduce the risk of future flooding in the area the following measures have been suggested in the Thames Flood Management Plan.

1 Land use planning – reduce the amount of building on floodplains

2 Sustainable approaches in dense urban areas – increase river corridors and open space near rivers wherever possible

3 Role of existing floodplain – increase the use of the floodplain to store excess water during times of flood

4 Flood defences – improved planning will reduce the need for defences

 D *Part of the Thames Flood Management Plan (adapted)*

Activities

1 Why are urban areas at increasing risk of natural hazards?

2 Explain why Los Angeles is called a multi-hazard city.

3 Why are people in urban areas in less developed countries often more badly affected by hazards?

extension Use the internet to find out why the Thames Flood Barrier was built and how it works.

Reducing deprivation in urban areas in more developed countries

What is meant by 'deprivation'?

It is clear that there are enormous differences in living conditions within urban areas. Travelling through almost any city it is possible to see modern office buildings and luxury apartments alongside run-down areas with boarded-up shops and vandalised housing (Photo **A**). These differences were clearly shown by a recent health study in London, which showed that life expectancy is nearly 10 years longer in Westminster (central London) than in Stratford (East London) – which is only 10 stations away on the underground!

A World Health Organization (WHO) report in 2008 stated that:

- a child born in one particular Glasgow suburb (Scotland) can expect to live 28 years less than another born only 13 km away
- in the USA there would have been 886,202 fewer deaths between 1991 and 2000 if **mortality** rates were the same for white and African-American urban dwellers.

What determines a person's quality of life?

The term 'quality of life' is used to describe the general conditions in which people live. It usually includes information about:

- economic conditions, such as level of income, unemployment rate, rate of home ownership
- social conditions, such as quality of local schools, housing quality, access to healthcare, **life expectancy**, crime rates

A *A deprived urban area*

- environmental conditions, such as levels of pollution, amount of green space, amount of **vandalism**.

Information collected about a number of different factors can be put together to form a **deprivation** index. This can be presented as a deprivation map and used to compare the quality of life in different parts of an urban area (Map **B**).

How can deprived areas be improved?

The World Health Organization (WHO) has suggested that the key to improving **deprived areas** is:

1 measuring and understanding the problems of the area
2 improving housing, health and education
3 building community spirit.

Key terms

Mortality: death rate, usually expressed as deaths per 1,000 of the population.

Life expectancy: average number of years a person may expect to live at the time of birth.

Vandalism: intentional damage of property.

Deprivation: where a person's quality of life falls below a level that is regarded as the acceptable minimum by the government of a country.

Deprived areas: places where economic/social and environmental conditions are very poor.

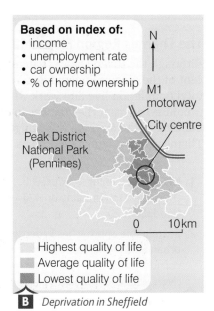

Based on index of:
- income
- unemployment rate
- car ownership
- % of home ownership

N

M1 motorway

City centre

Peak District National Park (Pennines)

0   10km

Highest quality of life
Average quality of life
Lowest quality of life

B *Deprivation in Sheffield*

The following examples describe improvements in two urban areas.

Bringing back community spirit in east London

Parts of east London have some of the highest deprivation rates in the UK, with people living in poor housing, with no safe places for children to play and high rates of vandalism and crime. The following statement was made by a 16-year-old boy who lives in Hackney in east London:

66 *I live in a tower block of flats in a two-bedroom flat with my parents, brother and two sisters. My young brother and sisters share a room and I sleep in the sitting room. We have been waiting for years for a larger place. From my window I can see the City of London with its high-rise office blocks and luxury apartments – only a few kilometres away but a different world!* 99

C   *New housing on the Nightingale Estate, Hackney*

The Nightingale Estate in Hackney has seen improvements in recent years which have improved the quality of life for local residents (Diagram **D**).

⚭ links

Use the internet to find out how the Nightingale Estate has been improved.

Some tower blocks demolished, others refurbished – security doors in entrance and caretaker employed in each block.

Community centre built – facilities for youth club, nursery and older citizens club

Litter collection and recycling system

New houses and low-level flats with gardens

Children's play area and open space

Landscaping and seating. Increased greenery and trees

Improved street lighting and security cameras

D   *Improvements to the Nightingale Estate, Hackney*

Improving health and housing

Torquay, a holiday resort in southern England, is regarded as an affluent area but has a number of housing estates where deprivation levels are significantly higher than the local average. In Watcombe, one of the poorest housing estates, a housing improvement scheme has been introduced. This included upgrading central heating, ventilation and insulation levels. Local residents have reported that their homes are now warmer, drier and cheaper to run. As a result general health and wellbeing have improved and there is a greater sense of community spirit.

AQA *Examiner's tip*

Be able to describe how deprived urban areas can be improved.

Activities

1   a   What is meant by 'quality of life'?

   b   Explain why quality of life is a mixture of economic, social and environmental factors.

2   Describe the quality of life in Sheffield (Map **B**) and suggest reasons for the patterns shown.

3   Suggest how the Nightingale Estate improvements might improve quality of life for its residents.

Did you know ??????

Slums are not only a problem in poor countries: 6 per cent of urban dwellers in wealthy countries live in slums (World Health Organization).

Birmingham – Britain's second largest city

The West Midlands conurbation (Map **A**) developed as one of Britain's industrial heartlands, and the city of Birmingham was known as 'the city of a thousand trades' because of the wide range of manufacturing industries found there. An example of the scale of its manufacturing can be seen in the Fort Dunlop building to the north of the city. In the 1950s this single industrial site employed over 10,000 people and was the largest factory in the world.

Connecting the industrial areas in the West Midlands was a series of canals with loading basins where barges brought in raw materials and took away finished products.

Industrial decline in the 1970s and 1980s left the area with rising unemployment and increasing urban **dereliction** as factories closed and canals fell into disrepair.

Redevelopment and regeneration

In the last 20 years Birmingham has been transformed by a number of regeneration projects. Some of these can be seen in Map **B**.

> **In this section you will learn:**
>
> how Birmingham has been redeveloped over the last 20 years
>
> about an example of a mixed use redevelopment scheme.

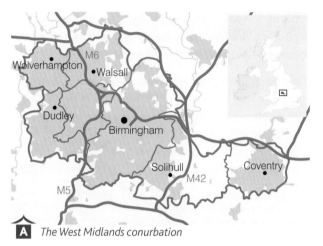

A　The West Midlands conurbation

City Hospital
A £35 million development that includes an eye hospital and a teaching unit

Eastside
- £40 million redevelopment of Matthew Bolton College (higher education)
- New technology institute
- The region's first IMAX theatre

Brindleyplace
- Redeveloped canal basin
- National Sea Life Centre– a 'family attraction of the year' in 2004

National Indoor Arena
Opened in 1991 – hosts sporting and musical events

International Convention Centre/Symphony Hall
Hosts up to 300 events a year

The Mailbox
Former Royal Mail sorting office – now a shopping centre and BBC headquarters

Find out ...

In the 1970s the Fort Dunlop factory closed. The building lay empty for 20 years before the whole site was redeveloped. Find out about the regeneration of the Fort Dunlop site.

New Street Station
A £550 million redevelopment scheme given the go-ahead in 2008 (the Gateway Plus Project)

Bullring Shopping Centre
Redeveloped shopping centre opened in 2003 – over 140 major shops including Selfridges. Over 35 million visitors a year

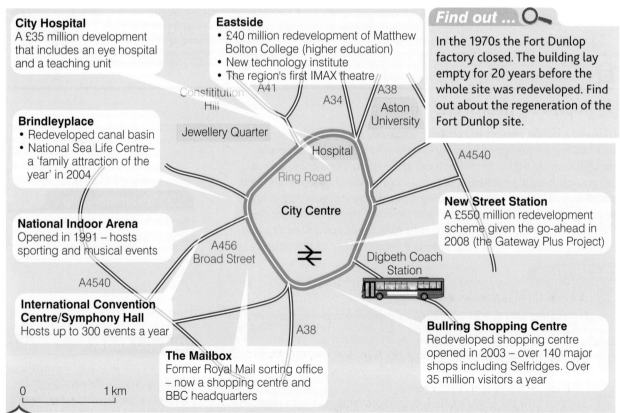

B　Major regeneration projects in Birmingham

Brindleyplace – an example of a mixed use redevelopment scheme

Brindleyplace was an area of derelict canalside warehouses and disused factories centred around one of the main canal basins in the middle of the city. Since the 1990s it has been redeveloped to create **mixed use** residential and commercial accommodation in the heart of the city. The major features of the **redevelopment** scheme can be seen in Photos **C** and **D**.

C *Canalside area, Brindleyplace, with the National Indoor Arena (NIA) events centre in the background*

D *Symphony Court residential area*

Key terms

Dereliction: previously used land/ buildings fallen into disuse and decay.

Mixed use: has a mixture of uses – commercial, leisure, residential, etc.

Redevelopment: renovation and improvement of areas that were previously run-down.

Did you know ??????

There are 10 universities in the West Midlands with a total of nearly 200,000 students.

Activities

1 Explain how the projects shown in Map **B** might improve the social and economic conditions in Birmingham.

2 Why are planners trying to encourage people to live in city centres?

3 a Why is Brindleyplace described as a mixed development scheme?

   b How has the Brindleyplace redevelopment scheme improved the local economy and environment?

   c Why might people wish to live in Brindleyplace?

∞links

Investigate a company that specialises in regeneration projects, turning disused buildings into business or residential spaces. For example, www.urbansplash.co.uk

2.6 Managing movement in urban areas

Why is traffic a growing problem in urban areas?

The growth of traffic is a major challenge for many urban areas around the world. As towns and cities grow, both in size and population and car ownership increases (Diagram **A**), more journeys are made by car. In the UK it is estimated that 80 per cent of personal journeys are made by car and 90 per cent of business journeys over 3 km are made by car.

The growth of traffic congestion increases air pollution and business costs, and adds to the pressure to build more roads.

The following examples illustrate different ways in which people movement is being managed in urban areas.

Cambridgeshire guided busway

What is a 'guided busway'?

A guided busway is a dedicated concrete track that can only be used by buses. Any bus can use it as long as it has two extra small drive-wheels.

What are the advantages of a guided busway?

- It requires less land, so land and environmental costs are lower.
- Land between the guide beams can be left open for drainage.
- No other vehicles may use the track.
- Smoothness gives an improved ride.

The Cambridgeshire guided busway (Map **B**) opened in 2009 at a cost of £116 million. It is built along the existing disused railway line that links St Ives with Cambridge. The aim of the busway is to provide a high-quality alternative to car use on the congested A14 corridor where nearly 50,000 new homes are planned in the next 10 years.

The main features of the guided busway

- It links a number of villages between St Ives and Cambridge.
- Each stop has a dedicated shelter and cycle parking.
- Park and ride facilities are available in St Ives, Longstanton and on the edge of Cambridge.
- It provides a fast service into Cambridge every 10 minutes.
- When buses reach Cambridge they turn off the guideway and use normal roads.
- There are paths beside the guideway for pedestrians and cyclists.
- The area is being replanted and landscaped after construction and wildlife areas increased.

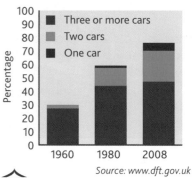

Source: www.dft.gov.uk

A Car ownership in the UK

links

Learn more about the Cambridgeshire guided busway at **www.cambridge.gov.uk** → transport

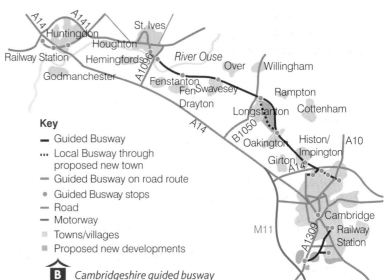

Key

— Guided Busway
··· Local Busway through proposed new town
— Guided Busway on road route
• Guided Busway stops
— Road
— Motorway
▪ Towns/villages
▪ Proposed new developments

B Cambridgeshire guided busway

Manchester Metrolink

Manchester Metrolink was Britain's first street-running tramway. It connects a number of smaller towns and suburbs to Manchester city centre, the redeveloped area of Salford Quays and Old Trafford, the home of Manchester United football club. Trains run every 6 minutes with extra units coupled together during rush hours.

All the stops have shelters with electronic signboards. In 2007 the Metrolink carried 20 million passengers. Three new routes are planned, costing £575 million. When these routes are completed they are expected to take 5 million car journeys off local roads each year and to increase the use of the Metrolink system from 55,000 to 90,000 people each day.

Curitiba's (Brazil) Bus Rapid Transport (BRT) system

Curitiba, a city of 2.5 million people, was the first Brazilian city to have dedicated bus lanes as part of its **integrated transport system**. The Bus Rapid Transport (BRT) system has four elements:

- direct line buses, which operate from key pick-up points and run directly into the city centre
- speedy buses, which operate on the five main routes into the city and have limited stops
- inter-district buses, which join up districts without crossing the city centre
- feeder mini-buses, which pick people up from residential areas and take them to terminal points for the main routes.

The system has a smart card payment system and bus terminals have shops, cafés and a post office. The BRT operates like a rail system but it is much less expensive. The local authority has recently introduced cleaner buses which use a mixture of diesel and **biofuel**, creating less pollution and also helping agriculture.

How effective is the system?

- 1.3 million passengers per day.
- 80 per cent of all **commuters** use buses.
- 30 million fewer car trips a year.
- The environment is cleaner and the roads safer.

C A BRT bus at a terminal

∞ **links**

Investigate metro systems in the UK, including Metrolink at **www.metrolink.co.uk**

Key terms

Integrated transport system: all parts of the system fit together to make it efficient.

Biofuel: burning wood and other vegetation to produce energy/heat/electricity.

Commuters: people who travel daily between their place of work and home.

Activities

1. Explain how the growth of traffic causes both economic and environmental problems.

2. What are the advantages and disadvantages of the Cambridge guided busway?

3. Manchester Metrolink was 'designed for both commuter and leisure users'. Explain this statement.

4. Why do you think the BRT in Curitiba has been successful?

extension Find out about the aims of the congestion charge in London and how it works.

Did you know ??????

In the UK it is estimated that:

- a quarter of all roads are congested every day
- traffic congestion costs businesses £24 billion every year
- only 12 per cent of journeys are made by public transport.

Urban growth in developing countries – challenges and opportunities

How does urban growth create challenges?

In 2003 the United Nations produced a report that said: 'One in three people in the world will live in urban **slums** in thirty years'.

It also concluded that 'in developing countries urban slums were growing faster than at any time in history'.

In Africa the rate of slum growth is fastest, but it is Asia that has the greatest number of slum dwellers, estimated to be nearly 600 million (Table **A**).

A Urban and slum dwelling populations (2005)

	Urban population %	Urban slum population (millions)	Slum population as % of urban population
Africa	39	187	61
Asia	50	598	42
South America	76	128	32
Europe	75	32	6

Providing adequate housing and basic services for the urban poor is a major challenge in many developing countries. The majority of urban dwellers live in **squatter settlements** where homes are made of makeshift materials, and basic services such as clean water and electricity are limited.

In these areas living conditions can be a serious threat to life. The following paragraphs describe the living conditions in parts of two developing cities.

B Open drains run through the streets of Kibera, Nairobi

Mumbai

Mumbai is one of the fastest growing cities in India. It has a population of about 15 million people, although no one really knows the actual population. About half the population live in shacks or slum areas, often without proper sanitation or access to clean water. It is estimated that about half a million people live on the street as 'pavement dwellers', where they have no facilities and have to exist alongside busy roads, where levels of air pollution are high and children are at risk of road traffic accidents. Because the city has grown so rapidly it is not able to cope with the increased traffic congestion throughout the day, and air pollution is a major threat to health.

Nairobi

In Nairobi, the capital city of Kenya, over 60 per cent of the population live in slums. One of the largest slums is Kibera, where living conditions are appalling (Photo **B**). Living in the slum is difficult: slum dwellers do not own the land, so could be thrown out at any time. The houses are made of any material people can get hold of, and are often built on unsafe land. Piles of rubbish are everywhere and open sewers flow through the area. This encourages rats and other vermin which contribute to the spread of disease. It is estimated that child mortality in Kibera is three times greater than in other parts of the city. In addition to these problems, Kibera also has very high rates of violent crime and people are afraid to go out after dark.

■ How can urban growth create opportunities for development?

Urban growth in developing countries is often seen as totally negative because the images associated with it are usually about shanty towns, illegal squatter developments, pollution and crime. However, despite all of their problems, urban areas can be a positive force for development.

The advantages of urban growth

- Urban areas can provide the first step towards a better life for some of the world's poorest people.
- Access to clean water, sanitation, education and health care is often better in urban areas.
- Opportunities for employment are higher in urban areas.
- Slums provide affordable housing for poor migrants, which is preferable to living on the street.
- The urban poor provide a massive labour force who carry out essential jobs that keep cities running.

Even in some of the poorest slum areas there are strong social and economic communities. The following article describes life in Dharavi (Photo **C**), a slum area in Mumbai, and shows how a slum can be an important part of a city.

The Other Side of Dharavi

Dharavi has been called the largest slum in Asia and has many of the problems of slum areas across the world. It is home to an estimated three-quarters of a million people, mostly living in corrugated tin huts. On the surface it looks like an area with little hope, but walking around the streets it is clear that this is more than just another slum. A local resident explained:

'Dharavi is a mixture of everything: there are community groups, small schools, and organisations helping orphaned children. There are hundreds of small businesses and workshops where people can earn a living and make products that are sold around the world. India's largest plastic and tin recycling facility is here – the place is a thriving industrial area. Along the main routeways there are shops selling just about anything, and a range of small family businesses producing a variety of different foods. Some of the largest businesses are the garment factories, many with computerised machinery making clothes and bags for the western market. Dharavi is an important part of Mumbai, all it lacks is decent housing.'

Activities

1 Using the data in Table **A**:

   a construct a bar graph to show the slum population as a percentage of urban population

   b describe the global pattern of slum populations.

2 Describe the living conditions in urban slums and explain why they present a 'challenge' to urban planners.

3 Suggest three ways in which life for the urban poor may be improved.

extension   Explain why slums have been called 'slums of hope' by some people and 'slums of despair' by others.

C *Dharavi*

Responding to the challenges of urban growth in developing countries

How can living conditions for the urban poor be improved?

Urban areas are often the driving force for development in poorer countries, providing a large supply of cheap labour and an ever-growing market for industrial products. Mumbai, in India, creates nearly a quarter of the country's wealth yet half of the city's population live in slums. In Rio de Janeiro, Brazil, slum dwellers provide most of the labour force for the construction industry across the city. In recent years, progress has been made in improving living conditions in many urban areas. This has been achieved with the help of government schemes, **self-help schemes** and **non-government organisation (NGO)** projects. The following examples look at a number of ways that conditions for the urban poor are being improved in developing countries.

> **In this section you will learn:**
>
> that improving living conditions in urban areas requires a range of strategies
>
> how improvement schemes are helping to manage urban poverty.

Curitiba – Brazil

In Curitiba, COHAB, the city's public housing programme, maintains that residents should have *'homes – not just shelters'*. They have introduced a housing policy that will provide 50,000 homes for the urban poor.

The city council has:

- bought a large area of land and supplied it with basic services such as water and electricity
- divided up the land into small housing plots. Each plot comes with two trees and the promise of 'an hour with an architect' to help plan each home. The architect draws the building plans.
- provided small loans to get people started on building, often done a room at a time once the shell of the house is built
- built 24 show homes using a wide range of techniques to give people ideas about what they can do.

A visiting planner said:

'This scheme encourages people to build their own homes. Many slum dwellers work in the construction industry so they know what to do; this scheme gives them the opportunity.'

A fully integrated bus service links the area to the rest of the city (see page 47) and each area of housing has a school, health centre and local shops.

Equator

North Atlantic Ocean

BRAZIL

Manaus   Belem   Fortaleza
                 Natal
                 Recife
         Salvador Macieó
    Brasilia   *South Atlantic Ocean*

São Paulo   **Rio de Janeiro**
            Curitiba
Port Alegre

Rio de Janeiro – Brazil

In Roçinha, one of the poorest parts of Rio de Janeiro, the city council, working with the local people, has introduced a number of self-help schemes. These have:

- improved housing quality in some parts of the shanty town
- introduced schools and health centres
- encouraged the development of small businesses, including hotels where visitors can stay and experience life in a shanty town.

A   *Improvements for the urban poor in Brazil*

> **AQA   Examiner's tip**
>
> Know a case study of a slum area that has been improved to give residents a better quality of life.

B   *New housing plots in Curitiba*

Improving the lives of the urban poor in Africa

The following example describes urban improvement schemes in a number of African cities.

Dalifont – Senegal
A settlement upgrading scheme has been introduced to improve basic conditions. Five hundred homes have been given water and sanitation systems, electricity and a rubbish collection and recycling facility.

Addis Ababa – Ethiopia
The city government is giving small loans to families for self-help housing construction schemes. Individual families can construct their own homes or work with others as a cooperative.
A small number of dwellings are being built by the government. These have running water, electricity and sanitation systems.

Cape Town – South Africa
The South African Homeless People's Federation (SAHPF) has formed a partnership with the government's housing department, which has agreed to transfer land to the poor and provide nearly a million pounds for housing projects. Their aim is to 'encourage self-help and self-reliance'. One project that has benefited is the Gugulelo Women's Cooperative ('Gugulelo' means pride). Working as a cooperative they have started a savings scheme and have taught local families basic financial management and building skills.
Helped by SAHPF they have built a small community of new houses (Photo **D**).

Kibera – Kenya
A scheme of slum upgrading has been introduced, jointly run by the government and an international charity. It is trying to respond to the most important problem – lack of clean water and proper toilets. It is hoped that this will reduce rates of disease and mean that slum dwellers do not have to buy expensive bottled water.

Dar es Salaam – Tanzania
The city council has introduced a waste collection system. Rubbish is collected from the streets and taken to recycling points or burnt. This has:
• created 2,000 jobs for slum dwellers
• reduced the amount of rubbish rotting in the streets
• reduced disease
• generated money from recycling that can be spent on urban improvements.

ETHIOPIA
SENEGAL
KENYA
*Atlantic
Ocean*
TANZANIA
SOUTH
AFRICA

C   *Some improvement schemes in Africa*

D   *A new home in Cape Town*

Activities

1   What does COHAB (Curitiba) mean when it says that residents 'should have homes – not just shelters'?

2   Improvement schemes are often called 'self-help schemes'. Why is this?

3   How might urban improvement schemes:
   ■ encourage people to take pride in their homes
   ■ improve the health of residents
   ■ help to develop a 'community spirit'?

extension   NGO projects have helped to improve living conditions in many urban areas. Use the internet to investigate urban projects being carried out by WaterAid. For each project:
   ■ describe what is being done
   ■ suggest how it will improve the living conditions for urban dwellers.

Did you know ??????

Access to clean water and sanitation systems would make a big difference to many slum dwellers.

In Bangladesh, water-related diseases are responsible for 24 per cent of all deaths.

Britain's first zero energy urban development – BEDZED

What is BEDZED?

Beddington Zero Energy Development (BEDZED) is a mixed-use solar urban village built on former **brownfield** land in the London borough of Sutton (Photo **A**). Completed in 2002, it was the UK's first major zero energy development and is the largest carbon-neutral eco-community in the country. The aim of BEDZED was to 'develop an energy-neutral urban village that would be a viable socio-economic community'. In order to achieve this the development has both residential buildings and work spaces for local businesses.

A *The BEDZED development*

⚭ links

Investigate the BEDZED development or visit **www.peabody. org.uk** or **www.bioregional.com**

What is the development like?

The residential part of BEDZED includes nearly 100 homes, with a mixture of town houses and flats. They are made of natural materials and have attractive modern interiors and fuel-efficient appliances (Photo **B**).

The BEDZED village includes a children's nursery, meeting rooms and an exhibition centre of renewable technologies.

The workspaces and offices are in the shade zone of the residential buildings, their roofs providing gardens for many of the flats.

All the buildings have large windows giving good levels of natural light and sunny rooms, without the problems of over-heating in the summer.

B *Interior of a BEDZED home*

What are the main features of BEDZED?

- Energy-efficient buildings – the buildings face south to maximise the amount of sunshine reaching each building. They have double glazing and high levels of insulation.

- Renewable materials – wherever possible the development was built using renewable materials. All the timber came from sustainable forests.

- Self-sufficient heating and power – a small-scale power plant, fuelled by tree waste, is used to provide hot water for the whole development. Solar power provides electricity.

- Low energy consumption – all the heat used for cooking and heating water is recycled and reused. All the buildings are fitted with low-energy appliances and low-energy lightbulbs.

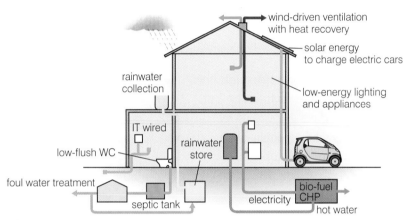

C   *How the BEDZED buildings work*

How environmentally friendly is BEDZED?

Compared with the average **ecological footprint** in the UK, BEDZED residents have a much reduced impact on the environment, even when they have a similar lifestyle. With an increased community lifestyle (see Table **D**), BEDZED residents can reduce their ecological footprint to below the global average (global average = 2.40 hectares).

D   *Ecological footprints*

Lifestyle	Description of lifestyle	Ecological footprint (hectares)
Average UK lifestyle	Owns car/drives to work; yearly holiday by plane; low level of recycling (10–20%); high level of energy consumption	6.19
BEDZED conventional lifestyle	Owns a car/commutes to work; yearly holiday by plane; high level of recycling (55–65%); average level of energy consumption	4.36
BEDZED community lifestyle	Part of a car sharing pool/works locally; holiday by plane every second year; very high level of recycling (80%+); low level of energy consumption	1.90

Key terms

Brownfield land: old industrial or housing area that has become rundown or derelict.

Ecological footprint: the impact of an individual on the Earth (measured in hectares per person).

Did you know ??????

A BEDZED home uses:

- 90 per cent less energy for heating

- 45 per cent less energy for hot water

- 55 per cent less energy for lighting

than an ordinary home.

∞ links

Learn more about sustainable building projects at **www.zedfactory.com** and **www.bedzed.com**

Activities

1   Describe the main features of the houses in the BEDZED development.

2   The BEDZED development is called a 'socio-economic' community. Why is this?

3   Suggest why residents of BEDZED have a smaller ecological footprint than the average for the UK.

4   What elements of BEDZED could be used to reduce energy in other residential areas?

Sustainable urban living – the Greenhouse development

What is 'Greenhouse'?

Greenhouse is part of the new South Leeds **urban regeneration** scheme, located within a 10-minute walk of Leeds city centre and close to the main railway station and motorway network (Map **A**). A disused former industrial building will be redeveloped (Photo **B**) to form part of the first **carbon-zero** mixed-use development in the UK which produces energy more than it uses. The development will have 172 one-, two- and three-bedroom **eco-homes** and offices, all set around a communal landscaped courtyard.

The Greenhouse development is part of a larger urban regeneration scheme which also includes:

- shops and cafés
- a medical centre and nursery
- parks with children's playgrounds
- a sports centre, with a swimming pool
- a conference centre with a full range of business facilities
- high-tech offices
- allotments where people can grow fruit and vegetables.

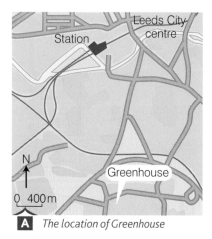

A *The location of Greenhouse*

B *Artist's impression of homes in the new Greenhouse development*

C *Rooftop solar panels like these will provide hot water for every home*

Key terms

Urban regeneration: improving social and/or economic conditions in run-down urban areas.

Carbon-zero: does not use resources that create carbon dioxide.

Eco-homes: homes that have a minimum impact on the environment.

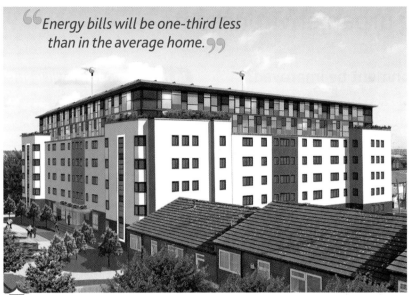

"*Energy bills will be one-third less than in the average home.*"

D *Artist's impression of the Greenhouse development with its wind turbines*

What makes the Greenhouse development sustainable?

In order to minimise carbon emissions and make the development as environmentally friendly and sustainable as possible, the following features have been included:

Energy generation

- Ground-source heat pumps draw water from 80 metres below the building and use heat-exchange technology to provide hot water, heating and air cooling.
- One large wind turbine will provide electricity for every home, as well as for local businesses.
- Smaller rooftop wind turbines will provide electricity to light corridors and outside spaces (Diagram **D**).
- Rooftop solar panels (like those in Photo **C**) will be used to provide hot water for every home.

Energy-saving technology

- A 'super-insulation' system will keep the homes warm in winter and cool in summer.
- Double-glazing units will reduce heat loss.
- Low-energy washing machines and appliances are provided in each home.

Transportation

- A car club of vehicles powered by renewable energy is available for residents to use.
- 'Green' cabs and buses using renewable energy run between the development and the city centre.
- Every home will have cycle storage, and free cycle hire will be available.

Resource management

- Allotments are available so that residents can grow their own food.
- Recycling facilities are provided.

Did you know ??????

Energy use in buildings is responsible for nearly 50 per cent of all carbon emissions in the UK. Reducing the use of fossil fuel energy sources and making buildings more energy efficient are therefore important ways of tackling climate change.

AQA **Examiner's tip**

Always try to use geographical words in your answers where possible.

∞ **links**

Learn more about the Greenhouse development at **www.greenhouseleeds.co.uk**

Activities

1   Explain how the Greenhouse development has created a local community rather than just a housing estate.

2   Why are the links to Leeds city centre seen as an important part of the development?

3   Using Diagrams **B** and **D** to help you, describe the main features of the Greenhouse development.

4   Suggest why energy bills will be one-third less than in the average UK home.

extension   On the advertising literature the developer uses the phrase 'eco-homes that don't cost the Earth'. Explain the point that the developer is trying to make.

How can the urban environment be improved?

In the past, large urban areas were often developed as industrial or commercial centres that required continued building development, usually at the expense of **green space**. At the same time urban waterways were frequently used as dumping grounds for industrial and human waste. Economic development was often seen as more important than environmental protection and as a result the environmental quality of many urban areas suffered.

In recent years many urban authorities have put restoration schemes in place in an attempt to improve the physical and built environment.

Why spend money restoring the urban environment?

Having a clean and attractive urban environment brings a number of social and economic advantages, including:

- improving living conditions for urban residents
- encouraging people to want to live in urban areas
- attracting new businesses and a more sustainable economic future
- encouraging visitors and the development of tourism.

The following examples show how urban environments can be made better places to live and work.

Cleaning up the Singapore River and the Kallang Basin

The Singapore River and the Kallang Basin are a major river catchment and port area on the southern part of the island of Singapore. Major industrial and population growth in the area during the 1960s and 1970s turned the river basin into what was described as 'a black, foul-smelling waterway devoid of any aquatic life'. The reasons for this were:

- raw sewage from squatter settlements flowing into the river
- the river basin being used as a dumping ground by farmers and residents
- chemical pollution from heavy industry and ships discharging polluted water into the basin.

What has been done to improve the environment?

The Singapore government put into place an environmental action plan to clean up the area. Included in the plan was the movement of squatter settlements into proper residential areas with sanitation facilities, the development of industrial estates with strict pollution controls, and the removal of chicken and pig farms from alongside the river.

Once the sources of pollution were removed the whole area began to recover. Riverside walkways and parks have been built and thousands of trees planted. The beach alongside Kallang Basin has been improved and recreational facilities developed (Photo **A**).

A *Kallang Basin today*

In 2008 the government announced a further plan to 'transform the waterfront into a gathering place for recreational and cultural activities' by building a national stadium, a range of leisure developments and further residential developments.

'Greening' urban areas

'Greening' urban areas is about increasing the amount of green space in towns and cities. It can be done by:

- developing green gardens on the roofs of buildings (Photo **B**)
- planting trees alongside roads, railway lines, canals and walkways (Diagram **C**)
- developing open spaces and parks.

B *A roof garden on City Hall, Chicago, provides a place to relax at lunchtime and cools the building down in summer*

⚭ links

Learn more about green spaces at **www.cnn.com/justimagine** → living spaces → parks in unusual places

C *A former train track in New York forms a ribbon of green space in one of the busiest parts of the city*

Why develop green spaces?

Developing green spaces in urban areas is not just about making a place look nice. It also has a number of other advantages including:

- increasing permeable surfaces helps to absorb rainfall, reducing the risk of urban flooding
- reducing noise pollution
- absorbing excessive heat in summer and making areas more comfortable
- providing community space and meeting places
- providing a more relaxing, cleaner environment that may improve people's health.

Activities

1 Suggest how the urban environment may be damaged if it becomes too developed.

2 a Using Photo **A** to help you, describe the main features of the Kallang Basin in Singapore.

   b Explain how the Kallang Basin environment has been improved.

3 Consider the idea that 'developing green spaces is not only about making an area look nicer'.

extension

a Describe and explain what is meant by the term 'urban heat island'.

b Suggest how your local urban environment may increase its green space.

What is an eco-town?

In 2007 it was announced that the government would give permission for a number of eco-towns to be built in England. These will be entirely new settlements of between 5,000 and 15,000 houses and will be the first large-scale **eco-settlements** ever built in the UK. Each eco-town will be carbon-neutral and community based, with its own shopping area and local schools. They will each have good transport links to surrounding towns and cities for jobs and services.

Fifteen sites across England were identified as potential sites for the first eco-towns. From these, ten have been selected for development. They include old industrial sites, disused airfields and former Ministry of Defence land (Map **A**).

Why are they being built?

The eco-towns will provide over 100,000 new houses and will be used as examples to show house builders how sustainable building methods may be used.

The eco-town debate

Supporters of the eco-town plan say that the settlements will provide healthy and sustainable environments and 'encourage community involvement'. However, local residents near a number of the proposed eco-towns are concerned because they feel that the development may damage existing countryside and increase traffic problems.

> **In this section you will learn:**
> about the characteristics of eco-towns
>
> that the development of eco-towns may create pressures and conflicts in some areas.

> **Key terms**
>
> Eco-settlements: settlements that do not harm the environment because they meet the needs of people without damaging the environment or exploiting resources.

> **Did you know** ? ? ? ? ? ?
>
> Using energy-efficient building techniques and rainwater recycling methods can reduce energy and water use by up to 50 per cent.

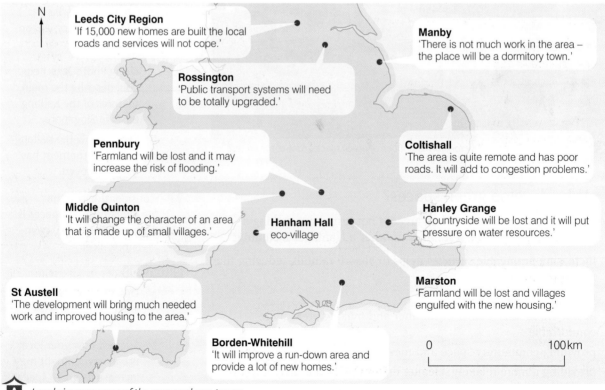

N

Leeds City Region
'If 15,000 new homes are built the local roads and services will not cope.'

Manby
'There is not much work in the area – the place will be a dormitory town.'

Rossington
'Public transport systems will need to be totally upgraded.'

Pennbury
'Farmland will be lost and it may increase the risk of flooding.'

Coltishall
'The area is quite remote and has poor roads. It will add to congestion problems.'

Middle Quinton
'It will change the character of an area that is made up of small villages.'

Hanham Hall
eco-village

Hanley Grange
'Countryside will be lost and it will put pressure on water resources.'

Marston
'Farmland will be lost and villages engulfed with the new housing.'

St Austell
'The development will bring much needed work and improved housing to the area.'

Borden-Whitehill
'It will improve a run-down area and provide a lot of new homes.'

0   100km

A *Local views on some of the proposed eco-towns*

Hanham Hall, the UK's first eco-village

The first eco-village to be built in the UK will be at Hanham Hall, a disused hospital site near Bristol. The house builder, Barratt, has been chosen to build the eco-village with the aim to 'create carbon-zero homes and eco-lifestyles' and show what may be done in the larger planned eco-towns.

Key features

The eco-village will be a community of 200 homes set in open parklands and will have the following features:

Community

- local shops, cafés and a restaurant
- local schools and nursery facilities
- a community hall
- farmers' shops selling local food
- office space for local businesses/home workers.

Transport and parking

- a car sharing club
- bicycle storage facilities
- car parking zones separating people from vehicles
- links to the local public transport network.

Energy

The development will be powered by a biomass power station producing energy and hot water.

Environmental management

Sustainable environmental management will include:

- recycling facilities
- open green space/play areas
- hedges around gardens/tree planting
- allotments for growing food
- cycle and walking routes.

The development will include 'The Sustainable Living Centre', a permanent exhibition and visitor centre.

⚭ links

Learn more about Hanham Hall at **www.hanhamhall.co.uk**

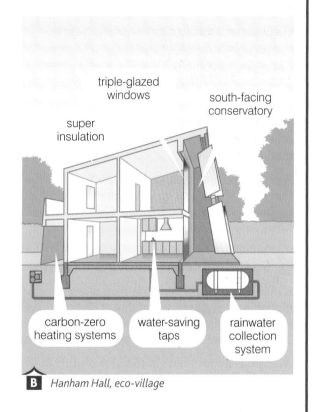

triple-glazed windows

super insulation

south-facing conservatory

carbon-zero heating systems

water-saving taps

rainwater collection system

B *Hanham Hall, eco-village*

Activities

1 a What are the advantages of the eco-town plan?
   b Explain why some people are unhappy about the eco-town proposals.

2 a Describe the main features of the Hanham Hall eco-village.
   b Explain why the Hanham Hall eco-village is considered to be environmentally friendly.

extension   What is meant by the term 'eco-lifestyle'?

AQA Examiner's tip

Be able to describe the main characteristics of an eco-settlement.

Can cities be sustainable?

For a city to be truly sustainable it needs to be capable of providing a good standard of living for its residents and have a neutral effect on its surroundings.

In order to achieve this it will have to:

- generate all its power from renewable methods
- recycle and reuse as much waste as possible
- collect and manage its own water supply
- develop a fully integrated transport system that creates a limited amount of pollution
- provide good-quality housing for its residents
- preserve and manage the environment and develop green space throughout the city.

Is all this possible?

Planners and architects say that it is not only possible to create more sustainable cities, it is vital because the world is going to become increasingly urban in the future. The following example from China shows how the cities of the future may look.

Sustainable urban living – China

In the last 10 years China has seen massive urban growth as millions of people move to industrial towns and cities seeking work. This rapid growth has created a number of problems for urban areas – today China has some of the most polluted cities on Earth.

The challenge for China in the 21st century is to provide urban areas that are environmentally sustainable and able to cope with the continued flood of migrants. In order to do this the Chinese government has announced plans for five eco-cities, each housing between 500,000 and 1 million people. The first of these planned eco-cities is Dongtan, which is being built on the island of Chongming, across the river from Shanghai (Map **A**).

The Chongming wetlands, where the eco-city is being built, is a site of environmental importance, so special care is being taken. A new 3.5 km 'buffer zone' is being left between the wetlands and the new city. The city will be connected to Shanghai by a 25 km bridge and a tunnel, providing both road and rail links.

In this section you will learn:

what is meant by the term 'sustainable city'

how urban planning can make cities increasingly sustainable.

Did you know ??????

Green areas in cities produce oxygen and absorb carbon dioxide, improving air quality. They also provide areas for storm drainage and wildlife habitats.

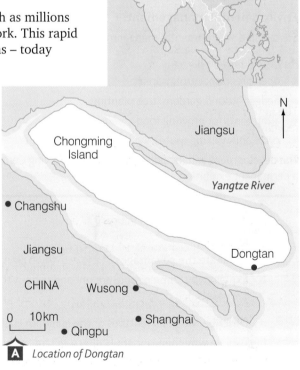

A *Location of Dongtan*

Key features of Dongtan

Work

Industrial and commercial areas will provide local employment opportunities (Diagram **B**).

Residential areas

Homes will be built alongside canals and will have wind micro-turbines to reduce energy bills. Housing will be based on small communities with local shops, schools, nurseries and a health centre (Diagram **C**).

The environment

Sixty per cent of the land will be green space; pollution regulations will be enforced.

Transport

Dongtan will have a fully integrated public transport system, solar-powered water taxis and hydrogen fuel-cell cars. Cycle paths and pedestrian walkways will reduce vehicle use.

Energy

Rice waste will be used to fuel a power station, creating 65% of energy needs. The remainder of energy needs will be supplied by solar and wind power.

Waste

The aim is to achieve 90% waste recycling, with human sewage processed for composting and waste water processed for use in farming.

B *Artist's impression of the harbour, Dongtan*   *Source: Arup*

C *Artist's impression of East Village and East Lake, Dongtan*   *Source: Arup*

The Dongtan development plan

2009: Bridge/tunnel link to Shanghai to be completed.

2010: First housing phase to be completed.

2020: Industrial/commercial phase to be completed, population at 80,000.

2050: City to be completed, population at 500,000.

Activities

1   Describe and explain the features that a city needs for it to be sustainable.

2   a   Describe the characteristics of Dongtan.

   b   Suggest why the transport link to Shanghai is an important part of the plan.

   c   Do you think that Dongtan will be sustainable? Explain your answer.

extension   Masdar is being planned as a totally sustainable city in the United Arab Emirates (UAE). Use the internet to investigate the plan – look at **www.hughpearman.com** → Articles → 2008 → Building the world's new eco-cities.

Find out ...

Dongtan is being planned by a British engineering company, Arup. Use the internet to find out more about this development.

3.1 The effects of earthquakes and volcanoes

Earthquakes and volcanoes are responsible for considerable loss of life, property and livelihoods (Table **A**). As they cannot be accurately predicted, the effects of earthquakes tend to be more destructive. However, on occasions volcanoes do erupt suddenly and with explosive force. They can send clouds of red-hot ash and dust hurtling down mountainsides at over 150 km/h. These pyroclastic flows are responsible for many of the deaths resulting from volcanic eruptions.

In this section you will learn:

about the primary and secondary damage caused by earthquakes and volcanoes

some case studies of the damage caused by an earthquake and a volcanic eruption.

A *Effects of volcanic eruptions and earthquakes*

Volcanic eruptions	Earthquakes
Primary effects (caused directly by the volcanic)	**Primary effects** (caused by shaking and ground movement)
Buildings destroyed by fires, explosions, weight of ash; crops/livestock destroyed	Buildings collapse, roads crack, bridges collapse, glass shatters, gas pipes break, electricity pylons fall, water pipes break
Secondary effects	**Secondary effects**
Mudflows, changes in landscape/climate, food/water supply disrupted, homelessness, businesses forced to close, cost of insurance claims, unemployment	Fires, explosions, floods, homelessness, tsunamis, diseases, landslides, businesses forced to close, cost of insurance claims, unemployment

The following case studies show some of the damaging effects of volcanic eruptions and earthquakes.

Case study

Tungurahua volcano in Ecuador erupts, August 2006

The Tungurahua volcano (Map **B**), whose name means 'throat of fire', blasted a 10 km high ash cloud into the sky (Photo **C**), along with larger pieces of rock called volcanic bombs. Huge flows of lava ran down the mountainside. The ash covered an area of 740 by 180 km with up to 5 cm of ash. Pyroclastic flows raced down the north-western slopes, destroying 7 villages and making 5,000 people homeless. Six people lost their lives and falling volcanic rocks injured many more. People tried to protect their heads by covering them with blankets and buckets, as they fled the area. Many suffered breathing difficulties due to the hot ash. The lava and ash covered the fertile farmlands, destroying the crops. Livestock were lost. Many farmers were left with nothing. Roads were impassable and rivers were clogged up with ash. The nearby hydroelectric plant was shut down, as were local airports.

AQA Examiner's tip

Be clear as to the differences between primary and secondary effects of both earthquakes and volcanic activity. Learn at least three examples of each effect.

Key terms

Primary effects: those resulting directly from the event itself.

Secondary effects: those that result from the primary effects.

Tsunamis: large ocean waves caused by an underwater earthquake.

Richter scale: a measure of earthquake strength.

Aftershocks: smaller tremors occurring after an earthquake.

B *Location of the Tungurahua volcano*

C *Tungurahua volcano*

Earthquake hits Yogyakarta, Java (Indonesia), May 2006

An earthquake measuring 6.3 on the **Richter scale** caused a huge amount of damage to Yogyakarta near the coast of Java (Map **D**). Almost 6,000 people lost their lives and 37,000 were injured, with many having to be treated at the roadside or in temporary clinics, as hospitals were damaged.

About 154,000 houses were destroyed and many more were damaged, leaving 1.5 million people homeless. People were trapped under the rubble of collapsed buildings, many of which were smaller, older houses (Photo **E**). A worker for a non-governmental organisation said: 'I was shaken from my bed … furniture was falling and concrete chunks started falling from my hotel room … people were running out in panic, in their bedclothes.' They feared that the earthquake might cause a tsunami like the one that followed the 2004 earthquake. Luckily this did not happen, but the earthquake did cause an eruption of the nearby Merapi volcano, which sent debris 3.5 km into the air.

Aftershocks forced medics to move injured people outdoors, for fear of further building collapse. Many survivors had gathered a few belongings and were sleeping outside. Plastic tents were set up on a nearby football pitch.

The area is one of great cultural importance and a Hindu temple complex was badly damaged, as were ancient royal palaces. This has resulted in a loss of income from tourism. Many small businesses such as silver handicrafts, earthenware pottery and weaving, were destroyed, and 82,000 people lost their livelihoods. The overall cost of the damage was put at US $3 billion.

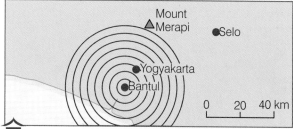

D   *Location of the Yogyakarta earthquake*

E   *Collapsed buildings in Yogyakarta*

Activities

1. a Describe the location of the Tungurahua volcano in Ecuador.
    b Draw a table to show the primary and secondary effects of the Tungurahua volcanic eruption.

2. a Describe the location of the Yogyakarta earthquake.
    b Draw a table to show the primary and secondary effects of the Yogyakarta earthquake.

extension   Conduct some research to investigate why the effects of earthquakes might be more damaging in a less developed country such as Indonesia.

Did you know ??????

The deadliest ever earthquake was in the Shaanxi Province of China in 1556. More than 830,000 people lost their lives. In recent times, the 2004 earthquake in Indonesia, which caused a **tsunami** in the Indian Ocean, claimed 283,100 lives.

∞ links

Learn more about earthquakes at **www.earthquake.usgs.gov**

3.2 The causes of earthquakes and volcanoes

The **Earth's crust** is divided into a number of **tectonic plates** (Map **A**). These plates float on the **mantle** and are moved a few centimetres each year by convection currents deep inside the Earth. Earthquakes and volcanoes occur in long, narrow belts at places where the plates meet (Map **A**). At some plate boundaries the plates are moving towards each other, at other places the plates are moving away from each other.

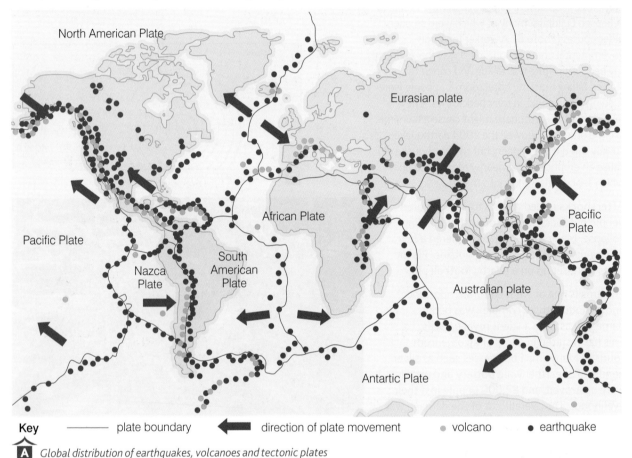

Key —— plate boundary ⬅ direction of plate movement ● volcano ● earthquake

A Global distribution of earthquakes, volcanoes and tectonic plates

What is a destructive plate boundary?

Where plates move towards each other, the thin oceanic crust is forced beneath the thicker continental crust to form a subduction zone. A deep ocean trench forms as the ocean floor is pulled downwards and the continental crust is buckled to form mountain ranges (Diagram **B**). As the oceanic crust is forced downwards, it starts to melt and form new **magma**. This is due to the friction between the moving plates and the intense heat in the mantle. The newly formed magma is less dense than that in the mantle and rises, reaching the surface through cracks in the crust and erupting to form volcanoes. Where the magma rises offshore, volcanic island arcs are formed. As the plates move against each other, pressure builds up. A sudden movement of the plate releases this pressure and the shockwaves cause earthquakes at the surface.

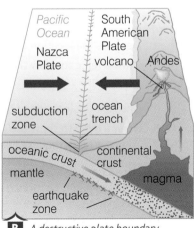

B A destructive plate boundary

■ What is a constructive plate boundary?

Where plates move away from each other, new crust is formed as magma rises from the mantle (Diagram **C**). Frequent volcanic eruptions form large ridges, up to 3,000 metres above the ocean floor. These are known as mid-ocean ridges, along which volcanic islands rise above the ocean surface. Along the Mid-Atlantic Ridge the seafloor is 'spreading' by between 1 and 5 cm each year. The Eurasian and African plates are moving away from the North and South American plates due to this process of continental drift.

■ What is a conservative plate boundary?

Where plates slide sideways past each other, no new crust is formed and no crust is destroyed. Therefore very few volcanic eruptions occur, but earthquakes are frequent and often very strong. The plates may lock together as they move and pressure builds up. As they snap loose, shockwaves cause violent earthquakes at the surface. An example of a conservative plate boundary can be seen on the western coast of the USA (Diagram **D**).

Key terms

Earth's crust: the solid, outer layer of the Earth.

Tectonic plates: large segments of the Earth's crust.

Mantle: the layer of the Earth between the crust and the core.

Magma: liquid rock below the Earth's surface.

Did you know ??????

- The strongest recorded earthquake was magnitude 9.5 in Chile on 22 May 1960.
- 500,000 detectable earthquakes occur in the world each year. 100,000 of these can be felt, and 100 of them cause damage.

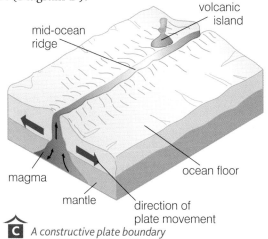

C *A constructive plate boundary*

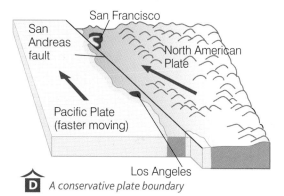

D *A conservative plate boundary*

Activities

1   Describe the distribution of earthquakes and volcanic eruptions.

2   What is meant by the term 'continental drift'?

3   Copy and complete the table below.

Type of plate boundary	Plate movement	Type of hazard found	Examples of plate movement
Destructive			Nazca plate meets South American plate
Constructive		Earthquakes and volcanoes	
Conservative	Plates slide sideways past each other		

AQA *Examiner's tip*

Learn the diagram of a destructive plate boundary and ensure that you can add at least four labels to it.

⊂⊃links

Learn more about plate boundaries at www.earthquake.usgs.gov/eqcenter/

extension   Explain the causes of the eruption of the Tungurahua volcano in Ecuador and the earthquake in Yogyakarta, Indonesia (see pages 62–3).

3.3 Living with tectonic hazards

Despite the hazards, many people continue to live in earthquake zones or areas close to volcanoes. As tectonic hazards occur relatively infrequently, they might feel that a major volcanic eruption will never happen in their lifetime, or that an earthquake will never strike their particular location. It may also be a case of 'there's no place like home'. After living in the same area for many generations, families develop a strong sense of heritage. Family and friends live in the area and they do not want to move elsewhere. In many less developed countries people simply cannot afford to move away, or it may be that as population pressure increases, more people are forced to live in areas of risk. In some cities building regulations do not allow development on areas that are at risk of **liquefaction**, but illegal shacks are sometimes built in these areas.

Volcanic areas offer many economic advantages (Diagram **A**). Many people live in these areas because the benefits outweigh the possible risks.

In this section you will learn:

the reasons why people live in earthquake zones and in areas close to volcanoes.

Key terms

Liquefaction: the loss of strength that can occur in the ground during earthquake shaking.

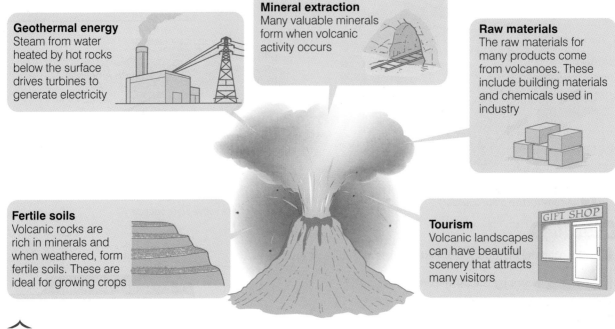

Geothermal energy
Steam from water heated by hot rocks below the surface drives turbines to generate electricity

Mineral extraction
Many valuable minerals form when volcanic activity occurs

Raw materials
The raw materials for many products come from volcanoes. These include building materials and chemicals used in industry

Fertile soils
Volcanic rocks are rich in minerals and when weathered, form fertile soils. These are ideal for growing crops

Tourism
Volcanic landscapes can have beautiful scenery that attracts many visitors

GIFT SHOP

 A Benefits of volcanic areas

Geothermal power

Geothermal power is widely used in places such as New Zealand, Hawaii and the volcanic island of Iceland, where it provides 70 per cent of energy needs. The Geysers field in northern California (USA) is the largest geothermal development in the world and provides enough energy for the city of San Francisco and its 765,000 people.

Geothermal energy is a renewable energy source which is clean and sustainable. Geothermal power plants release less than 1 per cent of the CO_2 emissions of a fossil fuel power plant and the steam and water are constantly reused.

Did you know ??????

- 500 million people live close to active volcanoes.

- Steamboat in Yellowstone National Park (USA) is the largest geyser in the world; it pulsates like a massive steam engine when it erupts, reaching heights of over 100 metres.

Tourism

Tourism is now an important activity in many volcanic areas. People get jobs in hotels and restaurants, in the making and selling of souvenirs, in transport and as tour guides. People flock to marvel at eruptions and there are trails, viewpoints and visitor centres provided for them. Other volcanic features also attract tourists; hot springs and mudbaths have long attracted people because of their health benefits. Geysers such as Old Faithful (Photo **B**) in Yellowstone National Park (USA) are major tourist attractions.

Agriculture

Lava breaks down quickly to form fertile soil, especially in a hot, wet climate. Hawaii produces crops such as sugar, coffee and pineapples on volcanic soils that have taken less than 100 years to form.

Minerals

In volcanic areas, heated groundwater concentrates traces of minerals such as copper, gold, silver, and tin into rich veins. These are mined, along with precious stones such as diamonds. Many worked-out goldmines have now become tourist attractions in their own right.

B *Old Faithful*

Is it worth the risk?

Many people living in areas of tectonic hazards believe that advances in science and technology will make life safer for them. Whilst many volcanoes are closely monitored and people are evacuated when there are signs of an eruption, it is still impossible to accurately predict when an earthquake will occur. Much research has been done on this subject – especially in Japan, where the entire population is at risk from earthquakes – but with little success. In California (USA), despite the history of earthquakes, increasing numbers of people want to live there. Attractions such as opportunities for well-paid jobs and a pleasant climate and lifestyle, make it worth the risk.

> **AQA Examiner's tip**
>
> There are potential benefits of living in areas that experience tectonic hazards. Learn some of these benefits in relation to specific locations.

> **Activities**
>
> Write a paragraph to explain how each of the following might benefit local people.
>
> **1** Volcanic scenery.
>
> **2** Material erupted from a volcano.
>
> **3** Heat beneath a volcano.
>
> **extension** Use the internet to find out more about the ways in which one volcano is of benefit to people, for example Vesuvius (Italy), Mount Merapi (Indonesia), Mount St Helens (USA).

⊂⊃links

Learn more about particular volcanic features in the USA and Iceland at **www.nps.gov/yell** and **www.energy.rochester.edu/is/reyk**

If people plan and prepare for earthquakes, then the risks can be reduced. Advances in building design means that many new buildings are 'earthquake proof' (Diagram **A**). Older buildings can be **retrofitted** to strengthen them in order to reduce the effects of earthquake shaking (Photo **B**).

In this section you will learn:

how people can plan and prepare for an earthquake

what actions people can take following an earthquake.

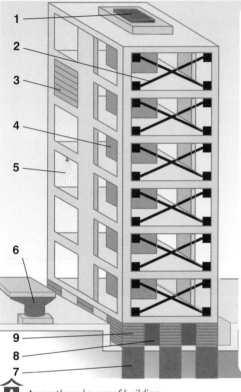

1 Computer controlled, movable roof weights to counter the shock waves.
2 Cross-bracing to give added strength and prevent twisting.
3 Automatic window shutters to prevent falling glass.
4 Sheer core of reinforced concrete and tensioned cables around lift shaft.
5 Automatic sprinkler system and gas shut-off to prevent fires.
6 Strengthened steel and reinforced concrete road supports.
7 Foundations set deep into the ground.
8 Rubber shock absorbers.
9 Base isolator allows sideways motion.

A An earthquake-proof building

B The building in the background has been retrofitted

Earthquake proofing and retrofitting are very expensive and may not be affordable in some countries. However, the use of **appropriate technology** can protect people in less developed countries. Over 1 billion people around the world now live in bamboo houses. This is because bamboo is very strong, yet bends easily and has been proven to withstand much earthquake shaking. In Costa Rica (Central America) 70 hectares of bamboo plantation will build 1,000 houses: to grow the same amount of timber would require 600 hectares. Also, only a tiny proportion of the energy needed to make steel is needed to process the bamboo. When a strong earthquake hit Costa Rica in January 2009, all of the bamboo houses at its **epicentre** survived without damage. In Gujarat, India, basic houses designed to withstand earthquakes are being built from local and recycled materials (Diagram **C**).

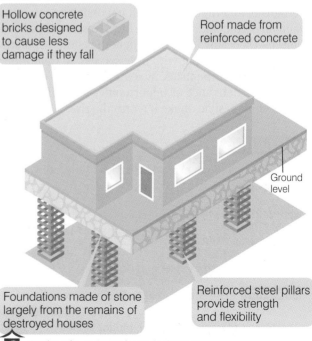

Hollow concrete bricks designed to cause less damage if they fall

Roof made from reinforced concrete

Ground level

Foundations made of stone largely from the remains of destroyed houses

Reinforced steel pillars provide strength and flexibility

C Earthquake-resistant house in Gujarat

■ What is earthquake preparedness?

If people are aware of what actions to take before, during and after an earthquake, then the number of casualties can be reduced (Figure **D**). In many areas earthquake preparation is taught in schools and there are regular 'drills' involving local people and the emergency services. In Japan 'Disaster Prevention Day' is held each year on 1 September, the date on which the Great Kanto earthquake struck Tokyo in 1923. People are reminded of what to do in the event of an earthquake.

Earthquake shaking maps can help with planning and responding to emergencies and targeting aid. Computer-generated scenarios show the intensity of ground shaking at different locations (Map **E**). People can be made aware of the level of risk in the area where they live and put in place the necessary levels of protection. The maps also help the authorities draw up **building codes**. In areas of intense shake, or areas at risk from liquefaction, codes would specify a high level of 'earthquake proofing' on buildings.

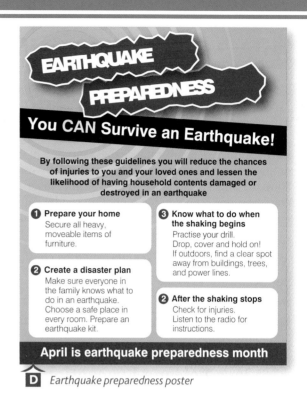

D   *Earthquake preparedness poster*

Key terms

Retrofitting: the addition of new technology to older buildings.

Appropriate technology: technology designed with consideration of the community it is intended for.

Epicentre: the point on the Earth's surface directly above the focus of an earthquake.

Building code: regulations which state how a building should be constructed in order for it to be safe.

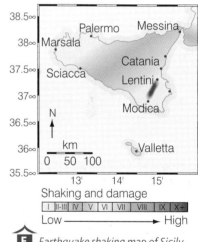

E   *Earthquake shaking map of Sicily*

Activities

1   Describe four ways in which buildings can be made to withstand an earthquake.

2   Suggest why the building methods used in Costa Rica and Gujarat are appropriate and sustainable.

3   Design your own poster to promote earthquake preparedness.

4   Give two ways in which earthquake shaking maps can benefit people.

extension   Suggest 10 items that you think should be included in an earthquake kit. (Page 76 may give you some ideas.) Explain why you chose each item.

AQA *Examiner's tip*

Be able to explain how both more developed and less developed countries have attempted to reduce the impact of earthquakes.

∞links

Learn more about preparing for earthquakes at www.earthquake.usgs.gov and www.fema.gov/hazard/earthquake

Reducing the effects of volcanoes

A volcanic eruption cannot be prevented, but the immense power of the volcano can be closely monitored. This reduces the risk of living near a volcano. Scientists look for increases in **seismic activity**, releases of volcanic gases and changes in the temperature or mineral content of nearby springs. The most noticeable sign that an eruption could occur are changes to the shape of the volcano. By using tilt meters to measure the angle of the slope of the volcano, **laser ranging** and aerial photographs, any bulges in the mountain can be detected. Mount St Helens (USA) bulged by 137 metres before it erupted in 1980.

If it is clear that a volcanic eruption is likely, then a course of action has to be decided upon. Several options could be considered, including:

- Restricting access to the area.
- Evacuating the area (see the article on Java and Map **C**).
- Reducing the effects of the eruption (see the article on Mount Etna and Photo **A**).

Java Volcano Evacuation Ordered

In May 2006, Indonesia's president ordered the **evacuation** of 17,000 people living near a volcano, which had been threatening to erupt. Mount Merapi, overlooking the city of Yogyakarta, was on orange code – the second highest alert level. As a precaution, the elderly, women and children in the danger zones were taken to emergency shelters. Two weeks later, the authorities raised the alert to the highest level – the red code – ordering the immediate evacuation of all residents on the mountain. In villages, horns were sounded to let people know they should leave. Army trucks were used to ferry thousands of people away from the danger zone. Some villagers did not want to leave their valuable farmland as they were worried about their property, cattle and crops being stolen. Most were eventually persuaded to evacuate.

Bulldozers move in on Mount Etna

Some 70 bulldozers have been used to build earth and rock walls to divert lava away from villages. Planes and helicopters have dropped water to cool the lava and slow it down,

A Bulldozers move in on Mount Etna

as they did in Iceland in 1983 when a lava flow threatened a nearby town. In the past the Italian authorities have used military bombing and dynamite to divert lava flows.

In this section you will learn:

how volcanoes can be monitored

how people can plan and prepare for a volcanic eruption

what actions people can take following an eruption.

Did you know ??????

Ash clouds may be so dense that they turn the sky pitch black. Ash severely restricts visibility and deadens sound. Very fine ash particles can stay in the atmosphere for many years, and be spread around the world by winds. Following the Mount St Helens eruption, ash travelled around the world twice. In the year following the eruption, the average global temperature fell by 1°C.

Key terms

Seismic activity: movements in the Earth's crust.

Laser ranging: using laser beams and mirrors to detect minute changes in the shape of the land.

Evacuation: movement of people away from a place of danger to a place of safety.

AQA Examiner's tip

Learn case studies covering volcanic eruptions in both more and less developed countries.

∞ links

Learn more about Mount St Helens at www.fs.fed.us/gpnf/mshnvm

■ How can people prepare for a volcanic eruption?

In areas where volcanoes emit large amounts of ash, a major risk is from roof collapse due to the weight of the ash. Improved building design can help to reduce injuries and lessons have been learned from areas that receive heavy snowfall. Flat-roofed buildings are most at risk of collapse and should not be constructed in areas where ash fall is common. Sloping roofs that are reinforced and made of smooth materials such as metal and glass are more likely to shed volcanic ash. Ash also corrodes roofs and suitable plastic coverings have now been developed. It can also damage computer and electrical systems and filter systems are increasingly installed in many buildings. Simpler methods include sealing doors and windows.

Through campaigns aimed at increasing awareness about what to do during a volcanic eruption, people are encouraged to keep towels and tape in an emergency kit, which should also include a torch, bottled water, wind-up radio, goggles and disposable breathing mask.

Thousands evacuated from danger zone

During the eruption of the Soufriere Hills volcano on Montserrat that began in 1995, access to the south of the island was restricted because of the danger (Map **B**). Around 5,000 people were evacuated to the northern part of the island and a further 7,000 left the island altogether.

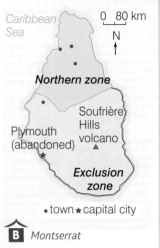

B Montserrat

Volcanic hazard maps (Map **C**) have been developed and are often available to local people on the internet, or are displayed in public buildings. They show areas most likely to be at risk from ash falls, lava flows or mudflows, for a number of different eruption scenarios. They can be useful for planning possible evacuation routes or future building projects.

C Hazard map for Mount Merapi (Indonesia)

Activities

1 Describe ways in which a volcano can be monitored.

2 Describe ways in which the actions taken by the authorities during the Mount Etna eruption differ from those taken during the Mount Merapi eruption.

3 a Suggest how each of the items included in the emergency kit might be of help to people in a volcanic eruption.

   b Suggest two other items that might be included in the emergency kit.

4 Suggest how volcanic hazard maps might be useful.

extension Find out why different actions are appropriate for different eruptions.

The high winds and torrential rain associated with a tropical storm are extremely damaging. Winds tear the roofs off buildings, or even cause them to collapse (Photo **A**). The poorer the construction of the building, the more likely it is to be destroyed.

A *Damage to buildings in Florida, USA*

During tropical storms trees are uprooted and fields of crops blown flat. Electricity lines can be blown down, causing power cuts in homes and businesses. Roads and other transport links become impassable, often hindering the emergency services.

The heavy rain causes extensive flooding, which can flush out sewers and lead to disease spreading. There can be much loss of life amongst people, livestock and wildlife. **Storm surges** can occur, flooding coastal areas (Diagram **B**). Table **C** shows some of the damaging effects of tropical storms.

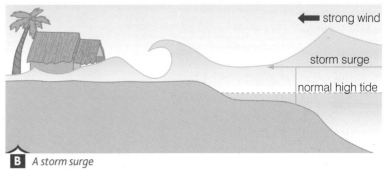
strong wind

storm surge

normal high tide

B *A storm surge*

C *Effects of tropical storms*

Type of damage	Effects
Physical and environmental	Structural damage to buildings, roads and other infrastructure, vehicles and other property destroyed, sensitive environments destroyed, loss of animal habitats, sea fish killed due to silting, freshwater fish killed in storm surges, fishing boats and other craft damaged
Social	People suffer trauma and stress, catch water-borne diseases, are displaced and communities broken up; food and water shortages, job losses due to damage to industries, civil unrest and looting
Economic	Costs of repair and insurance claims, loss of income as businesses close, crops destroyed and exports lost; oil prices may increase

Hurricane Hanna
Hurricanes batter Haiti

After being hit hard by Hurricane Fay on 15 August 2008 and Hurricane Gustav on 26 August 2008, Hurricane Hanna (Map **D**) unexpectedly made landfall with Haiti on 3 September 2008. As the hurricane was not expected to strike Haiti, people were unprepared and had no warnings to evacuate their homes. Consequently 550 people lost their lives. The city of Gonaives was badly damaged; many of the tin-roofed houses across the country were destroyed, leaving almost 1 million people homeless. Much of low-lying Gonaives was flooded, in some areas up to 3 metres deep. Thousands of people were left stranded on their rooftops. The ground was already saturated from the previous hurricanes and floodwaters rose quickly. Some roads and bridges were washed away and many roads were impassable. The only way out of Gonaives was by air or by wading through contaminated water (Photo **E**), which increased the risk of disease.

In other parts of Haiti, whole villages were buried as mudslides flowed quickly down hillsides. Already 98 per cent of the forests in the country had been removed and there was little natural defence from mudslides. Flimsy shacks were carried away and fields of crops destroyed, along with cows and goats, leaving many people without a source of food or income.

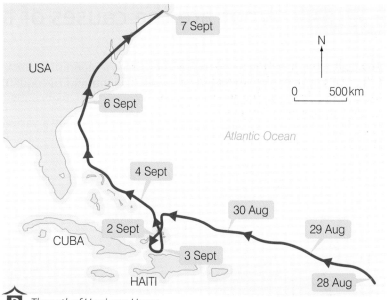

D *The path of Hurricane Hanna*

E *Flooding in Haiti*

United Nations troops had to supervise food aid distribution, fearing outbreaks of rioting, due to the large numbers of hungry people trying to obtain food. Three days later, Ike, a category 4 hurricane, also hit Haiti, claiming a further 74 lives and worsening the food crisis. The last bridge standing in Gonaives was washed away and the city was so badly damaged it was thought that it may have to be rebuilt elsewhere.

Activities

1 Group the effects shown in Table **C** into primary and secondary effects.

2 Describe the path of Hurricane Hanna.

3 Draw a table to show the physical and environmental, social and economic effects of a series of hurricanes on Haiti.

extension

a Find out about the effects of a recent tropical storm.

b Find out how heavy rainfall can lead to mudslides and landslides.

links

Learn more about predicting hurricanes at **www.nhc.noaa.gov**

Tropical storms occur in areas where sea surface temperatures are over 27°C. Most form between 10° and 30° north and south of the equator, rarely within 5° of the equator.

In different parts of the world tropical storms are known by a variety of local names (Map **A**).

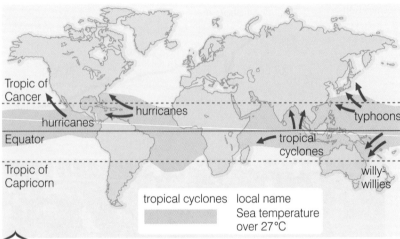

| tropical cyclones | local name |
| Sea temperature over 27°C |

A   Areas where tropical storms are found

Key terms

Tropical: situated in the area between the tropics of Cancer and Capricorn.

Eye: the calm, clear area at the centre of the tropical storm.

Track: the path taken by a tropical storm.

Tropical storms are large areas of low pressure or extreme depressions. On satellite images they show up as huge, swirling masses of cloud, with the **eye** clearly visible at the centre (Photo **B**).

How are tropical storms measured?

The strength of tropical storms is measured using the Saffir-Simpson scale (Table **C**). Diagram **D** shows the strength of tropical storms that occurred in different areas of the world during the 20th century.

C   The Saffir-Simpson scale

Category	Wind speed (km/h)	Effects
1	Strongest gusts 120–149	Damage to some crops, trees and caravans
2	Strongest gusts 150–79	Minor house damage, heavy crop damage
3	Strongest gusts 180–209	Some structural damage, power failure likely
4	Strongest gusts 210–249	Significant structural damage, widespread power failure
5	Strongest gusts greater than 250	Widespread destruction

B   Typhoon Aere moving over Taiwan in 2004

AQA   Examiner's tip

The formation of a tropical storm could appear in two types of question; one involving diagrams and the other asking for a more detailed written response. Make sure that you can tackle both tasks effectively.

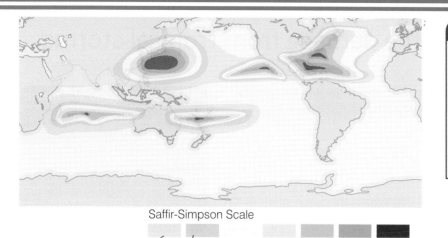

Saffir-Simpson Scale

tropical depression   tropical storm   1   2   3   4   5

D *The strengths of tropical storms in the 20th century*

∞links

Learn more about tropical storms at www.earthsci.org/flooding/unit1/ u1-05-01.html

What are the stages in the formation of a tropical storm?

The two essential ingredients needed for a tropical storm to develop are warm seas and warm, moist air. This is where they gain their energy (Diagram **E**).

1 Several thunderstorms drift over warm seas.

2 The warm air from the sea surface and the thunderstorms combine and warm air starts to rise.

3 More warm air rises and, due to the Earth's rotation, starts to move in a spiral. It cools and condenses, forming clouds, releasing much energy.

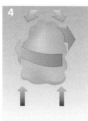

4 The air starts to rise faster and cooler air is sucked downwards. Wind speed starts to increase.

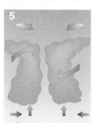

5 The tropical storm moves over the ocean, picking up warm, moist air. Wind speeds reach more than 120 km/h as more cold air is drawn into the eye.

E *Stages in the formation of a tropical storm*

The tropical storms **track** westwards and eventually make landfall. As they cross the land, they lose the source of their energy and start to reduce in strength.

Activities

1   Use an atlas to name two countries affected by tropical storms in each of the following continents: Asia, North America, Australasia.

2   By what name is a tropical storm known in each of the following areas: North Indian Ocean, North West Pacific Ocean, North Atlantic Ocean, South West Pacific Ocean?

3   Describe the location of the areas in which the most category 4 and 5 tropical storms occurred in the 20th century (Map **D**).

4   Draw a series of annotated diagrams to show how a tropical storm develops.

extension   Use the internet to find out how the weather conditions change as a tropical storm passes over a place. Explain why these changes take place.

In order to reduce the damage from tropical storms, people are advised to follow these three steps:

forecast → prepare → act

Forecast

The development and movement of tropical storms are closely monitored by agencies such as the National Hurricane Center (Atlantic) and the Joint Typhoon Warning Centre (Pacific). Warnings are issued to places where a tropical storm is likely to strike, but it is difficult to predict their movement with complete accuracy. The speed and path of a tropical storm are affected by many factors, which make them very unpredictable (see Hurricane Hanna on page 73). Map **A** shows the forecast for the path that Hurricane Katrina was expected to take after 26 August 2005.

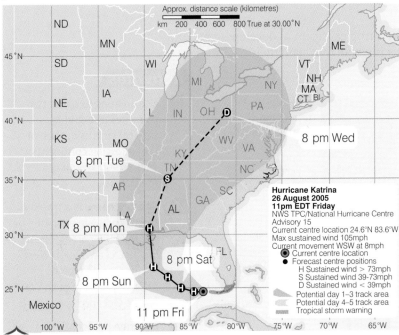

Hurricane Katrina
26 August 2005
11pm EDT Friday
NWS TPC/National Hurricane Centre
Advisory 15
Current centre location 24.6°N 83.6°W
Max sustained wind 105mph
Current movement WSW at 8mph
◉ Current centre location
● Forecast centre positions
  H Sustained wind > 73mph
  S Sustained wind 39-73mph
  D Sustained wind < 39mph
Potential day 1–3 track area
Potential day 4–5 track area
Tropical storm warning

A   *Forecast map for Hurricane Katrina*

Forecasts are available for residents to access on the internet, and are regularly updated. The forecast map includes an area or 'cone' of uncertainty, where the hurricane may strike within a 3-day or 5-day period. People who live within the area should prepare for the possibility that the hurricane could hit them.

Prepare

Many countries now have education programmes to try and raise awareness on how to prepare for and respond to a tropical storm. School lessons, posters and leaflets give advice on drawing up a family disaster plan, putting together an emergency kit and

Did you know ??????

Forecasters analyse large amounts of weather data and use complex computer modelling, but still only have a 20–25% chance of knowing exactly where a tropical storm will strike 48 hours in advance.

AQA Examiner's tip

Give examples to demonstrate how people can prepare for, and respond to, a tropical storm.

Key terms

Mandatory evacuation: an evacuation that is commanded by the authorities.

∞ links

Learn more about preparing for tropical storms at **www.redcross.org.uk** → overseas → preparing for disasters

B   *A hurricane emergency kit*

simple methods of protecting homes from strong winds and flying debris (Photo **B** and Leaflet **C**). In some areas, buildings are designed and built using materials that have been tested in storm simulators. Windproof tiles, water-resistant windows and strengthened building structures have now been developed, although these are very expensive. In areas at risk from storm surges, the ground floor walls of buildings are designed to wash out, leaving only the supports. This allows waves to wash through the building, rather than destroying it.

Most people in less developed countries, such as Bangladesh, are unable to afford the same protection as those in richer countries like the USA. With the help of non-governmental organisations (NGOs), simple yet effective measures are being put in place to protect people from the cyclones that strike the country (Photo **D** and Illustration **E**).

HURRICANE PREPAREDNESS WEEK
MAY 24th-31st

- Check for storm information on the internet. Listen to local TV and radio
- Board up windows or secure storm shutters
- Fasten roof straps
- Secure large items of furniture
- Turn off gas and electricity
- Put together a hurricane kit

BE RED CROSS READY   Get a kit   Make a plan   Be informed

C *Hurricane advice leaflet*

We are educating women in what to wear in case they have to swim during a cyclone.

We are building homes on stilts in case of a storm surge.

D *A cyclone shelter in Bangladesh*

We are building cyclone shelters (Photo **D**).

We are training local people to organise others in an evacuation.

 E *NGO schemes in Bangladesh*

▮ Act

When a tropical storm has been forecast evacuation plans can be put in place (Article **F**).

One million people along the coast of Texas in the USA were evacuated as Hurricane Ike approached in September 2008. In parts of Galveston, much of which is on low-lying islands, there was a **mandatory evacuation** order. Due to educational campaigns, those outside the danger area did not move out, leaving the highways clear for those in most danger. Over 1,350 buses helped transport people to higher ground.

 F *Evacuating a high risk area*

1. Suggest how forecasting the path of a tropical storm would help people who live in areas at risk.

2. Give five ways in which people might prepare for a tropical storm.

3. a Suggest how the items in the emergency kit (Photo **B**) might be of help to people in a tropical storm.

b Give two other items that might be included in the emergency kit.

4. Describe the cyclone shelter in Photo **D**. How would it protect people during a cyclone?

extension Using the internet, find information on a recent tropical storm. Describe how government, local authorities and NGOs helped the people affected.

3.9   More tropical storms to come?

There is disagreement as to whether or not the number and severity of tropical storms is changing (Illustration **A**). Many people believe that climate change, due to global warming, has caused an increase in the number of tropical storms and that this will increase further in the future. Others say that the number of tropical storms has stayed the same, but they are becoming more severe. Some scientists even go as far as saying that the number of tropical storms will start to decline in the future.

In this section you will learn:

how to make an informed judgement as to whether or not the number and severity of tropical storms is changing

about the nature of the changes to the number and severity of tropical storms.

▨ Why are opinions divided?

One reason for the uncertainty as to whether climate change is affecting tropical storms is that satellite technology has only been used to monitor them since the late 1960s. Before this, accounts from ships' logs, aeroplane research flights and simple weather recording instruments were used. This has led some scientists to believe that the number and strength of tropical storms in the past may have been greater than was actually recorded at the time. They also claim that there may have been some tropical storms occurring that we did not know about, as they did not hit land.

There appears to be a **natural cycle** of variations in the number of hurricanes. Graph **B** shows this cycle in the Atlantic Ocean.

The number of tropical storms has doubled in the last 100 years.

Due to global warming, the surfaces of tropical oceans have warmed up by 0.5 °C in the last few decades.

Technology predicts that the number of tropical storms will fall after 2080.

Short-term changes to the number of tropical storms may not be due to the actions of people.

Since 1995 hurricanes have become more frequent and intense.

Over the last 30 years, there have been more tropical storms with wind speeds of over 200 km/h.

We just do not have enough evidence linking global warming to changes in the number of tropical storms.

The changes to the number of tropical storms are part of the natural cycle. An active period started in 1995.

A   *Opinions about changes to tropical storms*

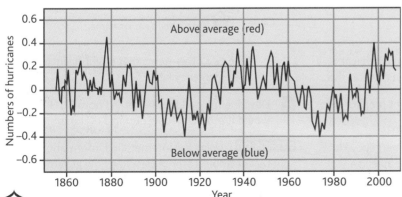

B   *Variations in the number of Atlantic hurricanes, 1856–2008*

Key terms

Natural cycle: series of events in nature that are repeated over and over again.

El Niño: a warming of the ocean surface off the western coast of South America.

Many believe that the actions of people are influencing the climate. They claim that in a period when the number of tropical storms is above average, they are becoming more powerful. Between 1995 and 2005, the average wind speed increased by 15 per cent and the length of the storms increased by 60 per cent. There are now more tropical storms reaching categories 4 and 5 than in the past (Graphs **C** and **D**). Perhaps it is the case that both global warming **and** natural variations affect the number of tropical storms.

■ Are tropical storms becoming more destructive?

Tropical storms do appear to be becoming more destructive, in terms of the costs of damage that they cause. In the USA, 6 out of the 10 most expensive hurricanes have occurred since 1990. In 2005, Hurricane Katrina caused damage estimated at over US $80 billion. In the past, coastlines threatened by typhoons or hurricanes were sparsely populated. Now, many people are more affluent and choose to live by or spend their holidays at the coast. The value of property by the coast has increased and much infrastructure is put in place as the population increases. With increased amounts of coastal development there is greater potential damage when tropical storms hit.

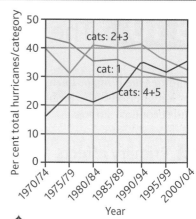

C   *Changes to categories of tropical storms*

∞ links

Learn more about predicting tropical storms at **www.gfdl.noaa.gov/global-warming-and-hurricanes**

Did you know ??????

The tropical storms with the highest ever winds speed of over 310 km/h were Typhoon Tip (1979), Typhoon Keith (1997), Hurricane Camille (1969) and Hurricane Allen (1980).

AQA *Examiner's tip*

Be able to argue both for and against the idea that the number of tropical storms, and the damaged caused is likely to increase.

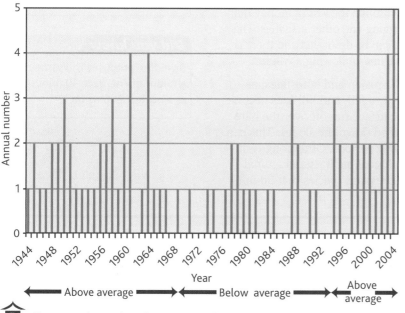

D   *Changes to the number of category 4 and 5 Atlantic hurricanes*

Activities

1   From Illustration **A**, draw a table to show the debate about change in the number and severity of tropical storms.

2   Suggest two reasons why data on tropical storms recorded before 1970 may be unreliable.

3   a   What evidence is there on Graphs **B** and **D** that there is a cycle of variation in the strength of tropical storms?

   b   What evidence is there on Graphs **C** and **D** that hurricanes are becoming more severe?

extension   Undertake research to find out how **El Niño** affects climate patterns. Is there a link to the number and severity of tropical storms?

3.10 The effects of wildfires

Wildfires are a major hazard as they can spread very quickly and burn for long periods. The problems they cause can be grouped into primary and secondary effects.

Primary effects

Primary effects include loss of life, injury, the destruction of property and possessions, and burning of vegetation and crops. They also include water and air pollution and health problems for people, such as breathing difficulties.

Secondary effects

Some examples of secondary effects include a loss of jobs and income for farm workers and those who work in other businesses that are affected by the wildfire. People are made homeless and the rebuilding of properties and infrastructure is costly and takes a long time. The many insurance payments made to people also push up the cost of insurance for others. The economy of an area can also be damaged through the loss of money that would have been earned from farming, logging and other activities. This can include tourism; attractive landscapes can be destroyed and there is often restricted access to some recreational areas following a wildfire.

Wildfires can also increase the risk of soil erosion and landslides, as there is less vegetation to intercept heavy rainfall, and hillsides become increasingly unstable. There is increased surface run-off over the bare surfaces and ash, soil and debris are washed down the slopes. This can continue to pollute rivers and lakes for long periods. Other long-term effects on the ecosystem can include the loss of habitats and animal species. Burnt areas are covered by invasive plant species that do not provide adequate food for local wildlife.

In this section you will learn:

about the primary and secondary effects of wildfires

about a case study demonstrating the effects of a wildfire.

Key terms

Physical effects: those affecting natural and built materials.

Social effects: those affecting people.

Economic effects: those affecting money and business.

Did you know ??????

A wildfire produces the same amount of energy in 10 minutes as a nuclear explosion.

Case study

Wildfires rage across California, USA

In October 2007 a series of 24 wildfires burned across California (Photo **A**).

They destroyed over 200,000 hectares of grassland and woodland in an area from Santa Barbara in the north to the Mexican border in the south, a distance of 370 km (Map **B**). The two largest fires were in the San Diego area, where 640,000 people had to evacuate their homes. At times the fires were so intense that fire tornados developed (Photo **C**). Nine people lost their lives in the fires and 85 were injured, many of them firefighters.

Over 1,800 homes were destroyed in the blaze (Photo **D**), including several multimillion-dollar homes belonging to film stars. Damage to property was estimated to be US $1.6 billion. Many people suffered severe mental trauma as they saw their houses and possessions reduced to piles of rubble and ash.

A *A Californian wildfire*

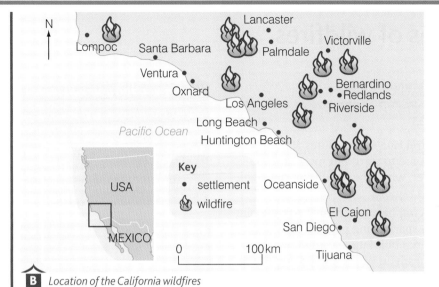

B   Location of the California wildfires

C   A fire tornado

Clouds of smoke from the wildfires blotted out the sun and could be seen from space. These drifted across the region and raised levels of air pollution to three times their normal level. This posed a health hazard to children, the elderly and people with breathing problems. People were advised to stay indoors and keep their windows closed. Businesses and factories had to close and the wildfires disrupted the important tourist trade. San Diego Zoo and Sea World were closed, as were restaurants and bars across southern California. In the San Diego area alone, $US 45 million of business was lost each day. Drinking water in the some cities became polluted and residents were advised to drink bottled water only.

Farms and their crops of avocados, melons, strawberries and vegetables were left smouldering. Some crops simply died due to lack of water, as the farm owners had been evacuated and were unable to irrigate the dry land. Farm workers lost their jobs and food prices rose. The wildfires were also extremely damaging to the natural vegetation. Even species of plants adapted to fire conditions were killed off, as the wildfires were so intense. Many species of animals were killed in the blaze, or lost the habitat they depend upon to survive. The US president declared Southern California a 'disaster area'.

D   Homes ravaged by the 2007 California wildfires

∞ links

Learn more about California's wildfires at **www.calfires.com**

Activities

1   Explain the difference between the primary and secondary effects of wildfires.

2   Make a large copy of Table **D**. Complete it by giving examples of each type of effect.

D   Effects of the California wildfires

Physical	Environmental	Social	Economic

extension   Find out how wildfires can lead to flooding and landslides.

Use the internet to find out more about the effects of the Australian wildfires of 2009

Did you know ??????

In February 2009, a series of wildfires burned across the state of Victoria in the south of Australia. Over 3,500 homes and other buildings were destroyed, leaving 7,500 people homeless. One fire-fighter was killed and a further 172 people lost their lives, with many more injured.

AQA   Examiner's tip

Learn a case study that describes the physical, environmental, social and economic effects of wildfires.

3.11 The causes of wildfires

The causes of wildfires are both natural and human.

Natural causes of wildfires

- Lightning is the biggest single natural cause of wildfires (Photo **A**). Some lightning strikes may cause a fire to start, but most of these are small and soon die out. However, when the conditions are right, fires started by lightning can spread rapidly.

- Spontaneous heating is where material becomes heated to the point at which it will catch fire without a spark being present. This occurs where large amounts of plant material build up and the flow of cooling air is restricted. It occurs mostly in warm, humid conditions.

- Volcanic eruptions emit red-hot lava and ash. These can also start wildfires.

Wildfires can spread very quickly when they occur during a period of hot, dry weather. Fallen branches and leaves dry out and can catch fire very easily. The situation can be made worse if there are also strong winds to fan the flames. Wildfires in California are most extreme when a period of **drought** is accompanied by the dry Santa Ana winds which blow from an area of desert (Photo **B** and Map **C**). These winds can gust up to 140 km/h.

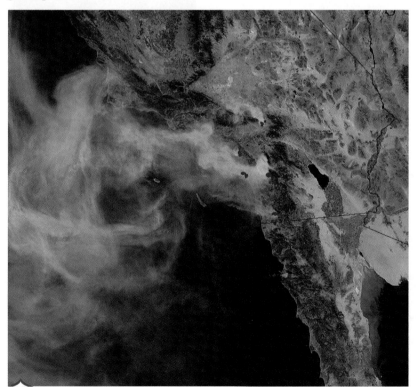

B *Satellite image of the Santa Ana winds fanning wildfires in California*

The physical geography of an area can also affect the speed at which wildfires spread. On south-facing slopes the sun dries the vegetation out, increasing the risk of fire. Steep slopes mean that fires spread quickly as the flames come into contact with vegetation upslope.

A *Lightning striking trees*

Key terms

Drought: a long period of low rainfall.

Did you know ??????

Lightning strikes the planet hundreds of thousands of times a day.

desert

mountains

Santa Ana winds

Los Angeles

Pacific Ocean

C *Santa Ana winds, California*

Human causes of wildfires

- Accidents are to blame for starting many wildfires. Children playing with matches, campfires that have not been put out properly and discarded cigarettes have all caused major wildfires.

- Broken bottles can act as a magnifying glass. The pieces of glass concentrate the sun's rays onto a small area. This can set fire to dry vegetation/leaves or litter that has been dropped by people.

- Slash and burn is a method farmers use to clear land to grow crops. Sometimes these fires can get out of control and spread.

- Arson is the act of deliberately starting fires. In some areas, it can account for up to 30 per cent of wildfires and was a major cause of the Australian wildfires in 2009.

- Other causes include sparks from train wheels or machinery, military training, household chimneys and barbecues.

Often wildfires start and spread due to a combination of both natural and human factors. One devastating wildfire in California was started when the Santa Ana winds blew down electricity power lines. The resulting sparks set the dry vegetation alight and the fire raged for nine days.

More and more wildfires are a result of the actions of people. The numbers vary from area to area, but in one state in Australia, arson was the biggest cause of wildfires (Diagram **D**). However, nature can still be a highly destructive force, as the following newspaper headlines show.

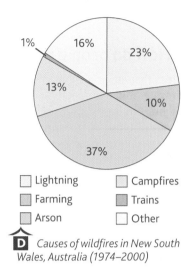

D   *Causes of wildfires in New South Wales, Australia (1974–2000)*

∞links

Learn more about wildfires at **www. usgs.gov/hazards/wildfires**

> **Lightning Storms Cause California Wildfires**

> **5,000 to 6,000 lightning strikes start 842 wildfires over a two-day period**

Activities

1   Draw a spider diagram to show the causes of wildfires.

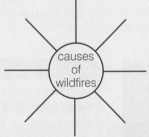

2   Explain three natural and three human causes of wildfires.

3   Suggest why the Santa Ana winds aid the rapid spread of wildfires in California.

4   In Diagram **D**, what percentages of causes were due to the actions of people?

extension   To what extent are wildfires a natural hazard? Investigate the causes of some recent wildfires.

Did you know ??????

The wildfires in Australia (February 2009) spread very quickly. They started during a period of drought and at a time when there were very high temperatures (over 40 °C) and winds of over 100 kph. The most destructive fire and several smaller ones were deliberately started by arsonists.

Reducing the damage from wildfires

■ How do people respond to a wildfire?

In areas that are accessible to fire engines, fire-fighting teams spray them with water and foam. Aeroplanes and helicopters are also used to allow firefighters to land at or even parachute into remote, inaccessible areas. They are also used for **air drops**, where water and fire-retardant chemicals are released from aircraft onto the wildfire. Areas ahead of the wildfire are also sprayed to stop it spreading. Helicopters are fitted with a large bucket that can be filled up from the sea or a nearby lake (Photo **A**).

Firefighters also create **fire lines** (also called fire breaks), which act as a barrier to stop the spread of the wildfire. They dig trenches, or clear areas of ground. This removes dry grasses, bushes, leaves and twigs which act as fuel for the wildfire. Without a supply of fuel the wildfire will eventually burn out. In accessible areas this is done using bulldozers, but it often has to be done by hand, using a tool called a **pulaski**. Sometimes a **backfire** is used to remove the fuel: this is where an area ahead of the wildfire is set alight and a controlled burning of the fuel supply takes place. This clears the area very quickly, but there is always the risk that the second fire could get out of control and spread.

In severe wildfires, where many lives could be at risk, people are made to evacuate their homes and move to safe areas. This called a mandatory evacuation, which can be enforced by arrest in some areas.

■ How do people prevent and prepare for a wildfire?

Volunteer groups remove dead leaves and branches from areas at risk from wildfires and controlled burns take place in order to remove dead plant material before any fires start. However, the best method of prevention is to educate the public through campaigns designed to increase awareness of how wildfires can start.

The Smokey Bear cartoon character (Photo **B**) has been used for over 60 years in the USA to advise people on how to build campfires and how to extinguish them safely. Advice on burning crop debris, reducing

B *Smokey Bear*

In this section you will learn:

the ways in which people can respond to a wildfire

the ways in which people can prevent and prepare for a wildfire.

A *An air drop*

Key terms

Pulaski: a tool that is a cross between an axe and a hoe.

Geographical Information System (GIS): electronic system used for storing, analysing, managing and presenting data, which is linked to a location.

Did you know ???????

Aeroplanes drop a bright pink sludge onto wildfires. In the USA, this is known as 'Sky Jell-O' (jelly).

AQA *Examiner's tip*

Be able to describe the measures people can take to prevent and prepare for wildfires.

the risk of sparks from vehicles and disposal of cigarettes appears on posters, leaflets and advertisements. In some areas, DVDs are sent to schools for use in lessons on wildfire safety.

When a wildfire does occur, the public is given information on what to do. Methods of making homes as fireproof as possible are suggested, along with tips for survival during a wildfire. Families are also advised to draw up detailed evacuation plans. **Geographical Information System (GIS)** wildfire risk maps are available online and detailed wildfire forecast scenario software is being developed to inform people of the safest evacuation routes if a wildfire should start in any given area.

Some responses to a wildfire in Greece are described in the following case study.

Case study

The deadliest blaze in Greek history, August 2007

A total of 42 wildfires raged for three days across southern and central Greece. They killed at least 57 people, and destroyed 110 villages and 2.5 million hectares of farmland, along with many more hectares of pine forest and olive groves. Arsonists started some of the fires and seven people were arrested. Once started, the fires spread quickly as strong winds fanned the flames across tinder-dry forests, which had not seen rain for several months.

Hundreds of people were evacuated by land and sea. Over 1,000 soldiers were called in to assist firefighters (Photo **C**) and create fire lines. Police blocked roads to prevent people from entering danger areas and firefighting planes dropped water onto the wildfires. Firefighters and aircraft came from 17 countries. The Greek government declared a state of emergency and offered compensation to people who lost relatives or property.

C *Greek firefighters*

Activities

1   Describe ways in which each of the following groups may respond to or help reduce the damage from wildfires: emergency services, armed forces, local authorities, local residents.

2   Suggest how education helps to reduce the risk of wildfires.

3   a   Give two causes of the Greek wildfires of 2007.

   b   Give three effects of the Greek wildfires of 2007.

   c   Give three ways in which people responded to the Greek wildfires of 2007.

extension   Suggest how GIS wildfire risk maps can be used to reduce the damage from wildfires.

links

Learn more about dealing with wildfires at **www.smokeybear.com** and **www.iccsafe.org** → public safety → wildfire safety

3.13 More wildfires to come?

It is not fully known whether significant changes to the pattern of wildfires are taking place. Long-term global records of the number of wildfires do not exist. However, scientists have identified several changes to **wildfire intensity**, and to the number of wildfires and areas experiencing them. By 2007, the length of the **wildfire season** in the USA had increased by 78 days compared with 1970. Also, the average size of wildfires and total area destroyed has increased steadily between 1960 and 2004 (Graph **A**). In the USA, detailed records of wildfires do exist. The graph does not show that in some periods the number of wildfires was below average and in other periods they were above average.

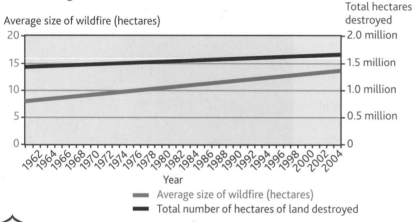

A Changes to the number and size of US wildfires, 1960–2004

It is clear that the climate does have a great effect on the number of wildfires. Periods of high numbers of wildfires coincided with periods of above-average temperature and early snowmelt in the mountains. Some scientists think that climate change, due to global warming, will mean that the number of wildfires will continue to increase (see the newspaper articles). They also think that areas in which wildfires are not common, the risk of them happening will increase. In these areas, the fires will be very intense and burn for longer, as large amounts of fuel (dead wood, leaves, etc.) have built up. This will release a lot of stored energy and large amounts of carbon dioxide into the atmosphere, further contributing to global warming.

Key terms

Wildfire intensity: the severity of burning.

Wildfire season: the period of the year during which wildfires occur.

NASA: National Aeronautics and Space Administration – the US space agency.

Wildland–urban interface: area where houses and other human developments are built on the fringes wilderness areas.

Did you know ??????

Across the world, over 350 million hectares of forest are destroyed by wildfire each year.

AQA Examiner's tip

Be able to explain why the damage caused by wildfires is likely to increase.

Experts Say Massive California Wildfires Caused by Climate Change

Experts say the fires sweeping southern California were predicted by climate change models. There may be many more such events in the future as vegetation grows heavier than usual and then ignites during long droughts. They said that this 'may be another piece of evidence that climate change is a reality'. The models suggest that parts of the United States may be experiencing several wet years in a row followed by several that are drier than normal. If you get a wildfire during these periods it can spread very quickly. 'In the future, huge fires may simply be a normal part of the landscape.' Droughts or heatwaves, the researchers said, would lead to wildfires larger than ever seen before.

Other scientists feel that periods of increased wildfires are part of a natural cycle where there are periods of higher temperatures and lower rainfall, similar to those factors affecting tropical storms (see pages 78–79).

Detailed studies of wildfires across the globe are now taking place, to monitor the problem and find out if changes to their numbers are permanent. Satellite images produced by **NASA** can now show the location and intensity of all wildfires (Photo **B**).

∞links

Learn more about the wildland-urban interface at **www.silvis. forest.wisc.edu/projects/WUI_ Main.asp**

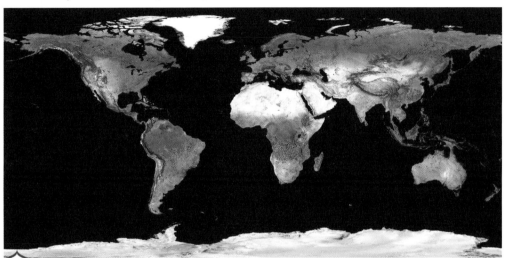

B *NASA satellite image of wildfires during 2002*

What is known for certain is that the cost of damage from wildfires is increasing, especially in more developed countries. Photo **B** shows that the greatest number of wildfires (areas in red) occur in dryland areas of Africa, South America and Australia. However, the wildfires that attract the most media attention are those in the USA and Europe; especially when the multi-million-dollar mansion of a movie-star is at risk (Photo **C**). In many areas, as people become more affluent, they choose to live or have second homes in remote rural areas. In the USA alone, over 10 million homes have been built in the **wildland–urban interface**. This increases the costs of fire fighting and prevention, insurance claims and the risk to human life.

C *A wildfire destroys a Malibu mansion in the USA*

Climate Change Could Lead to More and Larger Wildfires

Researchers say that the area burned by wildfires could double by the end of the century if the climate warms. Researchers have seen relationships between climate records and an 85-year record of wildfires during the 20th century and used them in state-of-the-art global climate models. They said:

'Models linking the size of area burned with temperatures during the fire season, predict that global warming will bring a five-fold increase in wildfires.'

Activities

1   Describe the changes to the average size and total damage created by US wildfires since 1960 (Graph **A**).

2   Suggest two reasons why the number and size of wildfires may be increasing.

3   Suggest one argument against the idea that the number and size of wildfires will continue to increase.

4   Give two reasons why the cost of damage from wildfires may be increasing.

extension   Use the internet to research the possible link between climate change and the number of wildfires.

4.1 Where are the hot desert environments and what are they like?

A desert is a region that receives little rainfall. Not all of the world's deserts are hot. Deserts such as the Gobi in Central Asia are very hot in summer, but very cold in winter. The true hot deserts are found around the tropics, usually between 15 and 30 degrees north and south of the equator. Most hot deserts are on the dry, western margins of continents. However, the Sahara and Arabian Deserts extend across northern Africa and south-west Asia (Map **A**).

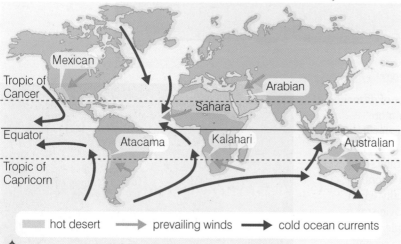

A The world's hot deserts

Key on map: hot desert → prevailing winds → cold ocean currents

Labels: Mexican, Tropic of Cancer, Arabian, Sahara, Equator, Atacama, Kalahari, Australian, Tropic of Capricorn

Photo **B** shows part of a hot desert. This is the way that most people imagine a desert to look – endless kilometres of sand dunes. Large areas of the driest deserts are made up of constantly shifting sand dunes. These are formed from wind-blown sand that prevents most plants from growing. However, many areas of hot desert are also very rocky and mountainous.

◼ Why do hot deserts have high temperatures?

As Graph **C** shows, hot desert regions have high temperatures and low rainfall throughout the year, resulting in high levels of evaporation. At the tropics, the sun's rays have to pass through less of the atmosphere than in the upper latitudes (see page 105). The solar energy is concentrated in a much smaller area and, therefore, temperatures are high. Also, the tropics are in a **high pressure** belt. Here, the air that was heated and rose upwards at the equator is descending. There are low levels of condensation and few clouds to reflect back the sun's heat. Consequently, rates of surface heating are high.

> **In this section you will learn:**
>
> the location of the main hot desert environments
>
> about the factors affecting temperature and precipitation in hot desert environments.

> AQA *Examiner's tip*
>
> Hot deserts are not located on the equator as many people expect. Learn where the world's hot deserts are located and why they are in these locations. Ensure that you can name and locate at least two hot deserts.

B Desert sand dunes

> **Key terms**
>
> **High pressure:** colder air is slowly sinking, pressing down on the Earth.
>
> **Prevailing winds:** the winds blowing most frequently from one particular direction.
>
> **Arid:** dry.

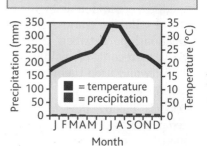

Legend: ◼ = temperature ◼ = precipitation

C *Climate graph for a hot desert region*

Why do hot deserts have low rainfall?

1 With high pressure at the tropics, the **prevailing winds** blow across the land towards areas of low pressure over the sea. They pick up little moisture and, therefore, bring little rainfall, as in the Sahara Desert (Diagram **D**, part A).

2 Cold ocean currents run along the western coasts of continents. When winds do blow from the ocean, they have to cross these currents. As they do so, they quickly cool down and any water vapour they are carrying condenses to form sea fog. As a result, the winds reaching the coast are dry winds and do not bring rainfall, for example in the Atacama Desert (Diagram **D**, part B).

3 When winds blowing across the ocean are pushed upwards by a range of mountains, the air cools and condenses, and rain or snow falls over the mountains. As the winds descend inland they become increasingly dry and form a 'rain shadow' area in the interior of the continent, for example in the Australian desert (Diagram **D**, part C).

⚭ links

Learn more about deserts at **www.oxfam.org.uk/coolplanet/ ontheline/explore/nature/deserts/ deserts.htm**
The term 'desertification' is defined on page 90.

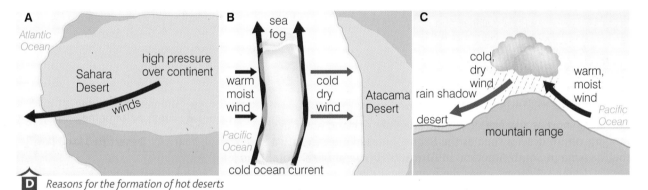

D *Reasons for the formation of hot deserts*

Semi-arid areas

As you move away from hot desert areas, rainfall increases and semi-arid conditions are found. It is often these areas that are at risk of desertification (Map **E**).

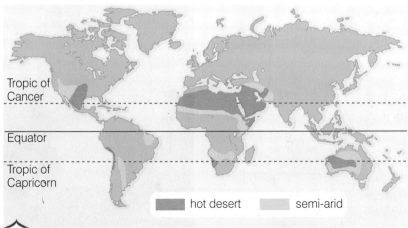

E *Semi-arid areas around the world*

Activities

1 Describe the global distribution of hot deserts.

2 Using Graph **C**, describe the climate of a hot desert region.

3 Using annotated diagrams, explain why some places have low rainfall.

extension Search for a climate graph for a semi-arid region. Compare the climate there with that of a hot desert region.

Many areas of the world are at risk from **desertification** (Map **A**). Up to one-third of the Earth's surface could become desert in the future. The amount of land which is becoming desertified is increasing (Table **B**) and the livelihoods of 1.2 billion people are under threat. This is especially true of rural areas of less developed countries, where people depend on farming the land to make a living.

Key terms

Desertification: the spread of a desert – the process in which land slowly dries out until little or no vegetation can survive.

Land degradation: a reduction in the ability of the soil to support life.

Overcultivation: growing too many crops, year after year on the same piece of land, without allowing the soil to regain its fertility.

Soil erosion: the wearing away of soil by water and wind.

Irrigation: the artificial watering of the land.

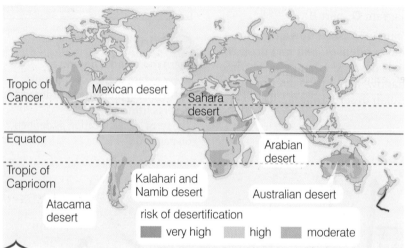

Tropic of Cancer — Mexican desert — Sahara desert

Equator — Arabian desert

Tropic of Capricorn — Kalahari and Namib desert — Australian desert

Atacama desert

risk of desertification
very high   high   moderate

A Areas of the world at risk from desertification

The areas most at risk from desertification are dryland areas at the margins of hot deserts such as the Sahara and Kalahari in Africa and the Atacama in South America. In Africa, 66 per cent of the total land area is dryland. In some areas the margins of the deserts are advancing. In other areas, patches of **land degradation** occur in dry areas that are hundreds of kilometres from the edge of a desert. These patches grow and join together, creating desert-like conditions (Photo **D**).

The problem of desertification is not just limited to less developed countries. In Europe, one-third of Spain is at risk of becoming desert (Map **C**), with 90 per cent of the land bordering the Mediterranean Sea under threat. In the USA 30 per cent of the land is at risk from desertification.

B Changes to the amount of desertified land in the world

Year	Desertified land (km²)
1970	1,004
1980	1,351
1990	1,600
2000	2,211
2010	3,800 (est.)

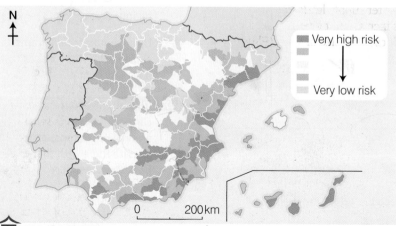

N

Very high risk

Very low risk

0   200 km

C Risk of desertification in Spain

D Signs of desertification in Sudan

What are the causes of desertification?

Desertification can be the result of both natural and human factors (Graph **E**). A period of drought does not always result in desertification, but it is more likely to do so if people also misuse the land. In areas such as the Sahel, one of the poorest parts of Africa, the need to feed the growing population has increased pressure on the land. This has resulted in:

- **overcultivation**, which exhausts the soil; nutrients are removed due to the continual growth of crops
- overgrazing, where too many animals are grazed on land that does not have enough grass for them to feed on
- the overuse of fuelwood, which leads to deforestation, further increasing the risk of desertification.

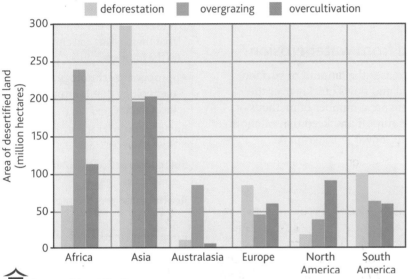

E *Causes of desertification*

These practices result in the removal of the protective vegetation cover. The soil becomes exposed and open to **soil erosion**. It is then easily washed away by heavy rainfall during flash floods. It can also dry out and be blown away as dust storms by the wind. The remaining infertile lower layers of soil become baked hard in the sun and few plants can grow, resulting in unproductive desert.

In some areas, overuse of the available water supply leads to desertification. Poor **irrigation** practices increase salt levels in the soil and also cause rivers to dry up, therefore reducing the size of lakes (Photo **F**). In Spain, the huge number of tourist and housing developments along the coast have greatly increased the demand for water. Most of this water is obtained from boreholes. This reduces the amount of water available to the interior areas of the country. Demand for water inland has also gone up due to an increase in the amount of crops, especially vegetables, being grown to meet the growing needs of both tourists and local people.

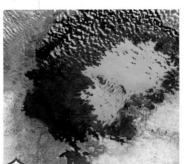

F *Lake Chad in Africa has been shrinking for decades*

AQA Examiner's tip

Ensure that you understand and can explain some of the human factors that are contributing to the expansion of hot deserts.

∞links

Learn more about desertification at www.unccd.int

Activities

1   Using Map **A**, describe the distribution of areas at risk from desertification.

2   a   Use the following data to draw a graph to show how human activities cause desertification: deforestation 30%, fuelwood gathering 7%, overgrazing 35%, overcultivation 28%.

   b   Put the causes into rank order.

   c   For each cause, explain how it leads to desertification.

   d   Using Graph **E**, describe the impact of human activity in each continent.

extension   Use the internet to produce a case study of the causes of desertification in the Sahel region of Africa.

Many of the areas that are at risk from desertification are in less developed countries. It is important, therefore, that methods used to reduce the problem are **sustainable** and use **appropriate technology** for that region or country. In order to reduce the rate of desertification, the problem of soil erosion by wind and rain must be tackled. This way the land remains green and fertile and does not become degraded. The methods used also aim to ensure that people do not misuse valuable soil and water resources, so that plants can grow. The prevention of desertification is much cheaper to undertake than it is to repair degraded land. Managing the fringe of the hot desert is crucial if the United Nations' Millennium Development Goals, of eradicating extreme poverty and ensuring environmental sustainability, are to be achieved.

■ How can soil be protected from water erosion?

Heavy rainfall, such as a flash flood, increases the amount of **surface run-off**. Rainfall cannot infiltrate the soil and flows quickly over the land, carrying the soil away with it. There are a number of methods of **soil conservation**. These reduce surface run-off and keep the soil moist, allowing plant growth. Some of these are shown in Diagram **A**.

In this section you will learn:

how soil erosion by water and wind can be reduced

why methods of reducing soil erosion are sustainable and appropriate.

Key terms

Sustainable: a use of resources that meets human needs while preserving the environment so that these needs can also be met in the future.

Appropriate technology: technology that is affordable to local people.

Surface run-off: the overland flow of water.

Soil conservation: protecting the soil for future use.

Reafforestation: the replanting of trees.

Coppicing: method of encouraging re-growth of trees by cutting them back to near ground level.

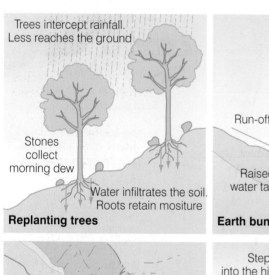

Trees intercept rainfall. Less reaches the ground

Stones collect morning dew

Water infiltrates the soil. Roots retain mositure

Replanting trees

Run-off

Water and soil collect behind earth bund

Raised water table

Earth bunds

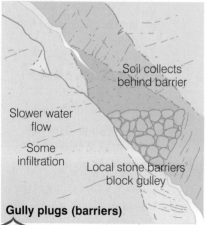

Soil collects behind barrier

Slower water flow

Some infiltration

Local stone barriers block gulley

Gully plugs (barriers)

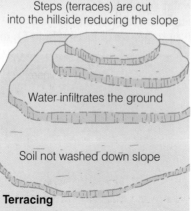

Steps (terraces) are cut into the hillside reducing the slope

Water infiltrates the ground

Soil not washed down slope

Terracing

A Methods of reducing soil erosion caused by water flow

B Building a stone line in Niger, Africa

Did you know ?????

Each year, soil that could be used to grow food to feed the population of Europe is eroded by rain and wind.

Soil is being lost much faster than it can be naturally replaced. It takes up to 1,000 years for fertile soil to form.

Other methods include contour ploughing (across the slope, rather than from top to bottom) and land levelling (filling in depressions in the ground using soil from raised areas in between).

How can soil be protected from wind erosion?

When vegetation is removed, the soil has no plant roots to bind it together and to retain moisture. It quickly dries out in the sun and is easily blown away by the wind. One method of reducing soil erosion caused by the wind is to replant the land with trees. Many countries are now undertaking programmes of **reafforestation**. Education of local people about the dangers of soil erosion is crucial to tackling the problem. In areas where many trees have been removed, people are taught to 'harvest' the trees and not remove them completely. By **coppicing** the trees, people can still use them for fuelwood, but they will continue to grow and protect the soil, reducing the risk of desertification (Diagram **C**). Other methods of protecting soil from wind erosion are shown in Diagram **D**.

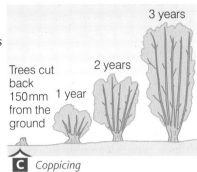

Trees cut back 150mm from the ground — 1 year — 2 years — 3 years

C *Coppicing*

∞links

Learn more about dealing with the problem of desertification at www.unccd.int

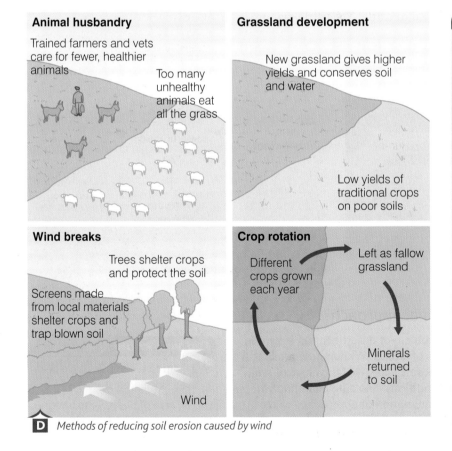

Animal husbandry
Trained farmers and vets care for fewer, healthier animals
Too many unhealthy animals eat all the grass

Grassland development
New grassland gives higher yields and conserves soil and water
Low yields of traditional crops on poor soils

Wind breaks
Trees shelter crops and protect the soil
Screens made from local materials shelter crops and trap blown soil
Wind

Crop rotation
Different crops grown each year
Left as fallow grassland
Minerals returned to soil

D *Methods of reducing soil erosion caused by wind*

Methods such as those shown in Photo **B** and Diagram **D** are not expensive to set up. They require little maintenance. They use local materials, technology and labour and are therefore appropriate and sustainable in less developed countries.

Activities

1 Suggest two reasons why it is important to reduce the risk from desertification.

2 a Using Diagram **A**, choose two methods of reducing soil erosion by water.

 b Using Diagram **D**, choose two methods of reducing soil erosion by wind.

 For each method, explain how it would help to reduce desertification. Use annotated diagrams to illustrate your answers.

3 Explain how coppicing (Diagram **C**) helps to protect the soil from erosion, yet still provides resources.

extension Use the internet to investigate three of the methods shown in this section. With examples, explain why each method could be regarded as sustainable and appropriate.

Some methods of managing the fringe of hot deserts focus on irrigation in order to make the land green again. Irrigation can enable two or more crops a year to be grown in order to meet the needs of a growing population. Even hot desert areas can become fertile if enough money is spent. In oil-rich Saudi Arabia, large areas of desert are under irrigation (Photo **A**). **Desalinisation** plants and deep wells provide the water required for the growth of crops. These methods are not always appropriate for less developed countries, as they use expensive technology and have high maintenance costs. Neither are they always sustainable, as much water is lost to evaporation and salts build up in the soil so that healthy plants cannot grow.

Some scientists argue that **genetically modified (GM)** crops will benefit poor, arid countries. Crops can be 'designed' to grow in hot, dry conditions. However, doubt remains as to their impact on the environment and some argue that it is simply wrong to tamper with nature. A more sustainable approach might be to introduce crops from other areas, which will grow in the increasingly arid conditions. The enset plant (or 'false banana') has been introduced into Ethiopia. The plant can be made into porridge to feed people, while the stem produces fibres and the leaves can be fed to cattle. The cattle manure is then added to the soil as a fertilizer.

> **In this section you will learn:**
>
> why not all methods of reducing desertification are appropriate and sustainable
>
> how methods of reducing desertification can be multi-dimensional in nature.

> **Key terms**
>
> **Desalinisation**: removal of salts from seawater.
>
> **Genetically modified (GM)**: crops that have had their DNA changed through genetic engineering.

A Irrigation in Saudi Arabia

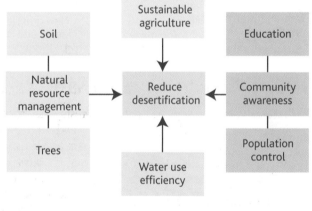

B Tackling desertification from all angles

What is a multi-dimensional approach?

It may seem that one solution to the problem of desertification is by tree planting or covering hillsides with lines of stones. Whilst these are useful methods, they are not the complete answer. Many NGOs run small-scale projects that take into account local conditions – no single method will solve the problem. Many feel that a combination of approaches to the problem must be taken. These try to address all the issues affecting desertification, not just one element such as soil erosion (Diagram **B**).

Many methods could be used in conjunction with stone lines, bunds and tree planting to give a multi-dimensional approach to the management of the fringe of hot desert areas. Diagram **C** and the article on the next page show how this approach has been applied in Mali, in West Africa.

> **Did you know** ??????
>
> - Irrigation techniques have been used since prehistoric times.
> - The area of desert land under irrigation in Saudi Arabia has increased from 162,000 hectares in 1976, to over 4 million hectares today.

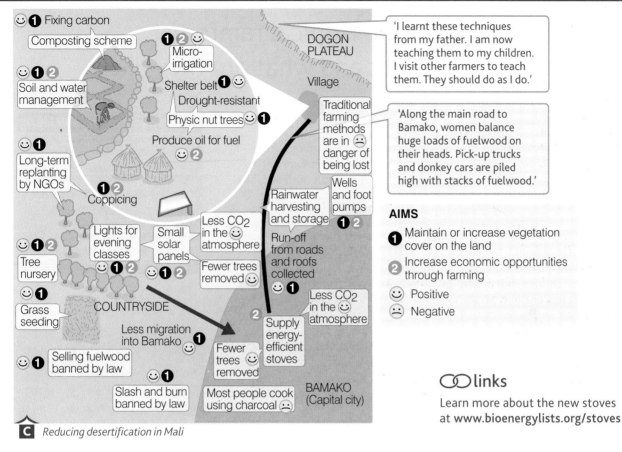

C *Reducing desertification in Mali*

Reducing the use of fuelwood

Stoking Stoves to Save the Trees

Houses have to replace open cooking fires with the latest in sub-Saharan high technology – energy-efficient wood-burning mud stoves.

Under Mali law, households without at least two stoves have to pay a fine. Ever-widening areas of deforested land now surround the capital Bamako. In a region where wood accounts for 90 per cent of energy use, foreign aid experts say there is a clash between shrinking forests and a growing population's demand for firewood.

'When I was a boy in the 1960s, people went 10 kilometres outside of Bamako to get firewood,' said the Director of Forestry in Mali. 'Today, they go 150 kilometres to find wood. People no longer give

forests the time to regenerate. Instead of waiting four to five years to cut again, they cut every year.' To slow this, tree-planting projects have been started by all of Mali's aid donors. For faster results, Mali has started a national campaign to place mud stoves in every household because they use one-quarter of the wood and save the children from burns. The ingredients for a mud stove – sand, clay and water – are plentiful.

A promoter of metal stoves for urban use often drives around Bamako wearing a shirt with a picture of a happy woman and such a stove. The caption reads: 'Joy of cooking with my improved stove'. The stoves soon pay for themselves in reduced wood purchases.

Activities

1   Irrigation and use of GM crops might not be sustainable and appropriate methods for a poor country. Explain why.

2   Explain how the use of new stoves can help to reduce desertification.

3   Explain why the methods shown in Diagram **C** make up a multi-dimensional development plan.

extension   Carry out research to find out more about three of the methods of reducing desertification shown in Diagram **C**.

4.5 | Where are the tropical rainforest environments and what are they like?

Where are tropical rainforest environments?

The world's tropical rainforests are found between 23.5 degrees north (the Tropic of Cancer) and 23.5 degrees south (the Tropic of Capricorn). However, most are found between 5 degrees north or south of the equator.

In Africa, the main remaining areas of tropical rainforest are to be found in the Congo basin and Madagascar. The rainforests of Asia are found mainly in the south-east of the continent in countries such as Burma (Myanmar), Indonesia (Photo **B**) and Malaysia. There are smaller areas of tropical rainforest in north-east Australia and Papua New Guinea, but a third of all remaining rainforest is found in the Amazon basin in South America (Map **A**).

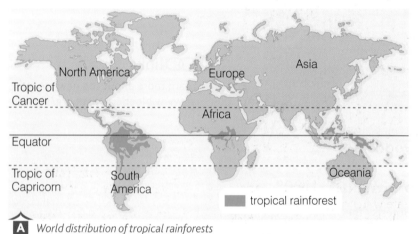

A World distribution of tropical rainforests

B A rainforest in Indonesia

What is the tropical rainforest environment like?

Tropical rainforest environments are characterised by a high annual rainfall (1,750–2,000 mm) and temperatures that are high throughout the year (Graph **C**). This is known as an **equatorial** climate; there are no seasons, and weather conditions vary little from day to day. As you move away from the equator, there is a short drier season, but annual rainfall and temperature remain high.

Due to these 'greenhouse-like' conditions, plants grow all year round and the rainforests contain the most luxuriant vegetation in the world. They are home to two-thirds of all the plant and animal species on Earth.

Did you know ??????

- Before people started destroying rainforests, they covered 15% of the Earth's land area. Today, they cover 6%.

- Tropical rainforests are the Earth's oldest ecosystems. In South-east Asia they have survived for 70 million years.

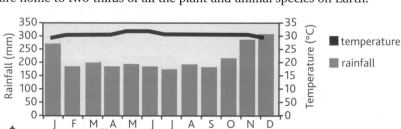

C Climate graph for the equatorial climate

Key terms

Equatorial: existing at or near the equator.

Ecosystem: the set of relationships between climate, landscape, animals and plants.

Temperatures are constantly high at the equator because the sun is always at a high angle in the sky. This concentrates the heat from the sun on a smaller area of the Earth's surface. Also at this point, the sun's rays pass through less of the atmosphere and less heat is absorbed by particles in the air (Diagram **D**).

∞ links

Learn more about tropical rainforests at www.oxfam.org.uk/coolplanet/ontheline/explore/nature/trfindex.htm

AQA *Examiner's tip*

Learn where the world's tropical rainforests are located and why they are in these locations. Ensure that you can name and locate at least two areas of tropical rainforest.

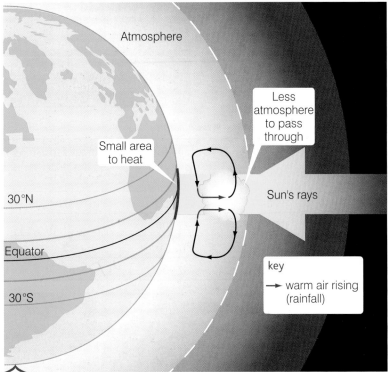

D *Factors affecting temperature and rainfall*

The heavy rainfall in equatorial regions is a result of low atmospheric pressure. The high temperatures evaporate water at ground level, which rises, cools and condenses to give the daily convectional rainfall, which is a characteristic of the tropical rainforest environment (Diagram **D**).

Although the tropical rainforest is abundant with many species of plants and wildlife, they have to be specially adapted to the hot, wet conditions.

The rainforest **ecosystem** is very fragile. The climate, plants and soil are in a very delicate state of balance. As the plants grow all year round, there is a constant supply of plant material falling to the forest floor. Due to the hot, wet conditions, this decomposes very quickly and gives the soil its nutrients. These are quickly taken up by the large numbers of fast-growing plants, but are replaced just as quickly (Diagram **E**). If this cycle of nutrients is broken, then the soil quickly loses its fertility. This occurs when deforestation takes place. Once the trees are removed, the land quickly becomes unproductive.

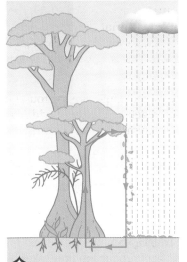

E *Rainforest nutrient cycle*

Activities

1 Describe the distribution of the areas of tropical rainforest.

2 On a copy of Map **A**, mark and label the following areas: Amazon basin, Congo basin, South-east Asia.

3 Describe the features of the equatorial climate (Graph **C**). Include information on the following in your description: total rainfall, average monthly rainfall, average monthly temperature, range of temperature.

4 Describe the factors affecting temperature and rainfall in equatorial regions.

extension With the help of Diagram **E** and your own research, explain why the rainforest is a 'fragile environment'.

The shrinking tropical rainforest

Over the last 50 years, the world has lost one-third of all its tropical rainforests due to deforestation. In the Amazon, the rate at which trees are being chopped down or burnt is decreasing slightly (Table **A**). However, on a worldwide scale the rate of deforestation is still increasing.

Almost all the areas of tropical rainforest are found in less developed countries. Here, for many years, poor farmers have removed the forest for **subsistence agriculture**. **Slash and burn** methods were used to clear an area, which was farmed for several years until the soil became exhausted. The farmer would then move on to another area and the forest grew back. Local people would also use the wood as fuel for cooking. In the past these activities did not cause great damage to the environment, but as populations increase, they are becoming more damaging. In some parts of Congo almost all the trees have been removed.

The governments of many less developed countries view the tropical rainforest as a valuable resource. As the number of people in the world increases and as many countries become more developed, the demand for natural resources becomes greater. Forest areas can provide these natural resources and they can be exported to the more developed countries in order to make money.

The causes of deforestation vary from country to country, but the main reasons are as follows.

Logging

Trees are removed for timber, which is used in the construction industry (Photo **B**). Tropical hardwoods such as mahogany and teak are used to make furniture. In some areas, logging is difficult to control and up to 80 percent of timber is removed illegally.

Agriculture

Areas are cleared so that crops can be grown. This is often done by large companies which are trying to meet the increasing demand for products such as soya. Large areas of the Amazon have been given over to this crop in recent years. In other areas, such as South-east Asia, oil palm trees have been planted and the oil used in food products and cosmetics. Up to 10 per cent of products found in British supermarkets contain some palm oil. Soya and palm oil, along with other crops such as sugar cane and corn, are used to make **biofuels**. The use of these fuels is expected to rise in the future and this could lead to further deforestation.

As the demand for meat increases, especially from rapidly developing countries such as India and China, more tropical rainforest is cleared for cattle pasture. Over 30 per cent of Brazil's beef production now takes place in the Amazon region.

> **In this section you will learn:**
>
> that less developed countries need to exploit natural resources to earn money
>
> about the type of activities that lead to deforestation.

A *Forest loss in the Amazon*

Years	Average forest loss per year (km²)	Forest remaining (%)
1970–77	6,000	97
1978–87	21,000	91
1988-97	17,000	90
1998–2007	17,000	82

B *Logging by clear-cutting in the Amazon rainforest*

> **Key terms**
>
> **Subsistence agriculture**: growing food to feed the family.
>
> **Slash and burn**: chopping down and setting alight an area of forest.
>
> **Biofuel**: fuel derived from plants as an alternative to fossil fuels.

Minerals

Beneath some areas of tropical rainforest are valuable deposits of minerals such as bauxite, copper and gold. The trees are cleared and the topsoil removed so that the minerals can be mined (Photo **C**). The in-migration of workers can also add to the amount of deforestation, as homes have to be built, farmland created and wood taken for fuel.

Roads

The building of roads into areas of tropical rainforest not only leads to the removal of trees during construction, but it opens up the area for other developments such as the building of settlements and farms, logging and mining. In the 1970s, the Trans-Amazon highway and other roads were built in Brazil. Following the construction of these roads, the amount of deforestation increased significantly (Photo **D**).

Hydroelectric power (HEP)

Areas of tropical rainforest are flooded when rivers are dammed for HEP schemes. In Brazil there are plans to build with a further 30 of these projects. The largest is on a 1,900 km stretch of the Tocantins River, consisting of 8 major dams and lakes and 19 smaller dams.

D   *A deforested area in the Amazon*

C   *Opencast mining in the rainforest*

AQA   Examiner's tip

Learn the definition of subsistence farming and the characteristics of the slash and burn method of clearing land for farming in tropical rainforest areas.

Activities

1   Describe the changes to the Amazon rainforest shown in Table **A**.

2   Explain why some countries continue to remove areas of tropical rainforest.

extension   Search Google Earth and find an area of tropical rainforest that has been deforested. Research the area and try to find out why the trees were cleared.

Use the internet to find two other localised examples of where tropical rainforest is being removed to sell trees, for agriculture, mining and for HEP schemes.

links

Learn more about rainforests at www.rainforestweb.org

AQA   Examiner's tip

Ensure that you can describe in detail some of the threats to tropical rainforest areas.

4.7 Managing the tropical rainforest environment (1)

■ Protecting tropical rainforest environments

The continued clearance of tropical rainforests, and the activities that cause their clearance, can lead to many problems for both people and the environment. It can seriously affect **indigenous people** and animal populations as well as affect local climate. There are also wider implications for continued deforestation, in that it can have global-scale consequences (Diagram **A**).

Loss of forest can contribute to global warming. Trees remove carbon dioxide (CO_2) from the atmosphere, through photosynthesis. If this 'carbon sink' is lost there will be more (CO_2) in the atmosphere

Fewer trees means less evapotranspiration and less moisture in the atmosphere. This can alter local climate. With less rainfall, there is a danger that the tropical rainforest could become grassland

Rainforest soils are infertile and large amounts of fertilizer are used if crops are to be continually grown. This can wash into rivers, affecting plant life and animals

Indigenous people will lose their homes and livelihoods along with their culture and heritage. Contact with 'outsiders' can lead to disease and death. They have no immunity to diseases such as measles

If habitats are lost, animal species become endangered. Up to 50,000 species a year become extinct through deforestation. This can disrupt the whole of the rainforest ecosystem

Flooding of land destroys animal habitats and displaces indigenous people. It affects the migration routes of fish and animals

The rainforest will have less value as a tourist destination if its beauty is destroyed

Large-scale cattle rearing and crop growing pushes other farmers deeper into the rainforest

Burnt and dead trees release CO_2 and other greenhouse gases into the atmosphere. Burning also releases other poisonous gases, which can cause health problems for local people

Fewer trees means less interception of rainfall and increased surface run-off. There are fewer roots to take up water and bind the soil together. This can lead to soil erosion, landslides and flooding

A loss of long-term income for governments, from logging

Increased surface run-off and soil erosion leads to silting of rivers, which makes them more likely to flood. The water becomes muddy and undrinkable

Mercury, used in gold mining, can run into the river, killing fish

Even if cleared areas are allowed to regrow, they will never be able to support as much life as primary forest

Heavy machinery compacts the soil

A *Reasons for protecting the tropical rainforests*

Restoring damaged environments

A Brazilian bauxite mining company operating at Trombetas in the Amazon has developed a forest restoration programme. Before mining started, the topsoil was removed, along with the ash from the burnt trees. This was then stored and replaced when mining had finished. Native forest tree species were used to replant hundreds of hectares of deforested land. Unless companies agree to recreate the original landscape and dispose of any toxic waste safely, mining permits are not issued.

Key terms

Indigenous people: people native to an area.

Ecotourism: the responsible development and management of tourism, which helps to preserve the environment.

The following case study shows how tropical rainforests can be protected.

Case study

Reafforestation in Madagascar

Much of the rainforest in Madagascar has been destroyed by slash and burn (Map **C**). With the help of a small non-governmental organisation (NGO), the reafforestation of over 400 hectares of land has taken place. Local people were trained in the collection of seeds and setting up tree nurseries, and 100,000 young rainforest trees were planted (Photo **D**).

Fifty-seven different varieties of plants were used, the seeds being taken from the original rainforest. Another aim of the scheme was to allow local people to help themselves and give them a new livelihood as forestry workers, tour guides and rangers. The development of **ecotourism** was an important element as it created a lasting income for the population. Trails were laid, and using wood made from local eucalyptus trees, small wooden bridges were built over the rivers, along with viewing platforms, two small campsites and cabins for the guards at the entrance. Rare orchids and animals such as lemurs attract tourists to the forest.

Maromiza was declared a nature reserve in 2007. It is estimated that every 250 hectares of the forest now stores 1,000 tonnes of carbon each year.

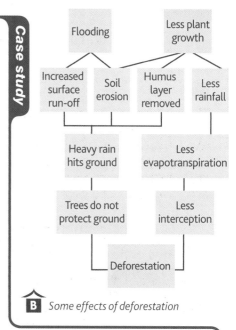

B *Some effects of deforestation*

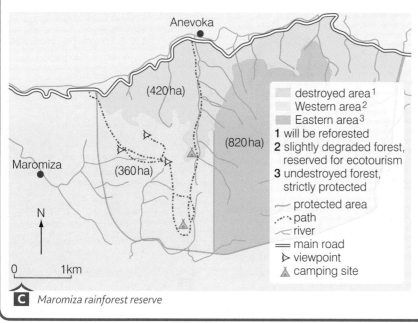

C *Maromiza rainforest reserve*

Map legend:
- destroyed area[1]
- Western area[2]
- Eastern area[3]
- 1 will be reforested
- 2 slightly degraded forest, reserved for ecotourism
- 3 undestroyed forest, strictly protected
- protected area
- path
- river
- main road
- ▷ viewpoint
- ⛺ camping site

D *Replanting trees in Madagascar*

Activities

1 With the help of Diagram **A**, explain why protecting the tropical rainforest is important for: local people, national governments, the protection of plants and animals, reducing the risk of global climate change.

2 Describe how the Maromiza scheme in Madagascar (Map **C**) benefits both local people and the environment.

extension Suggest why the Maromiza scheme is an example of sustainable development.

∞ links

Learn more about reafforestation of rainforests at **www.rainforest-alliance.org**

4.8 Managing the tropical rainforest environment (2)

How can the tropical rainforest be conserved?

Poverty is a major cause of deforestation. It is difficult to **conserve** the tropical rainforest if people or governments need to remove it in order to make money. Many people feel that some sustainable use of the tropical rainforest is the best way to conserve it. This offers an opportunity for a long-term income (Illustration **A**).

> We have few ways to earn money. We have to live off the land.

> We have to make the forest more valuable if it is left standing than it is cut down.

> Conservation must be in the interest of local people.

 A Some opinions on conservation

Methods of conserving the tropic rainforest

- Agroforestry is a farming technique that mimics the layers and diversity of the natural rainforest (Diagram **B**). Trees and a variety of crops are planted, some of which help to return nutrients to the soil. This technique can also help to repair deforested areas, which serve as a 'buffer zone' surrounding and protecting the remaining rainforest.

- Ecotourism is seen as a method of ensuring an income for local people and governments. There is also an incentive to conserve the natural beauty of the rainforest to attract tourists. As with any rainforest activity, ecotourism needs careful management to ensure that it does conserve the environment and not damage it.

- Local people can sell craft items to tourists. Some are now being produced on a larger scale and sold abroad as sustainable forest products. Scraps of timber left by loggers, and lianas (rattan), are used to make furniture; plants are tapped for perfumes and flavourings.

- Some governments are trying to control logging by issuing permits to companies and putting a limit or quota on the number of trees that can be removed. In some areas companies are given GIS equipment, so that the position of their activities can be known. If other breaks in the forest canopy are spotted on satellite images or aerial photos, the authorities can then remove the illegal loggers.

In this section you will learn:

about the conservation methods used in areas of tropical rainforest

how people can use the tropical rainforest in a sustainable fashion.

Key terms

Conservation: the protection and management of natural resources.

Watershed development: the management of the whole catchment area.

B Agroforestry

AQA Examiner's tip

Know different methods of conservation that can be used in rainforest environments.

Did you know ??????

People in rainforests can earn more from carbon credits than from selling timber.

What can we do to help preserve the tropical rainforest?

C How people from other countries can help to conserve the rainforest

Method	Description
Recycling	Materials derived from rainforest products (paper, cardboard) should be taken to a recycling centre.
Substitution	The demand for tropical hardwoods can be reduced by replacing them with alternative materials, e.g. plastics or timber from sustainable forests.
Education	People need to become aware of the beauty of the tropical rainforests and understand their importance. They are then more likely to support their **conservation**.
Ethical shopping	Look for a certification label on products. This shows that it comes from a sustainable source.
NGOs (non-governmental organisations)	Encouragement for countries to conserve their areas of tropical rainforest comes from organisations such as the United Nations (Commission on Sustainable Development) or the Forest Stewardship Council. Environmental pressure groups such as Greenpeace and WWF can also help raise awareness of conservation issues.

How could Borneo's tropical rainforest be saved?

The three governments of Borneo (Indonesia, Malaysia and Brunei) have agreed to work together to try and conserve the 'Heart of Borneo' (Map **D**). This is the tropical rainforest that covers one-third of the area. An international agreement was signed in order to try to stop illegal logging and plantations, which have reduced rainforest cover by half. Plans for a huge palm oil plantation in Borneo have been cancelled in favour of smaller sustainable developments.

An area of totally untouched forest in the Muller Mountains, which contains many rare species of animals, has been proposed as a World Heritage Site and is to be run as a national park. Other national parks and nature reserves have also been set up, including three forest reserves in Malaysia that, through sustainable forest management, help to protect endangered species such as the orang utan (Photo **E**) and pygmy elephant. Local government, with the help of NGOs, also runs smaller Conservation Districts. Local people are encouraged to protect the rainforest, by earning money for doing so. In Kapuas Hulu, many people are involved in a **watershed development**, whereby protecting and managing the forests on the upper slopes improves water quality and reduces flooding and the risk of wildfires on the lower slopes. Those who benefit, such as water companies, governments and industry, pay fees to fund and pay the local people.

Logging is now strictly licensed and companies are assessed to see if they meet the regulations on conservation and development. As an incentive for replanting and managing the forest, NGOs endorse products as being from a sustainable source and market them globally. Other forest initiatives include butterfly and orchid farms, which benefit research and conservation and provide income. They also attract tourists and many ecotourism tours to Borneo are now advertised. Lodges with canopy walkways are now found in many areas of the rainforest.

Forest lost 1900 – 2000
Projected loss 2000 – 2012
Possible forest 2012
Heart of Borneo proposed area

Kota Kinabalu
Bandar Seri Begawan
N
MALAYSIA
Kuching
Kapuas Hulu
Muller Mountains
Pontianak
Samarinda
INDONESIA
0   500 km

D The 'Heart of Borneo'

E The orang utan is under threat

∞links

Learn more about the Heart of Borneo at **www.wwf.org.uk/heartofborneo**

Activities

1 How can poverty lead to deforestation?

2 Describe three ways in which the tropical rainforest can be conserved.

3 Which of the methods of conservation used in Borneo would be the most effective? Give reasons for your answer.

extension Why is the Heart of Borneo scheme more likely to be successful with international agreement?

Where are the cold environments and what are they like?

Where are the cold environments?

There are three main types of cold environment (Map **A**).

- Polar (glacial) environments are the world's coldest places, with barren landscapes made up of **ice sheets** and glaciers (Photo **B**). These areas include most of Antarctica, the Greenland ice sheet and the frozen Arctic.

- Tundra is a cold environment that is not permanently covered by ice and snow (Photo **C**). It is too cold for trees to grow and the word itself comes from the Finnish *tunturia*, which means treeless land. Areas of tundra include parts of Alaska, northern Scandinavia, Siberia, the islands of the Arctic and the fringes of Antarctica.

- High mountain ranges such as the Himalayas, Andes, Alps and Rockies experience cold temperatures and have characteristics of both the polar (glacial) and tundra environments. These are known as alpine areas.

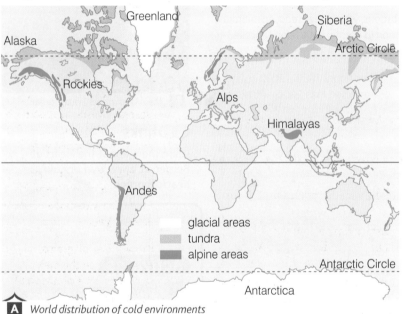

A World distribution of cold environments

Polar (glacial) environments and tundra occur in the high **latitudes**. They lie mainly to the north of latitude 66° 30'N (the Arctic Circle) and to the south of latitude 66°30'S (the Antarctic Circle). The main features of such environments are shown in Table **D**.

D Features of polar and tundra environments

Polar (Antarctica)	Extreme cold throughout the year. Barren, icy land upon which very few animals can survive. In the centre of Antarctica, precipitation is very low (less than 50 mm per year). Little evaporation. Snow builds up into thick ice sheets. Heavy snow along coastal fringes. Peninsula has areas of tundra.
Tundra (Alaska)	Permanently frozen ground (**permafrost**). A short growing season when upper soil layer thaws out. Water cannot drain away and bogs form. Sparse vegetation of shrubs, grasses and mosses. Animals such as Arctic foxes, polar bears and caribou are adapted to long, cold winters and a short breeding season.

In this section you will learn:

the location of the main cold environments

about the factors affecting temperature and precipitation in cold environments.

Key terms

Ice sheet: thick layer of ice covering a large area of land.

Permafrost: permanently frozen ground.

Latitude: distance in degrees north or south of the equator.

Katabatic wind: a strong, cold wind flowing downhill.

B Antarctica

C The Alaskan tundra

AQA Examiner's tip

Make sure that you can describe the differences between the three main types of cold environments: polar, tundra and alpine.

Did you know ???????

The largest ice sheet on Earth covers 99% of Antarctica. It is 50 times the size of the UK.

How do cold environments form?

The main factor affecting the climate of Antarctica and Alaska is **latitude**. In the high latitudes, the sun's rays have to pass through a greater thickness of atmosphere. This means that they lose a lot of their heat. The solar energy which does reach the Earth has a greater area to heat up than in the lower latitudes. This is due to the curvature of the Earth being greater towards the poles (Diagram **F**). Because of this, the Earth's surface in polar regions receives little heating. This is especially true during mid winter when they are in darkness for 24 hours a day, because the Earth is tilted on its axis (Diagram **F**).

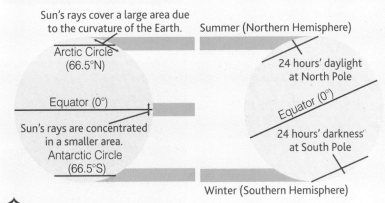

F The effect of latitude on climate

Antarctica has a colder climate than the Arctic. This is due to the following factors:

- Antarctica has more permanent snow cover. Snow cover reflects the sun's heat rather than absorbing it.

- Much of Antarctica is highland (temperature decreases by 1°C for every 100 m in height).

- The interior of Antarctica is a great distance from the warming effect of the ocean (the North Pole is in the middle of the Arctic Ocean). The land also loses heat more quickly than the ocean.

- Over the South Pole, cold air sinks and then flows outwards towards the coast. This causes constant, very cold **katabatic winds** that can reach speeds of over 200 km/h (Diagram **G**).

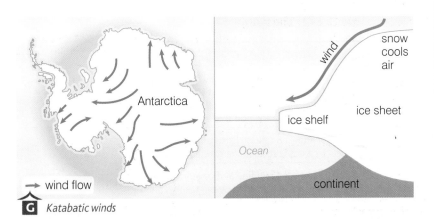

G Katabatic winds

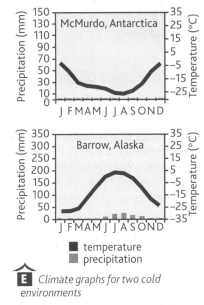

E Climate graphs for two cold environments

⨀ links

Learn more about tundra environments at **www. blueplanetbiomes.org/tundra.htm**

Activities

1. Describe the distribution of each of the cold environments on Map **A**.

2. Using Graphs **E**, compare the climate of McMurdo, Antarctica with that of Barrow, Alaska.

3. Draw spider diagrams to summarise the main features of the climate and vegetation in:

   a polar (glacial) environments

   b tundra environments.

4. Explain why Antarctica has a colder climate than the Arctic.

extension Search for, or draw a series of labelled diagrams, to show why Antarctica has a cold climate. Use the internet to research any other factors affecting the climate of Antarctica.

How does oil exploitation threaten Alaska?

The discovery of the huge Prudhoe Bay oilfield (Map **A**) in 1967 led to Alaska becoming the biggest oil-producing state of the USA during the 1970s and 1980s. The oil was transported over 1,200 km across the state, through the Trans-Alaska Pipeline, to the oil terminal at Valdez. From there it was shipped in tankers to the rest of the USA. There were always concerns raised by environmentalists that the fragile tundra ecosystem could be damaged in the event of an oil spill (Photo **B** and Table **C**).

In this section you will learn:

how oil exploitation can damage the environment of Alaska

about the arguments for and against any possible future oil exploitation in Alaska.

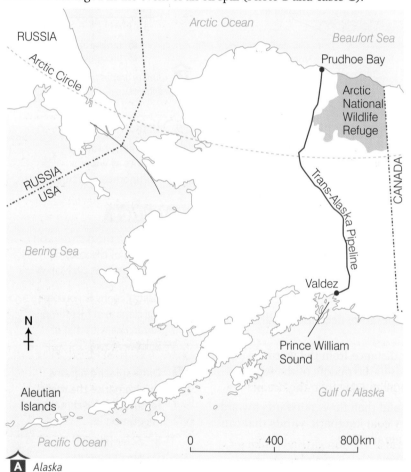

A Alaska

B Oil spill on an Alaskan beach in 2004

Did you know ??????

Crude oil is still polluting Alaskan waters today, many years after the tanker Exxon Valdez ran aground in 1989. More than 100,000 litres of oil remain in Prince William Sound.

Key terms

Extraction: removal of oil from below the ground.

Wildlife refuge: an area in which wildlife is protected.

C Effects of oil spills

Date	Place	Effects
March 1989	Prince William Sound	The super-tanker Exxon Valdez ran aground, spilling 42 million litres of oil onto 2,000 km of coastline. 390,000 seabirds are thought to have died, along with 300 seals, 250 bald eagles and 22 killer whales. Local salmon and herring fisherman were unable to fish due to the polluted waters.
December 2004	Aleutian Islands	A Malaysian tanker ran aground, spilling 1.8 million litres of oil. Sea otters, seals and other animals in a nearby wildlife reserve were killed.
March 2006	Prudhoe Bay	1 million litres of oil leaked from a corroded pipeline and covered 1 hectare of the snow-covered tundra. It polluted an area crossed by migrating caribou. Grasses and plants that grew in the short tundra summer were damaged.

The amount of oil produced in Alaska has fallen dramatically since 1988. There were slight increases with the building of some offshore platforms, such as Northstar (Photo **D**) in the Beaufort Sea. However, the oil that is available for easy **extraction** has mostly gone. The US government is looking into the possibility of opening up new oilfields on the coastal plain of the Arctic National **Wildlife Refuge** (Map **A**). Some of the arguments for and against this potential development are shown in Diagram **E**.

D *The Northstar oil platform*

For

We need the jobs the oil industry provides. We need money to make living in the harsh conditions easier.

We will only be drilling 3000 hectares of the 3 million hectares in the wildlife refuge.

The US needs this oil. We don't want to have to depend on foreign oil.

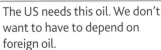

With modern technology, we can extract the oil without damaging the environment.

Against

Drilling would affect our culture and livelihood. It would affect the breeding of the caribou. We still need them for food.

Drilling will damage the fragile ecosystem. Birds, bears, wolves and moose will be badly affected.

More Alaskan oil would not reduce the world price of petrol. The area should remain as an unspoilt wilderness.

We should not be drilling for more fossil fuel. We should be investing in alternative forms of energy.

E *Arguments for and against new oil developments*

There are also worries about the safety of the Trans-Alaska Pipeline (Map **A**). Some people fear that the pipeline could be damaged and a major oil spill could occur because:

- The pipeline is a potential terrorist target.
- The pipeline is at risk of collapse because the supports are sinking as the permafrost melts. Some feel that this is due to global warming.
- The south of Alaska is at risk from earthquakes.

AQA **Examiner's tip**

Ensure that you know a case study of one cold environment that is under threat from the exploitation of resources.

links

Learn more about the Trans-Alaska Pipeline at **www.fairbanks-alaska. com/trans-alaska-pipeline.htm**

Activities

1 Describe how an oil spill might affect the following: plants, animals, local people.

2 Draw a spider diagram to show possible threats to the Trans-Alaska Pipeline.

3 Do you think that oil drilling should take place in the Arctic National Wildlife Refuge? Give reasons for your opinion.

extension

- Research the problems encountered in building the Trans-Alaska Pipeline.
- Research how climate change may lead to areas of tundra, such as Alaska, being opened up for further development.

What are the threats to Antarctica?

During the Antarctic summer, the temporary population may number 10,000. In 2007 there were visits by 37,500 tourists. Fishing boats are regular visitors to Antarctic waters. Some companies still think that there is a possibility of oil **exploitation** on the continent. All of these human activities pose a risk to Antartica's fragile environment (Diagram **A**).

Possible mineral exploitation

Scientific bases

Tourism

Fishing

A Some of the challenges in Antarctica

Key terms

Exploitation: taking advantage of a resource.

Glacier: a large body of ice slowly moving down a slope or a valley.

Impact: the effect of an action on an area.

Food chain: the feeding relationships between species in an ecosystem.

Ozone hole: the depletion of ozone in the Earth's atmosphere.

How do global problems affect Antarctica?

Many scientists believe that global warming is causing the melting of sea ice and the retreat of **glaciers** (Photo **B**). Others say that it is part of a natural cycle. However, the breaking up of the ice has an **impact** on the wildlife that lives upon it, or depends on it. Some seal and penguin populations have started to decline, as the **food chain** becomes disrupted. If sea temperatures rise further, this may create ideal conditions for predators such as sharks. Their arrival would cause chaos in the marine ecosystem. Ultraviolet radiation in Antarctica has increased, due to the growth of the **ozone hole**. This can also affect levels of sea plankton, which other animals feed on.

B Scientists at an Antarctic base

Antarctic Ice Shelf Breaks Apart

March 2002 UK scientists say the Larsen B shelf on the Antarctic Peninsula has broken into small icebergs in less than a month. It was 200 metres thick and had a surface area of 3,250 km². Researchers predicted that several ice shelves were at risk because of rising temperatures in the region – but the speed with which the Larsen B shelf has gone has shocked them. The ice would not raise sea levels because it was already floating. Sea levels would only be affected if the land ice behind it now began to flow more rapidly into the sea. There will be ecological changes, as life moves into the seabed no longer covered by ice.

Did you know ??????

If all the ice in Antarctica melted, sea level across the world would rise by 62 metres. This would flood many of the world's major cities.

AQA **Examiner's tip**

Be able to give reasons for the growth of tourism to Antarctica and be able to describe the impact of this tourist activity.

Case study

Tourism in Antarctica

Increasing numbers of visitors to Antarctica pose a threat to the environment. Visiting ships and aircraft increase the risk of water, land and air pollution and recreation activities can disturb wildlife.

The Antarctic Tour Company

Take a journey into an unspoilt wilderness. Gaze in awe and wonder at huge icebergs and glassy peaks. On a day that can last for 22 hours, see whales, penguins and seals in their natural habitat. Follow in the footsteps of the great Antarctic explorers such as Amundsen, Shackleton and Scott. Understand this delicate environment better with a first-hand visit and experience our on-ship lectures delivered by our expert expedition leaders.

FIVE AMAZING ANTARCTIC CRUISES ABOARD OUR LUXURY SHIPS.
BUT HURRY, THE PLACES ARE FILLING FAST!

EXPERIENCE THE WHITE CONTINENT

Weather permitting, you could see the blue-tinged icebergs up close, on one of our sea kayaking trips. It is a truly exhilarating experience. There are opportunities for climbers to scale peaks that few othes have visited. Stride out onto the Antarctic ice sheets, or visit an Antarctic base. It will be a once-in-a-lifetime journey that you will never forget.

We also practise environmentally safe travel, and you can be assured we follow all the international guidelines and that your visit will have a limited impact on Antarctica.

7, 10 or 14-day trips departing from Argentina

'The ultimate journey' Mr M Phipps (Devon)   *'Unbelievable'* Ms Chow (Leeds)

C | *An advertisement for Antarctic trips*

D | *A sinking Antarctic cruise ship, holed by ice*

⃝⃝links

Learn more about the Antarctic at **www.antarctica.ac.uk/about_antarctica**

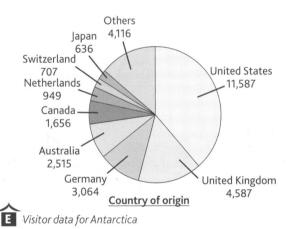

Country of origin:
- Others 4,116
- Japan 636
- Switzerland 707
- Netherlands 949
- Canada 1,656
- Australia 2,515
- Germany 3,064
- United Kingdom 4,587
- United States 11,587

Country of origin

Activity:
- Remote underwater vehicle 1,572
- Helicopter flight 2,934
- Scuba diving 5,869
- Walk 8,116
- Kayaking 16,775
- Station visit 34,296
- Small boat cruising 71,267
- Ship cruise 75,604
- Camping 1,445
- Aircraft flight 836
- Other 675
- Climbing 606
- Ice landing 525
- Skiing 8
- Small boat landing 187,144

Activity

E | *Visitor data for Antarctica*

Activities

1 Draw a spider diagram to show the threats to Antarctica.

2 Which human activity, taking place in Antarctica, poses the greatest threat to the environment?

3 Which human activity, taking place in Antarctica, poses the least threat to the environment?

4 Using Advertisement **C** and Pie Charts **E**, suggest why Antarctica is attracting increasing numbers of tourists each year.

5 Where do most visitors to Antarctica come from? Suggest reasons for your answer.

extension   Using Advertisement **C** and Pie Charts **E** and your own research, draw up a two-week travel/activities plan for a trip to Antarctica. Find out places to visit and the attractions of each. Describe the possible effects that tourism could have on the areas chosen.

Why should Antarctica be protected?

Antarctica is a continent of great natural beauty. It has been described as the last great wilderness on Earth. It contains places that remain untouched by people, yet it is a fragile and vulnerable environment.

As it is relatively undisturbed and unpolluted, it is of great value to science. It has been called a 'natural laboratory', a place that might help us to understand how our world works, and the effects that people can have on it. It is because of research carried out at a research base in Antarctica that scientists discovered the hole in the ozone layer. The ice sheets of Antarctica hold a 44 km thick 'library' of the climate on Earth over the past million years. This helps us to understand global climate change. These opportunities would be lost if the Antarctic were to become polluted and its delicate environment damaged. It is for these reasons that Antarctica is now one of the best-protected areas in the world.

In this section you will learn:

why the environment of the Antarctic should be conserved

how the environment of the Antarctic can be conserved.

Did you know ? ? ? ? ? ?

Antarctica is the best place on Earth to find meteorites. This can also help us to find out more about our world.

How is Antarctica protected?

Antarctica is protected by an international agreement. The first agreement was drawn up in 1959 and came into force in 1961. It was signed by 12 countries, which had research bases on the continent at the time. In 1991 the Antarctic Treaty laid down rules governing human activity, which became law in 1998. Its membership has now grown to 46 countries (Diagram **B**), which comprise about 80 per cent of the world's population. The Antarctic Treaty's Protocol on Environmental Protection covers the area south of latitude 60°(S). It views Antarctica as:

- a natural reserve devoted to peace and science (nuclear testing is banned)
- a place where all activities must be done in a way that limits their impact on the environment.

Some parts of Antarctica are so important that they have been given extra protection (Table **A**).

A *Special protection measures*

Name	Description
ASPA (Antarctic Special Protected Area)	Area of wilderness with great scientific value. Very strict management plan. A permit is needed to enter.
ASMA (Antarctic Special Managed Area)	Human activities are closely monitored and coordinated.
HSM (Historic Sites and Monuments)	Sites where remains of early Antarctic expeditions are preserved for the future.

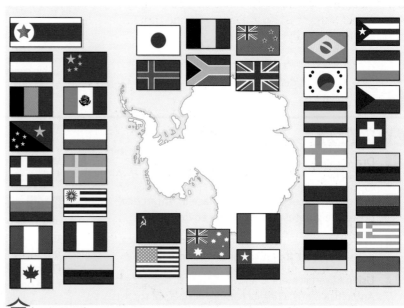

B *Flags of the Antarctic Treaty signatories*

Efforts are being made to reduce the impacts of human activities on the environment of Antarctica

Scientific bases

All the bases in Antarctica have been cleaned up and some removed. There are now strict regulations on creating as little waste as possible and preventing pollution. Most waste is now taken away from the Antarctic, but sewage and food waste is biologically treated and the resulting sludge put in an incinerator. Some bases are experimenting with alternative forms of energy. Wind power is one option, but the winds are often so strong that the windmills would be in danger of being blown over.

Mining

There was a voluntary agreement to limit mining as early as 1976. There was a massive campaign in the late 1980s, by **pressure groups** such as Greenpeace, for a complete ban. Now mining activities will not be allowed for at least the next 50 years.

Protecting animals

Seal hunting is now strictly controlled and kept to a low level. Some species are given special protection, e.g. Ross seals. No non-native species can be introduced to the continent and dog sleds are no longer used.

Fishing and whaling

These activities have not been banned, but are strictly regulated, with the aim of making them sustainable. All fishing boats have to report their catch so that the impact on the whole ecosystem can be assessed.

Tourism

There are no hotels in Antarctica yet, but some people have called for quotas on the number of tourists, so that the need for one never arises. Travel companies have joined together to form the International Association of Antarctica Tour Operators (IAATO) to promote responsible tourism. Visiting boats must be small, all tours must be guided and none should enter environmentally sensitive areas.

> **Key terms**
>
> **Pressure groups**: special interest groups that try to influence the views of others.

Who owns Antarctica?

Nobody owns Antarctica

We all own Antarctica

C *Opposing views on who owns Antarctica*

Activities

1. Describe four ways in which human activity can damage Antarctica.

2. Name the 12 countries that first signed up to the Antarctic Treaty. Name one other member from each continent. (Use Diagram **B** and/or search the internet.)

3. Design an Antarctic base for the future. What features would you include to ensure that the base has as little environmental impact as possible?

extension

a. Write an article for or against development in Antartica:

   Sometime in the future … 'The world is in desperate need of energy resources. Many countries now wish to explore Antarctica for oil.'

   Should Antarctica be protected at any cost?

b. Find out how Antarctica affects the world's climate and oceans.

> **AQA Examiner's tip**
>
> Ensure that you can describe some of the strategies used to manage and maintain the natural environment of Antarctica.

links

Learn more about the continent of Antarctica at www.discoveringantarctica.org.uk

Why should Alaska be protected?

The Alaskan tundra and ice shelf provide important habitats for many species of animals and birds, including endangered species such as the polar bear. A large percentage of the world's polar bears live in Alaska. It is a vast wilderness of outstanding natural beauty and the scenery inspires awe and wonder in the relatively few visitors that visit the area. Up until the discovery of oil in 1968, the area was untouched and unspoilt. Continued development threatens the fragile tundra and Arctic ecosystems, which could be lost forever.

Many people believe that extracting more oil from new Alaskan oilfields will not help with the drive to reduce the use of fossil fuels. They feel that burning fossil fuels contributes to global warming, which has many impacts upon Alaska. These include the melting of permafrost in many areas of tundra and the retreat of the ice shelves as the temperature rises. The thickness of the ice has declined by 40 per cent. This has huge impacts on the marine ecosystem and affects all life in the Arctic seas.

How is Alaska protected?

For many years environmental pressure groups such as Greenpeace have campaigned in support of conservation of the natural environment of Alaska (Statement **A**). For the US government, Alaska's oil is important to the economy. Conservationists recognise this, but argue for a compromise. They feel that further development of the oil industry in Alaska should be put on hold until the possible impacts on the delicate ecosystems are fully understood. Campaigns and protests have raised public awareness about environmental issues in Alaska. As a result, stricter regulations have been placed on the oil industry. The Trans-Alaska Pipeline (Photo **B**) has been described as an 'ageing giant' and essential maintenance is constantly taking place to prevent oil leaks. Pipelines were shut down in 2006 following an oil spill and the oil company was fined US$20 million. When it was first constructed, many safety and environmental features were incorporated into the pipeline's design (Table **C**).

In this section you will learn:

why the environment of Alaska should be conserved

how the environment Alaska of can be conserved.

GREENPEACE

66 *Alaska's Arctic ecosystem is doubly threatened by oil spills and global warming. The solution is the same: a future free of fossil fuels, built on safe, renewable energy sources. The Earth can no longer afford our addiction to oil.* 99

www.greenpeace.org.uk

A A Greenpeace campaign statement

B The Trans-Alaska Pipeline

C Trans-Alaska Pipeline safety features

Problem	Design solution
Migrating caribou	It is raised up to 6 m off the ground on stilts so animals can pass underneath.
Earthquakes	It is placed on Teflon shoes and built in a zigzag pattern to allow up-and-down and side-to-side movement. Stilts are driven deep into the permafrost.
Melting permafrost	As the oil is heated to stop it freezing, underground sections are encased in concrete and have insulated padding to keep heat in.
Oil spills	The pipe is split into 12 sections. In each there is a pump station that can shut off the flow of oil.

The Arctic National Wildlife Refuge

The Arctic National Wildlife Refuge (ANWR) was created in 1980 when a law was passed to preserve the landscape and protect wildlife (Map **D**).

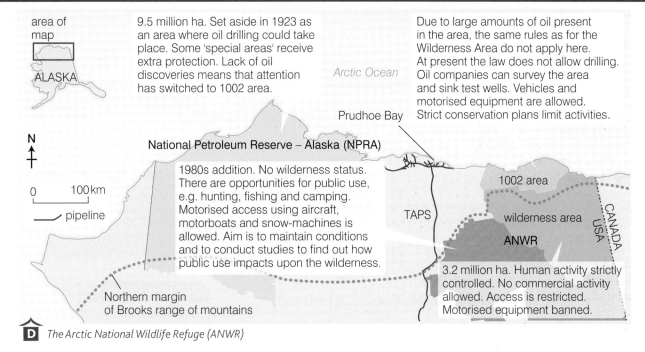

area of map

ALASKA

9.5 million ha. Set aside in 1923 as an area where oil drilling could take place. Some 'special areas' receive extra protection. Lack of oil discoveries means that attention has switched to 1002 area.

Arctic Ocean

Due to large amounts of oil present in the area, the same rules as for the Wilderness Area do not apply here. At present the law does not allow drilling. Oil companies can survey the area and sink test wells. Vehicles and motorised equipment are allowed. Strict conservation plans limit activities.

Prudhoe Bay

N

0   100 km

pipeline

National Petroleum Reserve – Alaska (NPRA)

1980s addition. No wilderness status. There are opportunities for public use, e.g. hunting, fishing and camping. Motorised access using aircraft, motorboats and snow-machines is allowed. Aim is to maintain conditions and to conduct studies to find out how public use impacts upon the wilderness.

TAPS

1002 area

wilderness area

ANWR

CANADA USA

3.2 million ha. Human activity strictly controlled. No commercial activity allowed. Access is restricted. Motorised equipment banned.

Northern margin of Brooks range of mountains

D *The Arctic National Wildlife Refuge (ANWR)*

The '1002 area' of the ANWR is an important breeding and feeding ground for both land and sea creatures. It is this area that is most under threat from oil exploitation (Photo **E**). Its long-term future is still undecided.

66 *I strongly reject drilling in the Arctic National Wildlife Refuge because it would irreversibly damage a protected National Wildlife Refuge.* **99**

Barack Obama

E *US President Barack Obama is against drilling in the Arctic National Wildlife Refuge*

Did you know ??????

- When permafrost melts, carbon dioxide and methane stored in the ground are released. These gases add to the greenhouse effect.

- Some scientists think that all the ice in the Arctic could melt within 70 years.

Activities

1 Give reasons why the environment of Alaska should be protected. Use the internet to find examples to illustrate your answers.

2 Give two effects of global climate change on Alaska.

3 Explain the importance of environmental pressure groups in helping to conserve the environment of Alaska.

4 Describe the location of the ANWR.

5 How and why is human activity restricted in the ANWR?

extension The Exxon Valdez disaster (page 106) caused lasting damage to the environment of Alaska. Use the internet to find out how new technology can be used to reduce the effects of oil spills at sea.

links

Learn more about the Arctic National Wildlife Refuge at **www.anwr.org** and **www.arctic.fws.gov/content.htm**

AQA *Examiner's tip*

Be clear as to the similarities and differences between the threats and management strategies that apply to Alaska compared with those for Antarctica.

5.1 The rise of the global economy

What is globalisation?

It is difficult to find a generally accepted definition of **globalisation** but most experts agree it is the way in which different countries and parts of the world are becoming ever more closely connected by:

- increasing trade
- the development of transport links
- the development of global communications and information technology
- global tourism (Map **A**).

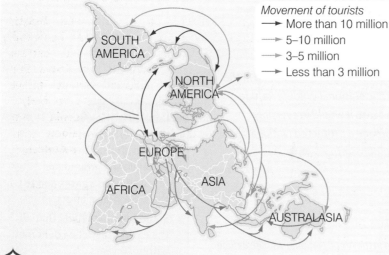

Movement of tourists
→ More than 10 million
→ 5–10 million
→ 3–5 million
→ Less than 3 million

A *Globalisation through worldwide tourism*

Countries are becoming increasingly **interdependent** and rely on each other for economic development. There are many different views on globalisation, two of which are set out to the right. Many people, like Guy Sorman, think it helps make everyone richer and more socially equal. Others, including Lewis Williamson, think it only helps richer countries or believe it is just a way of making everywhere the same as the USA and Europe.

How has everything become interconnected?

In the early and middle 20th century the world was a very different place. More developed countries made lots of different products and produced much of the food they ate. Trade was largely based on traditional **markets** so that, for instance, British products were sold to former British colonies.

In this section you will learn:

what is meant by globalisation

how globalisation affects your life.

Did you know ??????

McDonald's, a truly globalised company, has 31,000 restaurants in 119 countries on 6 continents and employs more than 1.5 million people.

❝ *What we call 'globalisation', one of the most powerful and positive forces ever to have arisen in the history of mankind, is redefining civilization as we know it.* ❞

Guy Sorman, French journalist, economist and philosopher

❝ *It is clear that globalisation has failed to rid the world of poverty. Rather than being an unstoppable force for development, [it] promises riches to everyone but only delivers to the few.* ❞

Lewis Williamson, journalist

∞ links

For more information on globalisation read the guide at **www.globalisationguide.org**

The World Bank answers questions on globalisation at **www.youthink. worldbank.org/issues/globalization**

As more countries have developed and become richer, international trade has grown and the process of globalisation has increased. As **trade** has grown so have other, more social, connections. Music and television programmes from many countries are transmitted all over the world. This process has increased rapidly as more and more countries are connected to the internet.

A globalised day

Globalisation affects us from the moment we get up until we go to bed. The article below describes a typical globalised day.

Although these connections with the outside world seem huge, they are a very small part of how we are affected by globalisation. Most cars, for example, will have mechanical parts and electrical components from 10 or more countries. The list also neglects to look at where the clothes we wear come from, who makes the beds and bedclothes we sleep in and which countries supply coal and oil to power all our electrical goods. There is no doubt that if we did not live in a globalised world our lives would be very different.

Key terms

Globalisation: the increasing international interaction in trade, politics, society and culture.

Interdependence: people, countries and businesses depending on one another.

Markets: the people and businesses that may want to trade with each other.

Trade: buying, selling and exchanging goods and services between countries.

AQA   *Examiner's tip*

Be able to define the term *globalisation*.

This morning, for breakfast, I ate Corn Flakes made from Argentinian corn and sweetened with Jamaican sugar, accompanied by some refreshing juice made from Brazilian oranges (Photo **B**). Getting into my Japanese car – built in France using Indian steel – I drove to work sitting on a seat made in Turkey. After a video-conference call to Singapore with Malaysian colleagues, I headed to McDonald's for lunch then washed my burger down with a Starbucks Ugandan coffee-based latte.

When I got home I helped my 12-year-old son access Bebo and Skype his friends in Lesotho, Guyana and Slovenia using our South Korean-assembled computer (Photo **C**) with parts from Taiwan and Singapore and software developed in Bangalore.

Dinner was a traditional British meal with Scottish roast beef and English potatoes, but with carrots and peas flown in from Kenya. For a treat we finished with an Italian tiramisu. Before heading to bed, I had a Ghanaian hot chocolate and relaxed watching Barcelona play Sparta Prague on the Indonesian-built plasma screen TV.

B   *Our daily breakfast drink could be coming straight from Brazil*

C   *A computer assembly plant in South Korea*

Activities

1   Describe your own globalised day.

2   Think about the products you like or the general names you see in the High Street. How many of these are from international companies?

extension   Investigate how globalisation affects you, using examples from around your home. In the kitchen, go to the cupboard and pick 10 kinds of food that you like to eat. Look at the labels and note down where they come from. Using a blank map of the world and an atlas, mark the countries your everyday items come from.

A hundred years ago, industry had few choices about where to set up. Transport was slow and it was expensive to take bulky products any great distance. Factories would locate near their **raw materials** – such as coal and iron ore – and close to the markets where they sold their products.

Nowadays, with increased global communications and vastly improved transport systems, companies have a much wider choice of locations. A trip around any **industrial estate** in the UK will find companies from all over the world (Photo **A**). Business parks in Surrey Heath near London, for instance, host offices and factories for Finnish mobile phone giant Nokia, Toshiba from Japan and global pharmaceutical company Eli Lilly.

Some countries, such as Ireland, have become very popular for big businesses wanting to set up in Europe. The area around Dublin with its well-educated population, beautiful natural scenery and excellent transport networks has proved particularly attractive to a number of international companies (Map **B**).

In this section you will learn:

about recent changes in industrial location

about the growth of transnational corporations.

A *Many global companies are located on industrial estates in the UK*

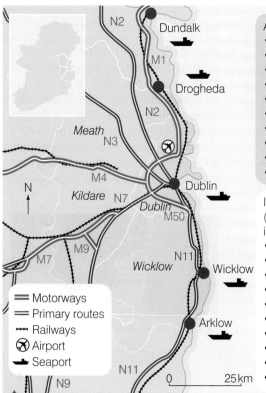

Advantages of Eastern Ireland for international companies:
- within Europe for good trade links
- 2 main seaports
- 450 flights a day from Dublin airport
- excellent road and rail networks to surrounding area
- 5 universities
- 4 technological institutes
- 9 designated business parks
- cultural history and historical monuments
- natural beauty, coastline and mountains
- Dublin social life with pubs, bars and restaurants

International companies (all from the USA) located in Eastern Ireland
- Intel
- IBM
- Hewlett Packard
- Wyeth
- Dell Direct
- Citigroup
- Microsoft
- Google
- eBay
- Merrill Lynch

Map legend:
- ═══ Motorways
- ═══ Primary routes
- ┅┅┅ Railways
- ✈ Airport
- ⛴ Seaport

0 ————— 25 km

B *Reasons why global companies are locating to the Dublin area*

Transnational corporations

Globalisation has encouraged the growth of **transnational corporations (TNCs)**, sometimes known as multinational companies. These are huge organisations, usually with their headquarters and **research and development** facilities in their country of origin. Factories, offices and shops are then spread throughout the world to take advantage of different locations.

Key terms

Raw materials: materials used to make another product, e.g. iron ore is a raw material in making a car.

Industrial estate: an area of land designated for industrial buildings.

Transnational corporations (TNCs): companies with branches and operations in several different countries.

Research and development: activities to improve old products and design/invent new ones.

Brand: a symbol or name that distinguishes a company from its competitors.

Corporate responsibility: how a company manages its impact on society and the environment.

Many of the largest TNCs are oil and gas companies such as Exxon Mobil and BP but there are also retailers including Wal-Mart (which owns ASDA) and electronics companies like South Korea's Lucky Goldstar (LG) (Table **C**). In a list of the world's top 100 economic powers there are more than 50 TNCs, making many of them richer than the countries where they operate (Table **D**). The vast majority of TNCs are American, Japanese and European companies, however, an increasing number are from China, India and other parts of Asia.

C *The world's biggest TNCs (2007)*

Company name	Business	Country of origin	Sales (US$ bn)
ExxonMobil	Oil	USA	339.9
Wal-Mart	Retail	USA	315.7
Royal Dutch Shell	Oil	UK/Netherlands	306.7
BP	Oil	UK	267.6
General Motors	Vehicles	USA	192.6
Chevron	Oil	USA	189.5
Daimler Chrysler	Vehicles	USA	186.1
Toyota Motor	Vehicles	Japan	185.8
Ford Motor	Vehicles	USA	177.2
Conoco Phillips	Oil	USA	166.7

Source: The Economist: Pocket World in Figures (2008)

Nokia – a global brand

Case study

The Finnish company Nokia is one of the biggest mobile phone businesses in the world and the fifth most recognised world **brand**. Some of the characteristics of the company are common to many TNCs:

- The company headquarters remain in Finland – the home country.
- There are regional headquarters around the globe in the USA, Singapore and Dubai.
- Research centres are located in Finland (headquarters), Germany, Hungary, China, Japan and the USA.
- Factories are dispersed worldwide with several of the biggest in less developed countries. Nokia has nine factories, in Finland, Germany, Hungary, South Korea, China, Singapore, the USA, Mexico and Brazil.
- Nokia offices and retail centres are found in more than 60 countries.

Like many TNCs, Nokia has faced criticism for some of its practices. The company has responded by pointing to its **corporate responsibility** programme which has given millions to projects that educate children in rural China, and combat HIV/Aids in Nigeria. Nokia's environmental work also includes the development of recycling practices and the responsible use of energy.

D *Economies of selected countries (2008)*

Country	Economy (US$bn)
USA	12,417
UK	2,199
Ireland	202
Bangladesh	60
Zimbabwe	3

Did you know ??????

If ExxonMobil was a country, it would be the 22nd richest in the world – wealthier than Saudi Arabia.

links

Learn more about Nokia and its corporate responsibility programme at www.nokia.com

Activities

1 Why has industry become increasingly globalised?

2 Explain how the factors shown on Map **B** might encourage international companies to set up in Dublin.

3 Suggest why TNCs such as Nokia have corporate responsibility programmes.

extension Pick two TNCs you are familiar with because you shop there or own something they make (examples could include Nike, Starbucks or Apple). Use the internet to find out where the companies operate and the products they make.

All countries are now part of the global economy. Some, such as the USA and the UK, make a lot of money from trade links with other countries while others, including many of the poorest countries, do not. In general, the more one country trades and connects with others, the richer it will become.

The world becomes a much smaller place

Over the last 50 years or so, many developments have worked together to increase global connections.

Increased mobility of people and companies

There has been a huge revolution in the way we travel and transport goods. Ships have become bigger and quicker so things can be transported increasingly cheaply by sea. Air freight means flowers, fruit and vegetables can be brought, for example, from southern Africa to Europe quickly and cheaply all year round. Increased air travel, especially **long-haul** movement and, more recently, the growth of budget airlines, means it is quick and easy to visit other countries (Photo **A**).

Technological developments

Global communication became easier firstly with a decrease in the cost of international telephone calls and then by almost instant messaging by telex and fax machines. More recent innovations, including the internet and mobile phone technology, allow us to do business with somebody in Nepal as easily as in London.

Politics, interdependence and government incentives

The growth of **market economies** in Eastern Europe, India, China and elsewhere has meant that there is greater cooperation in business between countries. Stable governments, which may offer financial **incentives**, are also able to attract TNCs more easily.

Labour costs and changing markets

Many businesses in more developed countries have moved away from making things (manufacturing) and towards services such as finance and insurance. Lower pay for workers in factories in less developed countries means that goods can be made more cheaply, for example in China, than in the UK. This has increased employment and wealth for many people in less developed countries who, in turn, become consumers and increase the demand for goods like cars, mobile phones and televisions.

Free trade

There are now more countries than ever before buying and selling on the world market. Many nations have relaxed their laws restricting trade and foreign investment (a process known as free trade). As a result, levels of trade around the world have increased rapidly.

In this section you will learn:

why countries are becoming increasingly connected

how TNCs are spreading around the world.

A Continuing developments in air travel, such as the Airbus A380, have increased global connections

AQA Examiner's tip

Be able to explain why transnational corporations (TNCs) often become established in less developed countries.

Did you know ??????

The fastest growing internet audience in 2006 was in India where the growth rate was 33% The USA, however, still has the largest internet population in the world and sends around 35% of all SPAM.

Key terms

Long-haul: travelling a long distance.

Market economies: where supply and demand determines the allocation of resources.

Incentives: something that encourages a company to do something.

More globalisation = more money

More globalised countries – that is, those that have developed the most global connections – are able to earn more money from trade. They then are able to attract more international business. It is no surprise that more TNCs locate in the USA than in any other country (Table **C**). As globalisation increases, TNCs are spreading their influence so that, for instance, the German postal service Deutsche Post now operates in more than a hundred countries (Table **B**).

B *The TNCs found in the most countries (2005)*

Company name	Number of host countries
Deutsche Post (Germany)	103
Nestlé (Switzerland)	96
Royal Dutch Shell (Netherlands/UK)	92
BASF (Germany)	79
Bayer (Germany)	70
Siemens (Germany)	69
Procter and Gamble (USA)	68
AstraZeneca (Sweden/UK)	67
Total (France)	65
IBM (USA)	64

Source: United Nations Conference on Trade and Development

C *Most favoured countries of the world's largest TNCs*

1	USA
2	UK
3	Netherlands
4	Germany
5	France
6	Italy
7	Brazil
8	Belgium
9	Switzerland
10	Mexico
11	Canada
12	Spain
13	Singapore
14	Poland
15	Japan
16	Czech Republic
17	Australia
18	Argentina
19	China
20	Hong Kong
21	Austria
22	Portugal
23	Denmark
24	Finland
25	Hungary

Source: United Nations Conference on Trade and Development

TNCs are always on the lookout for where their next market may be. As the following article shows, the latest competition is for a piece of the £140bn Chinese retail market.

The West Invades China

The newly rich middle classes of China are desperate to shop. While they want to retain traditional ways such as choosing and netting their own fish and turtles from the seafood counter rather than buying it pre-packed, they are also keen to do this in the style of a European or US-based supermarket shopping experience.

There is no shortage of TNCs wanting to take up the challenge. Already ASDA owner, Wal-Mart (the world's second biggest company), has announced plans to add to its 56 megastores in the country over the next five years and company chief Joe Hatfield has said he wants Chinese operations to rival the 3,700-store business in the USA.

Britain's Tesco and B&Q, Carrefour from France, Starbucks, Nike and Adidas are all hot on the heels of Wal-Mart – desperate for a big slice of the world's fastest-growing retail pie.

Did you know ??????

In 1950, it took three days to fly to Australia. A typical flight now takes around 21 hours.

Activities

1 Explain the reasons for increased globalisation.

2 How many of the countries most favoured by TNCs (Table **C**) are less developed countries? Explain your answer.

3 a Why do TNCs want to move into China?

   b What difficulties (such as cultural differences) do you think they may face?

extension Using the internet, see if you can find any more examples of TNCs that are opening (factories, businesses and stores) in China.

Find out ... ○⟋

There are lots of facts and figures about the global economy in the latest edition of *The Economist Pocket World in Figures*.

Patterns of global trade

World trading systems were mainly developed when European countries had colonies overseas in Africa, Asia and South America. The colonies exported **primary products** such as food and raw materials and the European countries (and some others, including the USA) sold more expensive **manufactured goods** back. This situation has changed over the last 50 years but recent figures (2006) show that:

- Seventy-five per cent of exports are from more developed countries and only 25 per cent from less developed countries (with 80 per cent of the world's population).

- More developed countries export mainly manufactured goods; 82 per cent of their total and 62 per cent of all world exports. They also sell services such as finance and tourism. Less developed countries' exports are often dominated by primary products.

- The share of global trade by less developed countries increased from 29 per cent to 37 per cent between 1996 and 2006. Africa's share, however, dropped from 6 per cent to 3 per cent.

These figures (and those on Map **A**) show that export from less developed countries, led by China and India, is increasing but trade is still dominated by more developed countries, particularly the USA. The differences in the industrial structure of three countries at different stages of development are shown in Table **B**.

Key terms

Primary products: food, agricultural raw materials and timber.

Manufactured goods: products made in large numbers, usually in a factory.

Fair Trade: a type of trade that guarantees reasonable incomes and long-term stability.

Cooperative: a company owned and managed by the people who work in it.

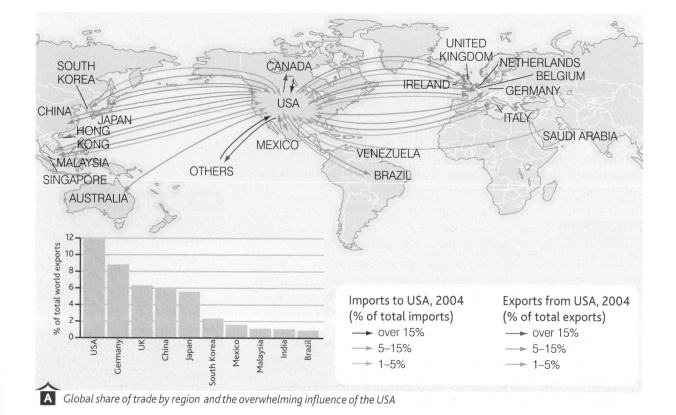

A   *Global share of trade by region and the overwhelming influence of the USA*

Why does trade appear unfair?

More developed countries buy primary goods and raw materials from less developed countries and decide how much they will pay. Prices are kept low and vary from year to year. It is difficult for farmers and businesses in less developed countries to plan for the future when they don't know how much money they will be getting for their products.

Traditionally, more developed countries have made manufactured goods from primary products and sold them back to less developed countries at high prices, earning more for their exports. Over time, the value of manufactured goods has increased more than primary products, and more developed countries have become richer while less developed countries have become relatively poorer. Even though TNCs are now locating factories in less developed countries, many have yet to see much benefit. In Asia, where many TNCs have factories, major profits are usually earned by the country of origin of the TNC.

Poorer countries often rely on one or two types of primary product, for example coffee in Uganda. If the price drops, the country has few other opportunities to make up the losses. Many people are campaigning for workers in less developed countries to be given better wages for the work they do and a higher price for the goods they produce. This has led to the growth of organisations campaigning for **Fair Trade**.

B *Difference in industrial structure between three countries at different stages of development*

Country	Total value of the economy (US$ bn)	Contribution to the economy of different types of industry (% income)		
		Agriculture	Mining and manufacturing	Services
USA	12,417	1	19	80
China	2,234	13	47	40
Cameroon	17	41	14	45

Source: The Economist Pocket World in Figures (2008)

AQA *Examiner's tip*

Know a case study that can be used to explain how Fair Trade works.

C   *Coffee farmers in less developed countries often live in very poor conditions*

Giving coffee farmers a chance with Fair Trade

Case study

Around the world, 25 million families are involved in growing coffee (Photo **C**) but the price they are paid has fallen so much over the last 30 years that many are now forced to sell their crop at prices too low to make a reasonable living. Prices are set by more developed countries which used to guarantee a fair price. Since 1990, however, price controls have been relaxed and new coffee-producing countries, including Vietnam, have flooded the world market. Prices paid to farmers have fallen by 65 per cent. The number of coffee shops such as Starbucks has increased hugely, but worldwide demand has stayed the same as people buy alternatives.

Coffee farmers have never been rich, but whereas they used to get enough money to buy food and send their children to school, many are now living in extreme poverty. In countries like Uganda, more than half of all rural workers are involved in coffee production and the current situation is disastrous.

Over the last few years, Fair Trade organisations have tried to help coffee farmers. They guarantee a living wage and promise to buy coffee for a number of years, making it easier for families to plan for the future. Farmers at one Ethiopian coffee **cooperative** receive more than double the money they would if they sold their crop on the open market. Fair Trade coffee also has environmental benefits as it is grown using more traditional methods.

Some TNCs are beginning to see the moral argument for buying Fair Trade coffee. Starbucks, for instance, has committed to buying 74 per cent of the coffee it uses at fixed, long-term prices to give farmers a more stable income.

Activities

1   What are primary products and manufactured goods? Give examples.

2   Briefly describe the basic characteristics of world trade, by referring to the text and Map **A**.

extension   Using the Fair Trade website, explain how Fair Trade can improve the lives of poor people in less developed countries.

Opportunities created by globalisation

Why are some countries richer than others?

There are many, reasons why one country is richer than another and these are often divided into natural and human factors. Some countries have greater reserves of natural resources. Iran and Iraq, for instance, have gained a lot of money from oil. Development in other countries has been restricted because of natural disasters such as floods and droughts or by civil wars and conflict. Political problems in Zimbabwe have held back an economy that was once one of the richest in Africa. Lack of technology, poor education and poor health also have negative effects on the development of a country.

How is development measured?

For many years the United Nations considered the amount of money a country earned the best way to judge the level of development. This was done using **gross national income** per person (known as the GNI). To calculate the GNI, all the money earned (in US dollars) from industry, mining, tourism and any other **economic activity** in a country is added together then divided by the total number of people living in the country. Sometimes the final figure is adjusted to take into account how much you can buy with the same amount of money in each country – rice, for instance, is much cheaper in India than in the UK.

Moving away from money – other development indicators

Judging a country by its wealth does not always give an accurate picture of quality of life and living standards. Just because a country has a high GNI does not make it a comfortable place to live. A country may have a relatively high GNI but the majority of the wealth may be in the hands of a small proportion of the population. The rest of the population may have little food and very poor living conditions. Brazil is an example of a country where there are huge differences in wealth between the richest and poorest (Photo **A**).

Instead of GNI, a much broader range of statistics, known as **development indicators**, is now used to compare levels of development. These are defined in the following terms:

- Social indicators – looking at health, education and **demography**. Statistics include life expectancy (the average age people are expected to live) and how many adults can read and write (adult literacy).
- Economic indicators – giving information about income by using data about how many people own mobile phones or have access to the internet. The number of people with the skills that will get them a job is a useful measure of economic development.
- Environmental indicators – examining air and water quality. For example, how many people have proper sanitation systems.

Did you know ??????

Although Cuba is a poor country it has very good health and education so its HDI rank is much higher than would be expected.

A *There are huge differences in living conditions for the rich (background) and poor (foreground) in São Paulo, Brazil's largest city*

Key terms

Gross national income (GNI): a way of measuring the wealth of a country.

Economic activity: all the businesses and activities that create wealth for a country.

Development indicators: health, wealth and social statistics that show the level of development of a country.

Demography: the study of population.

Human Development Index (HDI): a way of measuring development using information about income, education and life expectancy.

B   *Development indicators for selected countries*

Country	HDI rank	Adjusted GNI per person (US$)	School enrolment (%)	Life expectancy (years)	Adult literacy (%)	Mobile phones (per 1,000 people)	Internet users (per 1,000 people)
Iceland	1	35,814	96.0	81.6	100	1,024	869
USA	15	43,968	92.4	78.0	100	680	630
UK	21	32,654	89.2	79.2	100	1,088	473
Cuba	48	6,876	94.8	77.9	99.8	12	17
Brazil	70	8,949	87.2	72.0	89.6	462	195
China	94	4,682	68.7	72.7	93.0	302	85
India	132	2,489	61.0	64.1	65.2	82	55
Zimbabwe	151	2,038	52.4	40.9	89.4	54	77
Malawi	162	703	61.9	47.0	70.9	33	4
Sierra Leone	179	630	44.6	40.2	22.9	22	2

Source: United Nations Development Programme (2008)

More recently, the United Nations has used the **Human Development Index (HDI)** as an indicator of development. The HDI combines social and economic factors – life expectancy, educational attainment and GNI. Each of these variables is ranked, with 0 as the poorest and 1 as the best. The HDI is the average of the three scores and, using the final figure, it is possible to rank countries according to their level of development. Table **B** shows the HDI rank and selected indicators for a number of different countries.

Industrial growth, development indicators and the Millennium Goals

As countries develop they become wealthier and GNI increases. They can then afford to put more money into social facilities such as education and health which will improve general living conditions. This will be reflected in improving development indicators.

In 2000, the United Nations showed that living conditions for millions of people were unacceptably low. As a consequence it set eight Millennium Development Goals (Table **C**). These goals are intended to improve living standards for the world's poorest people, with a deadline of 2015 for the completion.

C   *The UN Millennium Development Goals*

Goal 1	Eradicate extreme hunger and poverty
Goal 2	Primary education for all
Goal 3	Equal treatment for women and men
Goal 4	Reduce infant mortality (death)
Goal 5	Improve health of pregnant women and new mothers
Goal 6	Fight HIV/Aids, malaria and other diseases
Goal 7	Environment sustainability
Goal 8	All countries to work together to help development

Source: United Nations Millennium Project

Activities

1   Suggest why one country may be more developed than another.

2   a   Using the data in Table **B**, draw a scattergraph with the GNI figures on the x-axis and either life expectancy or adult literacy on the y-axis.

   b   Describe and explain the relationship shown by your graph.

3   a   What indicators would you use to judge your quality of life?

   b   Use information from the HDI website to compare your quality of life with that of someone living in Malawi.

extension   Find out more about the UN's Millennium Goals. Do you think they will be achieved by 2015?

∞ links

Learn more about the Millennium Development Goals programme at **www.un.org/millenniumgoals** and **www.endpoverty2015.org**

Details of the Human Development Index and other development indicators for all countries can be found at **www.hdr.undp.org/en/statistics**

5.6   Can industrialisation reduce the development gap?

Closing the gap

All countries are developing but they are developing at different rates, so the gap between rich and poor countries is widening. This is called the **development gap**. In order to reduce it, less developed countries need to improve their social and economic conditions. The aim of the Millennium Development Goals is to reduce the gap. This can be done by cancelling debt, giving more aid to less developed countries, and making trade fairer. However, the development of industry in a country is often the driving force behind improved wealth and quality of life.

Advantages of industrial development

Setting up factories and developing industry produces employment and income. Finished products earn more money than raw materials when they are sold. A country with a large fishing fleet such as Haiti may never become rich because it has to sell the fish at low prices in local markets. Neighbouring countries such as Barbados have set up fish-processing factories to freeze or can the fish and sell the products all around the world, bringing in much needed **export revenues** (Photo **A**).

Countries need to think hard about what kind of industry they develop. Both Brazil and Malaysia, for example, sell wood products overseas but Brazil gets much less money for its pulpwood (used to make paper) than Malaysia does for its highly valued plywood and furniture.

A thriving industrial sector has many advantages for a country. The government gets taxes to spend on health and schooling, creating a strong, well-educated population who will have the knowledge to set up more industries. There will be more money available to build roads, ports, power stations and other **infrastructure**. The country may then attract more industry and foreign investment and generate more wealth.

As industry expands, so does the number of people employed in factories who have a regular income. These people spend more money in their local communities and shops and businesses spring up to serve them – this is known as the **multiplier effect**. The demand for consumer goods such as televisions and cars increases and these may be made in new local factories. People can afford increased education opportunities for their children. Other advantages of economic development include:

- less tension between rich and poor as the population becomes wealthier – this results in a more stable society
- a greater mixing of cultures as people travel and more tourists visit a country
- as society develops there is more time and money for people to express an interest in local culture such as music and art
- more awareness of the importance of the environment and the desire to develop technology and laws to protect it.

In this section you will learn:

about the advantages that industrial development can bring to a country

how industrial development can help to reduce the development gap between rich and poor countries.

Key terms

Development gap: the difference between the economic development of the world's richest and poorest countries.

Export revenues: money a country gains by selling products to other countries.

Infrastructure: the basic systems that a country needs to work, such as transport and power supplies.

Multiplier effect: industrialisation creates extra employment and earnings, giving employees more money to spend in their local communities and creating more jobs and services in those communities.

Industrial development: increasing the amount of industry in a country.

Biotechnology: using living things such as cells and bacteria in industrial processes.

Call centre: business information centre where customers can get advice on the phone.

A *Processing fish makes them much more valuable as an export*

One city showing the benefits of **industrial development** in a less developed country is Bangalore in southern India (Photo **B**), as can is described in the following article.

B *Bangalore is now a modern, industrialised and wealthy city*

Bangalore – Silicon City and Call Centre Capital

Bangalore's mild climate and hard-working population began to attract transnational corporations (beginning with US computer giant Texas Instruments) from the mid-1980s onwards. Since then it has established itself as the 'Silicon Valley' of India and now controls 33% of the country's IT exports. The growth of the university sector has also led to a boom in **biotechnology** companies with almost half of India's total based there. Meanwhile the well-educated, English-speaking population has attracted **call centres** relocating from the UK and USA.

Money brought in by rapid industrialisation has seen many Bangaloreans becoming increasingly wealthy, with at least 10,000 millionaires and an economic growth rate of over 10%. Many companies now use the city's shoppers as a testing ground for what fashions will become popular throughout the country and 83 per cent of all households have a television set – a very high number indeed for a city in a less developed country.

With more super-rich than any other city in India, the benefits of industrialisation are easy to see. It has not helped everyone, however, and the extreme poverty in some parts of the city shows that there can be a development gap within countries as well as between countries.

Facts and figures

Bangalore has the richest people in India with an adjusted GNI per person of over US $6,000 (compared with around US $2,500 for India as a whole).

Bangalore has more international sportsmen, models and university-graduate doctors than anywhere else in India.

Adult literacy is 85% (the average for India is 61%).

Bangalore has the highest density of traffic in the world, with over 5 million vehicles on the roads.

Bangalore has the highest number of pubs and cigarette smokers of any city in India.

Source: www.bangalorecityvisionindia. com and the United Nations Development Programme

AQA Examiner's tip

Be able to explain how industrialisation may improve the level of development of some countries.

Activities

1. a What are the reasons for the widening development gap?
   b Suggest ways in which the development gap can be reduced.

2. Explain how the multiplier effect can increase living standards.

3. Draw a flow diagram to show how industrialisation helps a country to develop.

extension Why are call centres relocating to countries like India? Explain how this creates both advantages and disadvantages.

∞ links

Case studies of businesses in Bangalore can be found at **news. bbc.co.uk/1/hi/business/6293291. stm**

In more developed countries there has been an increasing movement towards high revenue, technology-based industries (called the quaternary industrial sector). Companies involved in these industries sell knowledge in science and business to other countries and to transnational corporations (TNCs). Many of these new industries locate near to towns and cities on **greenfield sites** which have good transport links.

High-tech industries all in one place

One highly specialised development has been the growth of **science parks** – centres where many technological companies are found together. These have developed with industries such as biotechnology and telecommunications that have close links to research institutes and universities and employ a large number of graduates.

The idea of a designated industrial estate for science and research and development was first tried near Stanford University in California in the 1940s. In the 1970s the first UK science park was set up by Trinity College in Cambridge, 5 km from the city centre (see the case study below). There are now over 100 science parks in the UK accommodating more than 1,700 companies (450 of these are TNCs).

Building a science park costs a lot of money. The recently launched 10-year plan to build 'S-Park' near Bristol and Bath – described as a 'world-class environment for science and technology' – has a proposed budget of around £300 million (Photo **A**). The economic benefits of schemes such as this are huge. S-Park is expected to create around 6,000 highly paid professional jobs, with obvious knock-on effects for the UK economy through taxes paid and money spent in the local area. Already science parks in the UK employ around 70,000 people, a figure that has more than doubled since 2000.

Science parks in less developed countries

The huge costs involved mean the vast majority of the world's science parks are found in more developed countries, but there are increasing numbers in **newly industrialised countries (NICs)** – places like Brazil that are becoming wealthy but still have a lot of problems normally found in less developed countries. Science parks in NICs include BioRio and Tecnopolis in Brazil as well as many others in the Asian countries of Malaysia, Thailand and China.

Recently, sub-Saharan Africa's first science park – The Innovation Hub – was built at Pretoria in South Africa (Photo **B**). The centre is working with TNCs from more developed countries to develop into a regional centre for high-tech industries and research for the whole of southern Africa.

In this section you will learn:

the reasons for the growth of science parks

about the characteristics of science parks and the types of industry they attract.

∞ links

The plans for S-Park can be seen at **www.s-park.org.uk**

A *State-of-the-art buildings will be introduced at Bristol's 'S-Park'*

B *The Innovation Hub – a science park in a South Africa*

Cambridge Science Park – a European leader

Being associated with Cambridge University – one of the world's foremost educational centres – has been a very powerful way of attracting companies to Cambridge Science Park. Companies locating here know they will have access to the staff and facilities at the university and there will be a highly educated graduate workforce always looking for well-paid jobs. The original site had a lot of flat land that could be easily developed and from Cambridge there are excellent transport links to London and its airports and onward across Europe and the world.

From the start, the park has tried to attract the most able people by offering excellent working conditions. Building is low density with plenty of room for trees and landscaping. Car parks are screened from offices to keep the pleasant views (Photos **C** and **D**). Facilities for workers include a gym and fitness club, travel to work clubs, childcare, bars and restaurants.

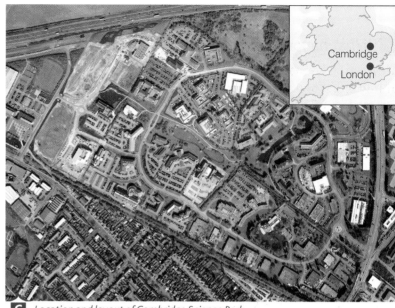

C *Location and layout of Cambridge Science Park*

The park has become the centre for a huge expansion in the number of research and development and technological companies around Cambridge. By the start of the 21st century over 1,200 companies employed 35,000 people in the Cambridge area. Within the science park there are world-famous biotechnology companies such as Bayer CropScience and Xenova Biomanufacturing. Nearby, Microsoft has located one of its major research centres.

However, people around Cambridge are now beginning to wonder if the success of the park has not come with too heavy a cost. The increasing number of workers need additional housing and property prices have soared for local people. Traffic congestion in the area has become a problem, leading to noise and air pollution and there has been pressure on the authorities to make more greenfield land available for further development. This has brought a number of complaints from environmentalists.

D *Cambridge Science Park has been designed to include lots of green space*

∞ links

More details about the Cambridge Science Park can be found at www.cambridgesciencepark.co.uk

Activities

1   Why are science parks often linked to universities?

2   Using the photos on these pages, describe the buildings and the general environment of science parks.

3   a   Why are there fewer science parks in less developed countries?

  b   Why might the number of science parks in less developed countries increase in the future?

extension   Using the Cambridge Science Park timeline (www.cambridgesciencepark.co.uk → about → timeline), describe how the landscape around the park has changed over the years, and what it is like today.

Key terms

Greenfield sites: former countryside, often on the edge of a town, now being developed.

Science parks: industrial estates set up near a university or research centre to attract and develop high-tech industries.

Newly industrialised countries (NICs): countries that are going through a rapid process of industrialisation.

The challenges of industrial change

What happens when industry declines?

There are both winners and losers in the globalisation of industry. The growth of TNCs and home-grown industries in China and India is creating millions of job opportunities. In other countries, especially more developed countries, there are areas suffering from industrial decline. When an area is dominated by a narrow range of industries, this can have very serious effects on the local communities and environments (Photo **A**).

The decline of the American automobile industry

An example of what can happen when industry starts to fail is the car industry in the USA (Table **B**). As petrol prices have risen, buyers have turned away from gas-guzzling vehicles in favour of smaller cars built more cheaply overseas. It is now very difficult for US companies such as General Motors and Ford to compete with Toyota and Nissan (from Japan). The only option left for these companies is to make their workers **redundant** and the effect this can have on their once-prosperous communities is devastating, as the article below illustrates.

A Industrial decline

B *Manufacturers' share of the US car market (%)*

	1955	1965	1975	1985	1995	2005
US manufacturers	100	90	85	75	65	52
Japanese manufacturers	0	2	10	20	30	43
European manufacturers	0	8	5	5	5	5

The Death of the Flintstones

Fifty years ago Flint, near Michigan, was one of the most prosperous places in the world.

Claire McClinton's grandparents, like many others, moved to the city to work for General Motors and the other automobile giants. For them, it was like arriving in another world.

'None of their children ever went hungry, we all had a good education, we had good jobs, and owned our own home. We thought we were living the American dream,' she said.

In the 1950s, workers in Flint had the highest incomes in the USA and the highest rate of home ownership but, today, the story is very different. Now, there are only 6,000 workers left at the GM factory – from a high of 100,000. The town and the people are suffering and the company has told its remaining workers it wants to cut back on the benefits it once promised them.

'Flint has the highest rate of unemployment, poverty and homelessness in Michigan,' Claire told me.

She works in a shelter feeding the poor and is not sure how much longer she will have a job – and if she retires, whether she will have any benefits.

A manufacturing map of the UK shows many areas, like Flint, where industries have closed down. Textiles companies have left the East Midlands and shipbuilding yards have closed in Cumbria. In some areas new industries have been attracted to replace those that have left – light industry has relocated from London to East Anglia, for instance. Other regions are struggling to cope with the loss of jobs and the effect this has had on local communities. The case study below features West Lothian in the central belt of Scotland, an area that has suffered many cycles of industrial change (Map **C**).

C *The major industrial centres of West Lothian*

The West falls and rises and falls and rises again

West Lothian – once the oil capital of the UK and known as the Texas of Scotland – has had more than its fair share of industrial decline and revival (Table **D**).

Following the end of the shale oil industry in the 1950s, efforts were made by the government to attract industry by paying them grants to set up factories and reduce unemployment. The incoming vehicle and electronics factories did not last long and, by the late 1980s, the main town of Bathgate had one of the highest unemployment rates in the UK.

More government grants followed and electronics firms such as Motorola and NEC moved in. A zone of high-tech industries spread across Scotland in an area known as 'Silicon Glen'. A global downturn in electronics at the start of this century left many companies looking to close factories and, for NEC and Motorola, the relatively highly paid Scottish workers were the ones to lose out.

Job losses were equal to 27 per cent of the total manufacturing employment and this devastated the local economy. Shops shut as local people had less money to spend and the local council reduced taxes so local services were cut, making the area less attractive to new business.

Slowly people managed to get new jobs, although this was difficult for older workers and the almost 50 per cent of employees who were unskilled. Many women, in particular, were forced to change from full-time to part-time work. One major effect was that, a year after closure, 70 per cent of Motorola and NEC employees were earning less than they had been and this affected the amount of money being spent in the local community.

The story may yet have a happy ending as the area rises again and West Lothian goes through yet another change in its industrial structure. The NEC site is now Tesco's national **distribution centre** for Scotland because of the excellent communication network and a huge local market (Map **C**). Over 100 other distribution centres, including Aldi and Morrisons, have moved into the area and the former Motorola factory is now a call centre for the Inland Revenue. However, many of these jobs are less well paid than those that previously existed in the area.

Key chronology	
early 1700s	Weaving and lime-making
1850s	Shale oil and coal industries opened
1940s on	Shale oil closures because of cheaper oil imports
1961	British Leyland set up truck factory
1984	Last coal mine closes
1986	British Leyland closes factory
Late 1980s	Electronics firms NEC and Motorola move to West Lothian
2001	NEC/Motorola close factories
Early 2000s	Tesco and Aldi sets up major distribution centres
2004	Inland Revenue set up large call centre

D *The changing industrial shape of West Lothian*

1 a Use the information in Table **B** to draw a multiple line graph showing the changes in the US car industry.

 b Describe the changes shown in your graph.

2 Suggest how industrial decline might affect local communities.

∞ links

Learn more about the background to West Lothian's industrial heritage at www.westlothian.gov.uk/tourism/attractions/history-culture/IndHerit

extension Use the internet to investigate the decline of a manufacturing industry region within the UK. Find out what the effects of the decline has had on the local community.

Over the past 20 years, many developed countries have seen a decline in their manufacturing industries, resulting in factory closures. International companies, many of them with their headquarters in these more developed countries, have realised they can make products cheaper in NICs such as the Philippines, Indonesia and Brazil.

Many companies within the NICs have also expanded to become huge TNCs. South Korea's Samsung began as a company selling dried fish for export but is now a global business. It is involved in everything from television manufacture to oil exploration and aerospace. Increasingly this process is taking place in other less developed countries, especially China and India.

Rapid industrialisation can create a number of problems, putting pressure on the countries where it is taking place. Some of these problems can affect the global environment. The following case study describes the challenges of rapid industrialisation in China.

In this section you will learn:

about the challenges of rapid industrial growth in less developed countries

how China manages the challenge of rapid industrialisation.

Key terms

Urbanisation: the increasing proportion of people living in towns and cities.

Acid rain: rainwater that contains chemicals as a result of burning fossil fuels.

Case study

China and the challenge of rapid industrialisation

China has one of the world's fastest growing economies. Between 1995 and 2005 it grew at an average rate of 9 per cent a year, compared with 3.4 per cent in the USA and 2.7 per cent in the UK. The country has gained huge benefits from economic growth with improved quality of life and advances in education and health care. However, such rapid growth has not been without its costs. Other countries will need to learn the lessons from China as they embark on their own path to industrial development.

Urbanisation out of control

China has some of the world's biggest cities and **urbanisation** – the growth of towns and cities – sees more people arrive in them every day (Table **A**). As industries develop, more and more people are attracted from the countryside by the relatively high-paying jobs. The population of Beihai, for instance, is expected to increase by more than 10 per cent each year between now and 2020. There are currently around 500,000 people living in the city so next year there will be 50,000 extra people. Those 50,000 people will need houses, water, sanitation, doctors, schools for their children and a transport infrastructure to get them to work. It is almost impossible for city authorities to cope with urbanisation on such a rapid scale. In many Chinese cities annual growth is between 2 and 3 per cent – causing problems with the growth of slum settlements, crime rates, water pollution, congestion and air pollution from the increasing numbers of factories, buses and cars.

Rural depopulation

As people in the countryside see and hear about the opportunities in the cities, more and more of them want to migrate. While this adds to the problem of urbanisation, it also causes problems in the countryside

 A   *China's biggest cities*

	Population 2006 (millions)
Shanghai	12.64
Beijing	10.85
Tianjin	9.39
Hong Kong	7.28
Wuhan	6.18

B   *China's power stations could be contributing to global warming*

they have left behind. China has so far managed to increase food output to compensate for the loss of people who previously worked on the land, but there may come a time when there are too few agricultural workers left to produce the food required. China may then have to import increasing amounts of food from other countries.

Many of the urban migrants are young men and this has other effects on the villages they leave, as a gender imbalance develops with too few men.

Environmental pressures

There are concerns that China's industrial growth is putting pressure on the environment – both in China and globally. Reports suggest that China opens one coal-fired power station each week to provide the power for its industrial development. Many of these power stations pump out pollutants that contribute to climate change (Photo **B**). Since energy is needed for industrial development, it will be difficult for the Chinese government to slow down the development of power stations.

Superdams built to increase hydroelectric power have also been criticised for flooding large areas of land, some of which has world-renowned natural beauty such as the Three Gorges on the Yangtze River (Photo **C**). Thousands of people have had to leave their homes because of such projects, many of them farmers who have been forced to move to areas where agricultural land is poor.

As China becomes richer, more people are becoming concerned about the cost to the environment and there is increasing pressure from environmental groups such as Greenpeace on the Chinese government to do something about protecting the environment.

Recently there are signs that the Chinese government is starting to think more about the environmental impacts of industrial growth. The country is vulnerable to increased flooding caused by changing weather conditions. There are also reports that around one-third of the country's agricultural land could be affected by **acid rain**. This is very important in a country that produces most of its own food. These factors are making the government think seriously about trying to control levels of pollution from its factories, vehicles and power stations.

C *The beautiful Three Gorges Valley has been flooded to create a hydroelectric dam*

Did you know ??????

The Yangtze River superdam could save lives by stopping the frequent flooding that has seen millions die over the last 100 years.

⊙links

Learn more about the Three Gorges Dam at **www.guardian.co.uk/ gall/0,,835373,00.html**

Activities

1. Why are many TNCs moving their manufacturing to NICs?

2. Using examples, describe the problems caused by rapid urbanisation.

3. What are the effects of China's industrial growth on the environment?

extension Describe and explain the social and environmental impacts of the Three Gorges hydroelectric power station on the Yangtze river in China.

AQA Examiner's tip

Industrial growth in China has had consequences for the people and for the environment. Ensure that you can give an account of these consequences.

Recent industrial growth in many less developed countries has mainly been due to the presence of transnational corporations (TNCs) who have their headquarters in more developed countries (Photo **A**). Motor manufacturers from the USA, including General Motors and Ford, were amongst the first to shift parts of their business to other countries. By doing this they could reduce costs because of lower wages and cheaper raw materials. Relocation also helped them extend their markets to other parts of the world.

Many companies followed the lead of the car manufacturers, especially those involved in computers, electronics and technological products. TNCs from Japan and other Asian countries, such as South Korea's Lucky Goldstar (LG), have set up factories in neighbouring countries. As they became more successful they expanded into countries further away. Many TNCs have come to the UK, for instance, to produce goods for sale within the European Union.

How have TNCs affected less developed countries?

TNCs have brought many advantages to their host countries but there are disadvantages as well, especially for less developed countries. Some of these are shown in Table **B**.

In this section you will learn:

how TNCs have affected less developed countries

about the moral obligations TNCs have in these countries.

A *TNCs from many different countries now operate all over the world*

B *TNCs and less developed countries*

Advantages	Disadvantages
Brings employment for local people	Numbers employed may be small
Local people get a regular wage and can be relatively well-paid	Labour force is sometimes poorly paid and does not have much job security
Wages are spent on **consumer goods** and other services in local communities which encourages further development	Consumer goods may be imported from overseas and not produced in the local area, adding little to the local economy
Local people learn new skills that can be used in other industries	Many jobs are not skilled and do not develop the skill base of the country
TNCs pay tax to the government which is spent on improving roads, airports and services such as education and health	Much of the profit is sent back to the country where the TNC is based and may not always benefit the host country
TNCs bring in modern equipment for their factories	Mechanisation means fewer people need to be employed in factories
Export earnings may increase	The environment may be exploited

Many organisations and anti-globalisation protestors have campaigned against TNCs (Photo **C**), saying they do not look after their workers. They give examples of TNCs forcing employees to work 14-hour days, 7 days a week, firing them if they complain and even sacking female workers when they become pregnant. For many people, however, working for a TNC gives them money to feed their families and pay for their children's education so that the next generation will get better jobs. Increasing the wealth of a country in this way leads to improvements in social conditions and can help reduce the development gap.

Did you know ??????

Nike has over 30,000 employees worldwide employed in factories and offices in almost 50 countries.

The moral obligations of TNCs

Following criticisms that they are exploiting the world's poor, many TNCs have developed 'corporate responsibility programmes'. These pay for development projects such as clean water, health care and schools. The publicity for projects like these influences customers in more developed countries who feel better about buying products from companies that put money back into poorer countries. If the TNCs do not do this, their public image may suffer and people may be less inclined to buy their products.

TNCs involved in particular types of business, such as health care, are sometimes criticised for being **exploitative**. Many people believe that pharmaceutical (drug) companies, for instance, should be selling treatments for diseases such as HIV/Aids much more cheaply to less developed countries. The drug companies say they have spent a lot of money developing their products and need to make a reasonable profit.

Harder to justify morally are the tobacco companies which have expanded their markets in Asia, Africa and South America as changing laws and increasing taxes have reduced their sales in Europe and the USA. Although responsible for an estimated 6 million deaths (and many more illnesses) worldwide every year, the tobacco industry still sells more than 5,000 billion cigarettes annually to its 1 billion global customers, see below.

C   *Some anti-globalisation protestors are violently opposed to TNCs*

The global tobacco industy

BAT is a US/UK company which sells 17.1% of the world's tobacco. The company says its 'Social Responsibility in Tobacco Production' programme helps 250,000 tobacco farmers around the world use good farming practices to help preserve the environment. It is also 'active in eliminating child labour' and does not buy from areas where trees are cut down to grow tobacco plants.

In addition, the company stresses it does not try and sell cigarettes to people who do not already smoke but merely gives a choice to those who have already 'chosen to be tobacco consumers'.

When asked if it is selling cigarettes to less developed countries to make up for the decline in smoking in the Western world, the company replies that it has been in these countries for over 100 years and is selling more because 'as disposable income grows, smokers want to trade up to higher quality, international brands'.

⚭**links**

Read about UK-based drugs company GlaxoSmithKline's work in less developed countries at **www.gsk.com**

Activities

1   Why might TNCs set up in less developed countries?

2   Suggest how the development of TNCs might help to reduce the development gap.

3   Explain the possible disadvantages of TNCs locating in less developed countries.

extension   Find out more about the global health programmes of pharmaceutical TNC GlaxoSmithKline. Do you think the company could do more to help combat major global diseases such as malaria and HIV/Aids?

5.11 Can economic development be appropriate and sustainable?

Can industry be sustainable?

Companies are increasingly looking at ways to reduce their environmental impact. This not only enhances their reputation but helps them reduce costs and increase profits. Many companies are trying to make their operations increasingly sustainable. This is not always easy when they use large amounts of natural resources and energy.

The dark side of traditional industry

Heavy industries such as mining, manufacturing and energy generation have always been big polluters. Pictures of traditional industrial areas show smoke billowing from factory chimneys while chemicals escape into waterways and cause health problems. In more developed countries there are now laws to prevent this, but some industries still pollute. In the USA, for instance, an increase in opencast mining has caused significant environmental damage (Photo **A**).

Industrialisation in less developed countries is putting increased pressure on the environment, but the need for money means that environmental concerns are often ignored. In China, agricultural land is being lost to acid rain caused by burning coal in its own power stations. Mining for aluminium ore in Jamaica is contaminating the local drinking water, and illegal gold mining in Brazil has increased the rate of mercury poisoning in the Amazon basin.

Can modern industry work in harmony with the environment?

As concern about the environment grows in more developed countries, new ways to reduce damage are being developed. The following are some examples:

- Coal mining laws in Australia state that any soil removed during the mining process has to be stored, mixed with fertilizer and replaced when mining is completed. The land is then replanted with vegetation.
- At the Japanese electronics giant Sharp's 'Super Green Factory' at Kameyama, 9,000 tonnes of water are recycled every day. Trees were also removed from the site while it was being built, then brought back and replanted when the site was landscaped.
- Landscaping and gardens around Marks & Spencer's lingerie factory in Sri Lanka have reduced the local temperature by up to three degrees, so less air-conditioning is needed.

Governments are encouraging industries to *reduce* the amount of waste they produce, *reuse* more and *recycle* the rest. Recycling aluminium, for instance, saves huge amounts of electricity. Recycling a single aluminium can saves enough energy to watch television for three hours.

In this section you will learn:

how traditional industries pollute the environment

what modern industry is doing to reduce its environmental impact.

A *Opencast mining is causing irreparable environmental damage*

Did you know ??????

16 of the world's 20 most polluted cities are in China.

Key terms

Sustainable: meeting the needs of the present population without destroying the environment for future generations.

Greenhouse gas emissions: gases, both natural and from industrial pollutants, that add to the risk of global warming.

Biodegradable: able to decay naturally and harmlessly.

The growth of the environmentally responsible company

Many companies have seen the benefits of promoting themselves as environmentally friendly and attracting consumers who want to buy from responsible companies. Car companies have led the way. Volkswagen, for instance, uses recycled materials to build more economical cars in low-emission factories. Honda has its own environmental website and spends billions trying to develop cars that run on alternatives to petrol – it even replaced all the advertising logos on its Formula One cars with huge pictures of the Earth (Photo **B**).

The following case study describes how Germany's chemical giant BASF is taking huge steps to reduce environmental damage at its industrial plants.

B   *Honda's Formula One 'Earth' car*

BASF – a carbon negative company

BASF has set goals to cut its **greenhouse gas emissions** by 25 per cent by 2020. Progress is already being made (Diagram **C**).

As well as cutting down on its own emissions, BASF provides environmentally friendly products to other companies. It says these products can save three times the air pollution given off while they are being made. This is achieved by making:

- thermal insulation products to reduce heat loss from buildings
- lighter plastics to reduce the weight of cars and reduce fuel consumption.

BASF has also developed:

- technology to cut emissions of greenhouse gases
- technology to cut down on releases of gases from agriculture
- alternative energy projects
- **biodegradable** plastics.

BASF is working with less developed countries to cut down on environmental damage. In Ethiopia it has planted 15,500 hectares of forest to reduce soil erosion and improve water quality. In Honduras it has built a hydroelectric power station to provide people with energy, cut down on fossil fuel use and create jobs. BASF is also contributing to the Millennium Development Goals (see page 123), for instance by starting education programmes in Brazil, benefiting 10,000 children.

66 *Climate change is one of the key challenges facing society. BASF has taken up the challenge and offers a variety of solutions to help protect our climate.* 99

Eggert Voscherau, Vice-Chairman of BASF SE

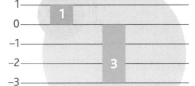

Greenhouse gas emissions
tons per year
87 million

Greenhouse gas savings
tons per year
252 million

C   *BASF's 'Factor 3' carbon balance*

Did you know ??????

Air pollution affects over 2 billion people living in 3,000 cities worldwide.

AQA   Examiner's tip

Be able to describe ways in which some companies are becoming more environmentally responsible.

Activities

1. Describe the ways in which industry can harm the environment.

2. Suggest how industry can work in harmony with the environment.

3. BASF is working to protect the environment.
   a   How is it doing this?
   b   Why do companies such as BASF want an environmentally friendly image?

extension   Write a report on how Sharp has created its 'Super Green Factory' at Kameyama, using the information on the website **www.sharp-world.com/corporate/eco/factory/kameyama.html**

Find out ... 🔍

Learn more about BASF's environment programme at **www.basf.com** and Honda's at **www.world.honda.com** → environment

5.12 Responding to economic change

Globalisation has led to changes in industrial location, with many heavy industries moving from the more developed countries where they originally started to less developed countries where wages and raw materials are cheaper. Industrial decline has left many areas with derelict industrial sites and rising unemployment. There has been a need to attract new industry through government **investment**. In the UK, for instance, millions of pounds were spent to ensure that Nissan located one of its biggest car factories in Washington near Newcastle upon Tyne. The factory has proved very successful and has employed workers made redundant after the closure of local coal mines and shipbuilding yards.

In this section you will learn:

how EU countries are trying to attract industry

how industrial estates and business parks are being built to boost declining areas.

Attracting industry to declining areas

All European Union countries spend money trying to encourage companies to set up factories within their borders. In the UK, 'assisted areas' have been identified (Map **A**) where businesses are encouraged to relocate. Businesses coming into these areas can apply for grants from the government to help them set up. These areas are in need of help because they have:

- declining existing industries
- rising unemployment rates
- low levels of adult skills
- high numbers of people claiming benefits and growing social problems
- limited economic opportunities
- poor infrastructure.

Elsewhere the government gives grants to help new companies set up and to expand existing businesses. Money is also available to improve research and development facilities and to help companies develop new technological ideas.

N

A Assisted areas in the UK (dark green), 2007 to 2013

B Investment in infrastructure around Canary Wharf has attracted many businesses

Key terms

Investment: money spent on buildings and equipment to make a business more effective.

Greenbelt: countryside around urban areas where there are stricter building regulations.

Companies need a strong infrastructure such as roads, railways and regional airports. Developing these is an important factor in attracting industry. Business at London's Canary Wharf (Photo **B**) was given a huge boost by the building of the Docklands Light Railway. Together with money spent improving facilities at the nearby London City Airport, this had a great effect on improving transport links, making the area the most important financial centre in Europe.

At a local level, councils also play their part. They set up development agencies to help businesses coming into the area and can also improve infrastructure such as public transport. In many areas councils also provide ready-made and serviced factories, offices and workspaces.

The modern landscaped industrial estate and business park

Industry can be brought into declining areas by providing purpose-built industrial estates and business parks. These have clean, attractive environments with green spaces, good parking and other facilities. Newer service industries such as call centres (where people sit at computer screens and answer phone calls from customers) and financial services have started to locate in these business parks. Some companies, such as the Royal Bank of Scotland (RBS), have built their own business parks to provide a quality environment with good working conditions and is consequently able to attract highly skilled workers. The following case study describes the RBS headquarters in Edinburgh.

Did you know ??????

Canary Wharf was named after the Canary Islands – from which many imports arrived in the 1930s when the area was a major London dock.

Number One Canada Square – the towering financial centre that dominates Canary Wharf – has 32 passenger lifts, 3,960 windows and 4,388 steps.

∞links

You can learn more about Canary Wharf from **www.canarywharf.com**

AQA *Examiner's tip*

Learn how governments have attracted industries to specific locations.

Case study

RBS world headquarters, Edinburgh

The £335 million Royal Bank of Scotland HQ (Photo **C**), built on **greenbelt** land just outside of Edinburgh, was not finished without controversy. Many thought the area should remain untouched, but the city council allowed the development to go ahead in order to make sure that Scotland's capital remained one of the world's leading financial centres.

Huge efforts have been made to motivate the 3,350 employees by providing the best facilities. The complex features a gym, swimming pool and crèche for working families. Inside, there is a small medical centre, a Tesco Express, a florist, a dry cleaner's, a hairdresser's, a bookshop and a Starbucks – everything a busy financial executive desires!

The site is surrounded by landscaped grounds with lakes and woodland, providing a peaceful environment for employees, and new habitats for wildlife.

C   *RBS world headquarters built on once-protected greenbelt land near Edinburgh*

Activities

1   Explain how governments encourage companies to set up in a certain area.

2   Using an atlas, describe the distribution of assisted areas in the UK shown on Map **A**.

3   Suggest why people might be attracted to work at the RBS headquarters in Edinburgh.

extension   Use Map **A** and Photo **B** (and other information researched from the internet) to explain why financial businesses have been attracted to Canary Wharf.

5.13 Can appropriate technology reduce the development gap?

Despite the globalisation of industry and trade, the gap between the world's richest and poorest countries continues to grow. In 2007, the United Nations stated that there was no evidence to suggest poverty was decreasing in the poorest 50 countries of the world, even when exports and foreign investment were increasing. The 800 million people living in these countries continue to suffer from hunger, disease and poor living conditions.

Reducing the development gap

The use of **appropriate technology** (AT) is seen as a way of reducing the development gap. This involves small-scale projects that reuse and recycle local materials, consume limited amounts of energy and use the knowledge and skills of local people. Examples can be seen in both agriculture and industry.

Simple, low-cost solutions for agriculture

Many AT solutions are aimed at improving agricultural production. Mushroom production in Zimbabwe, for instance, uses water hyacinth, a common weed, as a base on which to grow the mushrooms. In Kenya, the charity 'Excellent Development' builds sand dams (Photo **A**) by placing concrete walls across seasonal rivers. Water collects in the sand that builds up behind the wall and can provide enough for up to 1,200 people to drink. People are saved a long walk to get water and can spend more time on farming, increasing food production. This gives people more food to eat and they can sell any surplus, earning much needed money.

A Sand dams provide water for communities in Africa

Small-scale industrial development

In many less developed countries, electricity supply is unreliable and expensive but essential for those setting up their own businesses. In hot countries, sunlight is a plentiful resource so solar power has become an increasingly popular form of energy. In areas with plentiful water supply, schemes such as the Pico Hydro plant (see the article opposite) have been developed for small-scale electricity generation.

With a cheap and reliable power supply, small-scale industries can develop. In Bangladesh, the charity Practical Action has built workshops and power plants for pottery workers and provided them with loans to buy materials. Other small-scale industrial developments in less developed countries include:

- engineering workshops in Uganda
- a processing plant which dries and sells packets of herbs in Peru
- blacksmiths' workshops in Sudan.

Over time, these industries may develop, employ more people and create more wealth. One **entrepreneur** in India employed local women in a small factory sewing clothes (in which they were already highly skilled) and sold them at local markets. The business has developed quickly into an international operation with a large number of factories throughout the country.

Key terms

Appropriate technology: a technology that is suitable and sustainable for the place where it is to be used.

Entrepreneur: someone who starts their own business.

Turbine: a type of machine that uses the flow of water or air to produce electricity.

Did you know ??????

The ultimate example of appropriate technology could be the wind-up laptop computer. Plans for the computer could see it on sale to less developed countries for as little as £60.

As wealth increases, local people can afford to buy more from local shops and shopkeepers become wealthier. More families can pay for their children's education so the next generation will have more opportunities to improve their quality of life. This is a long process but in parts of Bangladesh it has been very successful. The country's 5 per cent annual increase in GNI has come about because of the efforts of people within the country, rather than through investment from overseas.

◼ Appropriate technology and the environment

AT projects are more beneficial for the environment than most traditional industries. Recent developments in small-scale wind power and the search for less polluting forms of transport show how appropriate technology can help the environment. More examples are shown in Figure **B** and Photo **C**. The following article describes how 'Pico hydroelectricity' is making a difference to people in Vietnam.

Getting the Most Out of Water

In the mountains surrounding the Vietnamese capital Hanoi, many rice farmers cannot afford electricity from the new pylons that line the valleys. Instead, they are turning to a low-priced alternative.

Pico Hydro is a small-scale version of conventional hydro-electric power (HEP) generation (Photo **D**). With a constant water supply they can drive a **turbine** fast enough to generate electricity, providing houses with a direct power supply. In some villages nearly every household has one of the US $20 turbines.

❝ *Using Pico Hydro is really easy. With better lighting, my wife can work and clean the house more easily, and my children can have better light to do their homework.* ❞

Ban Van Giang, Hanoi

Pico Hydro has proved exceptionally popular in Vietnam with 120,000 units installed so far.

D *The Pico Hydro plant is bringing power to thousands of people*

Building construction using:
- blocks of compressed earth
- adobe made from clay, sand, straw, water and earth

Power generation using:
- solar panels
- micro hydro
- wind power

Water supply including:
- collecting water from deep wells
- the roundabout playpump which pumps water as children play on it (Photo **C**)

Transportation including:
- bicycles
- animal-powered vehicles
- zero-emission cars

B *Examples of appropriate technology*

C *The roundabout playpump*

∞ links

Information and videos about Practical Action's appropriate technology projects can be found at **www.practicalaction.org.uk**

Also see videos showing appropriate technology projects in Africa at **www.excellentdevelopment.com**

Activities

1. Using examples, explain what is meant by appropriate technology.

2. Explain the advantages of appropriate technology for less developed countries.

3. Describe how appropriate technology can improve living conditions in less developed countries.

extension   Use the websites shown here to find other examples of appropriate technology in less developed countries. Write brief notes to describe how the projects work and the benefits they bring for local people.

6.1 Investigating global tourism

Tourism for the rich

Tourism has a long history but it is only in the last fifty years that foreign travel has been available to a wide range of people. Before that almost all foreign travel involved a journey by sea, with tourists staying in places for a number of weeks.

The growth of the 'all-inclusive' **package holiday** in the 1950s and 1960s opened up the possibility of cheap foreign holidays for millions of people. The development of air travel meant that increasing numbers of people could fly to areas like the Mediterranean coast within two or three hours.

Technological developments brought down the cost of flights so that even **long-haul** journeys, such as those to Caribbean countries and the USA, became increasingly affordable.

> **In this section you will learn:**
>
> about the development of global tourism
>
> why there has been a global growth of tourism.

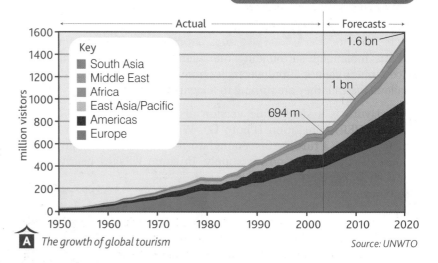

Key
- South Asia
- Middle East
- Africa
- East Asia/Pacific
- Americas
- Europe

A *The growth of global tourism*

Source: UNWTO

Tourism for all

The continuing development of air travel has reduced flight times and made travel increasingly affordable – even to such faraway places as Australia and New Zealand. In the past decade, the increase in budget airlines such as EasyJet and Ryanair has meant that many more people can afford to fly, especially on **short-haul** journeys. There are a number of reasons for the continuing global growth of tourism (Graph **A**) including:

- Increasing wealth – in many countries people have increasing amounts of disposable income to spend on holidays.
- Increased leisure time – employees now get more paid holiday time than they used to. On average a UK worker gets at least three weeks' paid leave each year. This allows people to take more than one foreign holiday each year.
- Improved transport facilities – better roads and increased car ownership mean that people can drive to nearby countries; regional airports make it quicker and more efficient for people to travel by air (Photo **B**).

B *Regional airports have encouraged more people to fly*

- Advertising – holiday programmes on television and in magazines, brochures and commercials have all increased exposure to, and knowledge of, different countries.
- Changing lifestyles – early retirement, student lifestyles and gap years have increased the amount of time available to travel.
- Increased motivation – the modern world is seen as being very stressful and holidays are a useful escape from day-to-day activities, often being seen as a necessity rather than a luxury.
- There is an increasing range of trips on offer, such as activity holidays and eco-holidays.

The importance of mass tourism

Despite the growth in destinations and types of holidays in the last few decades, **mass tourism**, where large numbers of people visit a particular area is still as popular as ever. In the 1960s, films and books such as the James Bond series glamorised the coastal areas of the Mediterranean encouraging increasing numbers of people to visit the area.

Cheap short-haul flights made the resorts of Spain, Italy and Greece much easier to reach. Holiday companies began to offer package holidays to the rapidly growing holiday resorts with their clean, attractive beaches and guaranteed sunshine. Although other parts of the world have become increasingly popular, areas like the Spanish Costas and the French Riviera are still very popular destinations, mainly for northern Europeans.

The new tourist

Increasing numbers of people from more developed countries are able to take overseas holidays – for those living in the UK, this often costs no more than holidaying at home. Many less developed countries are seeing the benefits of this increase in tourism as the money they receive from visitors increases their opportunities for economic development.

The number of people from less developed countries taking holidays is also starting to rise. China's developing middle class, for instance, wants to show its wealth by holidaying both within their huge country and elsewhere. With disposable income increasing by around 12 per cent a year, holidays such as elephant and temple tours of Thailand (Photo **C**) are proving irresistible, with trips to Paris, Rome and Sydney following closely behind. By 2020 China could even take over from Germany as the world's number one supplier of tourists.

Did you know ??????

Europe is the biggest tourist market in the world. More than 200 million foreign visitors holiday in France, Spain, Italy and the UK, accounting for 25% of the global market.

C Thailand is a popular holiday destination for wealthier Chinese

AQA Examiner's tip

Be able to explain the factors that have led to an increase in global tourism.

Activities

1 Describe the trends in the growth of global tourism as shown in Graph **A**.

2 What have been the main reasons for the growth in global tourism since the 1960s?

3 Suggest how economic development leads to the development of global tourism.

links

Learn more about Thomas Cook and the history of tourism at **www. thomascook.com/about-us/ thomas-cook-history**

kerboodle!

21st-century tourism

The business of tourism has changed significantly over the last decade with the increasing influence of the internet and the growth of **specialist holidays** and global tourism companies.

The tourists are doing it for themselves

As with many other aspects of modern life, the internet and direct advertising (sent straight through your door and to mobile phones and computers) has changed the way tourism companies operate. Only 20 years ago, most holidays would have been booked through specialists at high street travel agencies. Nowadays, increasing numbers of people find out about the places they want to visit on the internet and then book transport, accommodation and activities directly online.

Companies and organisations like the Jamaica Tourist Board have had to develop their own dynamic and attractive websites in order to attract customers. Using the interactive flash module map on their website, www.visitjamaica.com (Screenshot **A**), potential holidaymakers can tour the island and view sun-drenched beaches and spectacular scenery – this gives a powerful image to somebody sitting in a dark, rain-swept house in the depths of a British winter!

A   *The internet has revolutionised travel*   Source: www.visitjamaica.com

Advertising has also changed, with countries trying to find unique ways to market themselves. Scotland's 'Perfect Day' campaign and Ireland's 'Discover' series have both proved popular. Slogans can be very successful. Las Vegas's 'What happens in Vegas, stays in Vegas' gave the city four years of increased tourist numbers. However, it can be difficult to get it right. Scotland's recent 'Best Small Country in the World' was criticised for being boastful, while its successor 'Welcome to Scotland' was seen as 'too boring'.

Specialist holidays

Many countries are now selling themselves to certain kinds of tourist. New Zealand sees itself as the 'adventure tourism' capital of the world with its white-water rafting, mountain biking, bungee jumping and trekking (Photo **B**).

In this section you will learn:

how the business of tourism is changing

about the growth of specialist holidays and global tourism operators.

Key terms

Specialist holidays: holidays based on a particular area, interest or activity.

Fair Trade tourism: makes sure the benefits go directly to those whose land, natural resources, work, knowledge and culture are being used.

Event tourism: travel based around specific events whether sporting, cultural or historical.

Wilderness: an undeveloped and isolated environment.

Did you know ??????

Following Hurricane Katrina, there was a brief growth in 'disaster tourism' in New Orleans. This was later criticised as unethical.

AQA *Examiner's tip*

Know the arguments for and against people planning their own holidays using the internet rather than through a travel company.

B   *New Zealand is one of the world's top adventure tourism destinations*

South Africa leads the way in **Fair Trade tourism** and has set up a special award for activities that help local communities and the environment.

Event tourism is also becoming popular. Scotland marked 2009 as its 'Homecoming', inviting visitors around the world with Scottish connections to return 'home' and join in the celebrations. Sporting events such as the World Cup and the Olympics can bring in huge amounts of money for the host countries, as shown by the 2005 FIFA World Cup in Germany which brought in 20 million extra tourists. These large-scale events are also seen as redevelopment opportunities for run-down areas. The 2012 Olympics in London, for instance, is being used to transform the Lower Lea Valley, with increased sports facilities, jobs, housing and transport connections for local people (Photo **C**).

With increasing concern for the environment, **wilderness** holidays to places like Antarctica and Alaska are proving popular, and many people tour the National Parks of the USA such as Yosemite and Yellowstone. The world's most visited national park, Mount Fuji in Japan, attracts millions of visitors. For people seeking a really dramatic natural experience there are even companies specialising in tours of active volcanoes.

C *Redevelopment of the Lower Lea Valley for the London Olympics 2012*

The growth of global tour companies

As tourism has increased, some companies have grown to take control of the huge sums of money on offer. The UK's big four – Airtours, Crystal Holidays, First Choice and Thomas Cook – serve 80 per cent of British holidaymakers overseas. As an example of the worldwide spread of these companies, First Choice now take customers everywhere from Lapland to Cuba and Brazil, and offer family, clubbing, winter, summer and Santa holidays amongst others. There are also many smaller specialist companies, including adventure tour companies, that have a huge global reach (Table **D**).

D *Examples of adventure tour companies*

Tour company	Number of tours	Number of countries	Examples of countries	Examples of holidays
Explore Worldwide	More than 550	130	India, Peru, China, Oman, USA	Walking, Sailing, Cultural, Solar Eclipse
Exodus	More than 500	90	Cambodia, Papua New Guinea, Mali, Bolivia	Cycling, Winter Adventure, Polar Escapes, Wilderness
Journey Latin America	Variable including many tailor-made	More than 30	Aruba, Costa Rica, Falkland Islands, Brazil	Honeymoon, Family, Rafting, Walking, Cultural
Overland Africa	Variable including many lasting several months	11	Botswana, Zanzibar, Malawi, Uganda, Tanzania	Long-distance overland truck journeys

Sources: www.explore.co.uk, www.exodus.co.uk, www.journeylatinamerica.co.uk, www.overlandafrica.com

∞links

More about the regeneration of areas of London for the Olympics can be seen at **www.london2012.com/plans**

Specialist adventure tour companies include Explore **www.explore.co.uk** and GAP **www.gapadventures.com**

Activities

1. Explain the advantages and disadvantages of booking holidays using:
   a travel agents
   b the internet.

2. What economic opportunities does event tourism bring to the host country?

3. Devise a punchy slogan that could be used by the London Olympics 2012 to encourage people to visit.

extension Find a selection of advertisements for a variety of different tour companies from magazines or newspapers. How do the various companies try to ensure that people book with them?

Many of the world's most popular destinations and attractions are found in the northern hemisphere and involve short-haul journeys. Cruise ships, meanwhile, take people to destinations throughout the world. Event tourism and specialist holidays are on the increase with long-haul trips to the southern hemisphere for African safaris and tours of the historical Inca monuments of Peru. Even more specialised are the growing number of health tourism trips to places like India as people take advantage of the cheaper rates for dental work and operations. Examples of these trips and other popular destinations are shown on Map **A**.

In this section you will learn:

about the world's most popular holiday destinations and attractions

which countries may become popular over the next decade.

B *The world's top tourist destinations, 2008 (shown in pink on Map A)*

Country	Visitor numbers (millions)
France	81.9
Spain	59.2
USA	56.0
China	54.7
Italy	43.7
UK	30.7
Germany	24.4
Ukraine	23.1
Turkey	22.2
Mexico	21.4

Source: UNWTO 2008

C *Selected most-visited tourist attractions from around the world, 2007*

Location of attraction (and reference number on Map A)
1 Times Square, New York
2 Disney World's Magic Kingdom, Florida
3 Trafalgar Square, London
4 Niagara Falls, Canada and the USA
5 Fisherman's Wharf, San Francisco
6 Disneyland and DisneySea, Tokyo
7 Disneyland Paris
8 The Great Wall of China
9 Everland, South Korea
10 Pleasure Beach, Blackpool, England

Source: Forbes magazine (2007)

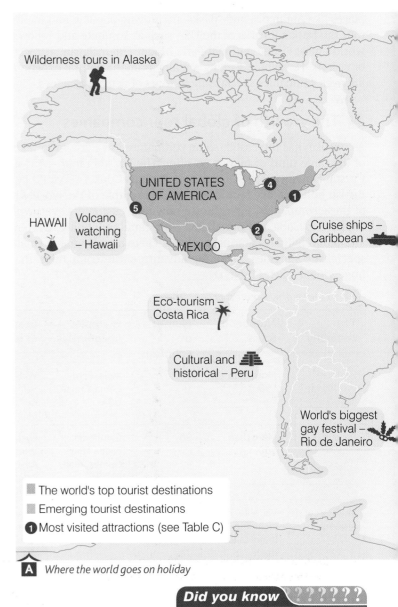

The world's top tourist destinations
Emerging tourist destinations
❶ Most visited attractions (see Table C)

A   *Where the world goes on holiday*

Did you know ??????

Ten times as many people visit Hawaii every year as actually live there.

The next big things?

As people look for exciting new places to visit, countries such as China and India and some Eastern European countries look set for huge increases in the number of visitors. Some countries, such as Montenegro, receive unexpected publicity – in this case because it featured in the James Bond film *Casino Royale* in 2006.

∞links

Facts and figures from the World Tourism Organization are available at www.world-tourism.org/market_research/facts/menu.html

D Top 10 emerging tourist destinations (shown in blue on Map A)

Country	Expected annual tourist growth up to 2017 (%)
China	9.1
Montenegro	8.6
India	7.9
Croatia	7.8
Democratic Republic of Congo	7.8
Vietnam	7.5
Romania	7.4
Namibia	7.1
Hong Kong	7.0
Chad	7.0

Source: World Travel and Tourism Council (2007)

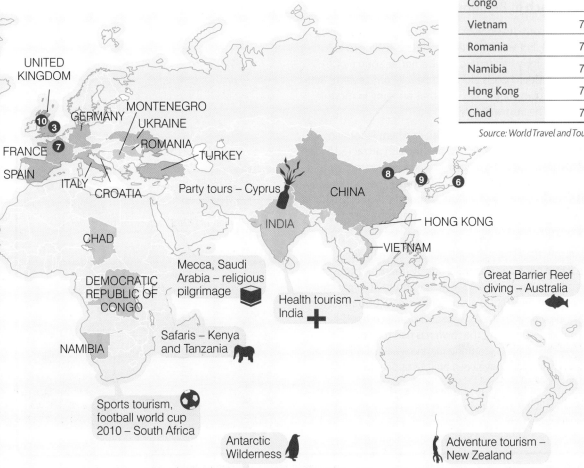

Activities

1. Describe the distribution of the world's top tourist destinations and the top 10 emerging destinations.

2. Suggest reasons for the growth of specialist holidays in less developed countries, as shown on Map **A**.

3. Give examples of countries you have seen on television, in films or on the internet that may become popular in the same way as Montenegro.

extension   Use the internet to find further examples of event tourism taking place around the world.

6.4   Different environments, different opportunities

Not everyone wants to go on holiday to the same place or do the same things. The growth of specialist holiday destinations is helping to cater for very different sections of the population. Nowadays people can do anything from cultural holidays viewing ancient ruins to gambling holidays hitting the slot machines.

Countries need to look at what they have to offer before developing their tourist industries and try to make the most of their natural and human resources. The following case studies present two vastly different examples of tourist destinations.

In this section you will learn:

how different places attract different kinds of people

why less developed countries are becoming increasingly popular holiday destinations.

Case study

Sun on the beach in Benidorm

For centuries Benidorm was one of the centres of Spain's fishing industry (Photo **A**), but with the decline of tuna fishing in the 1950s, the town quickly had to find an alternative source of income. There had been hotels along the beachfront Levante area since 1925 so the town council decided that bringing in more tourists would be the best way forward.

Slowly, the tourist industry expanded, with northern Europeans (especially from Germany, Scandinavia and the UK) attracted by the hot summer temperatures, the huge beach and all-day bars and all-night clubs. The main contributing factor to the huge tourist boom of the 1970s was the opening of Alicante airport in 1967, with the result that by 1977 the town received 12 million visitors – although the permanent population of the town was only 60,000.

A   Benidorm (1963) before the tourist boom

Benidorm was the model that all early mass tourism holiday resorts were based upon and it is still a hugely important tourist destination today. It has over 1,000 restaurants and 30 night clubs while visitors stay in the 20,000 apartments and 35,000 hotel beds that the resort provides (Photo **B**). With increasing competition from other tourist destinations, the town has had to expand its attractions, and theme parks featuring marine wildlife and ancient Mediterranean civilisations have been built to appeal to families.

Despite a recent downturn in the numbers of tourists travelling to Spain, Benidorm still has around 4 million visitors a year and there are reports suggesting that tourists spend around £500,000 each hour, accounting for 1 per cent of Spain's national income.

B   Benidorm today

∞ links

The official Benidorm tourist information site is at **benidorm. comunitatvalenciana.com**

Case study

Poles apart

While millions of people head to the Mediterranean each year, there are increasing numbers heading north and south to experience the opposite extremes of the world's climate. Polar tourism, starting from virtually nothing 15 years ago, is now a multimillion-pound industry. During the 2007 season almost 40,000 people visited Antarctica. The more accessible Arctic Circle, meanwhile, attracts over a million visitors every year.

Polar tourism costs a lot of money, with a trip to the Antarctic costing up to £7,000. Arctic tours are cheaper but still relatively expensive. For those interested in getting close to nature and unspoiled wilderness the costs seem worthwhile. Whale-watching, ice-sheet treks, polar bear viewing and dog-sled racing are just a few of the activities that make the most of the natural environment. Iceland leads the way for those who want to experience an active volcanic landscape and, in Sweden, guests can (for the winter months anyway) view the impressive Northern Lights from a hotel built entirely of ice (Photo **C**).

Specialist travellers are also catered for, with cultural tourism becoming increasingly popular, using local inhabitants as a resource in addition to the natural landscape. Tourists are encouraged to visit traditional Inuit villages, learning about the local people and their age-old way of life.

C *An ice hotel in Sweden*

The growth of tourist destinations in less developed countries

As people learn more about possible holiday destinations through television, newspaper travel supplements and the internet, the demand for global tourism is increasing.

Many less developed countries, with their unique environments and attractions, are benefiting from this. Panama in Central America, for example, saw a 20 per cent increase in tourists in 2006, with many people being attracted to the rainforests, with its large numbers of birds and exotic plants. Other Latin American countries such as El Salvador, Honduras, Guatemala, Chile, Colombia and Peru all feature historical, cultural and environmental attractions and have also had significant increases in visitor numbers.

Some less developed countries are now selling themselves as winter sun destinations, including the South-east Asian resorts of Thailand and Sri Lanka, and Goa in southern India. Traditionally these were seen as low-cost destinations and attracted students and travellers who did not spend much money. Nowadays these areas have large luxury hotels and attract families and couples with much higher disposable incomes.

There are some areas – such as the Maldives in the Indian Ocean – that market themselves as the ultimate romantic or honeymoon destination. Many couples even hold their wedding on these idyllic tropical islands and spend large sums of money making sure they have the perfect start to married life (Photo **D**).

∞ links

Information about Arctic adventure tourism can be found at **www.guardian.co.uk/travel/2007/apr/29/travelnews.climatechange**

Did you know ??????

Tourists can now parachute, ski, ride a motorbike or fly a helicopter across the Antarctic continent. Environmental organisations are increasingly worried about the damage these activities may cause.

D *Many couples get married on the tropical beaches of the Maldives*

Activities

1   What were the main reasons for the growth of tourism in Benidorm?

2   Describe the potential cultural and environmental impacts of polar tourism.

3   How does tourism encourage economic development in less developed countries?

extension   Choose an area in a less developed country which has a growing tourist industry. Using the internet, find out how natural and human features are attracting visitors.

AQA   Examiner's tip

Learn a case study of a tourist area in a less developed country and be able to explain why it has become popular and the benefits tourism brings to the country.

The good side of global travel

How can tourism help a more developed economy?

In 2006, tourism generated £400 billion worldwide. More than half of this went to European countries (Table **A**). The economic benefits of tourism for more developed economies are huge and the money generated by direct and indirect employment increases local tax revenue. This can then be spent on **infrastructure** such as roads and services including education and health.

The positive effects of tourism for the UK

The following facts about tourism in Britain in 2007 come from the Visit Britain website (Figure **B**):

- Tourism was worth more than £85 billion to the British economy, half of which came from money spent on day trips by UK residents.

- The 32.6 million visitors who came to Britain spent more than £16 billion.

- More than 3 million visitors came from each of the USA, Germany and France – Ireland sent slightly under 3 million.

- Occupancy rates of rooms in UK hotels were 62%.

- British residents took almost 54 million holidays of one night or more.

- British people spent £4.8 billion on almost 50 million overnight trips visiting family and friends within the UK.

Source: www.visitbritain.co.uk

B *British tourism facts and figures (2007)*

In the UK (2007) tourism created employment for over 2 million people. Other benefits of tourism for the UK include:

- Increased contact between different countries and cultures. Sitting at a café during the Edinburgh Festival, Germans and Americans talk to Irish at the next table while Spanish and French discuss with the city's Scottish residents events they have seen. People mixing socially in this way breaks down national barriers and increases cultural understanding.

- More interest in the cultural aspects of a country, such as museums, art galleries, castles and stately homes. This helps pay to keep them open and means that local people can enjoy them too.

- Increased protection for the environment. Large areas of Ireland and Wales, for instance, attract visitors because they are 'unspoiled'. The income from tourists helps to maintain the environment and the unique social characteristics of areas including the many National Parks throughout the UK.

Tourism can also improve a country's image around the world. The UK is a small country but has a worldwide reputation because of its natural beauty and history. **Heritage tourism** – travelling to see historical and cultural aspects of a country – means that the Queen and the royal family are big selling points for UK tourism. Although very few people actually see the royal family while visiting, millions head to Buckingham Palace and other royal residences every year (Photo **C**).

In this section you will learn:

about the positive social, ecomonic and environmental effects of tourism

how tourism can help to improve cities and rural areas.

A *Who gets the money from global tourism?*

Region	Percentage share of international tourism revenue (2007)
Europe	53.6
Asia	19.2
North America	10.6
Middle East	5.3
South America	5.2
Africa	4.9
Oceania	1.2

Source: UNWTO 2008

AQA Examiner's tip

Be able to explain the importance of tourism to more developed countries. Ensure that you can give specific details in relation to the named country.

C *Many tourists visit royal residences throughout Britain*

Regenerating cities and stopping rural decline

Some areas in more developed countries rely on tourism to generate jobs and income. Paris, Rome and Athens attract tourists from all over the world and employ huge numbers of people in the tourist industry.

Tourism can also help to regenerate areas that have suffered from industrial decline. When cities are awarded titles such as the **European City of Culture** it promotes them to new audiences. This attracts investment in new facilities and creates jobs for local people. Liverpool – the designated City of Culture in 2008 – invested millions of pounds on projects including the building of hundreds of new homes to revitalise the area of Garston.

The countryside can also benefit from increased visitor numbers. Many national parks and rural areas that attract tourists have few other opportunities for local employment. For years, the population of the Scottish islands has been declining as young people move away to find work. With tourism increasing on islands such as Skye, Gigha and Islay, there are increasing opportunities to earn a living in jobs which provide services to visitors.

It is clear that tourism can bring economic advantages but it can also create cultural and environmental pressures. The following article shows how such problems have increased on the Mediterranean island of Cyprus which receives huge numbers of visitors each year.

Key terms

Infrastructure: basic networks such as transport, power supplies and telecommunications.

Heritage tourism: visiting historical aspects of a country.

European City of Culture: a city designated by the European Union for one year.

D *Cyprus has suffered as well as benefited from tourism*

The impacts of tourism on Cyprus

In 1975, fewer than 50,000 people visited Cyprus but, by 2008, the country was receiving more than 2.5 million a year. Over half of these come from the UK with Greece, Germany and Russia also sending substantial numbers. These tourists contributed £1.4 billion to the economy of the country in 2007, bringing much-needed employment and a boost to the local economy.

However, there have been negative aspects to the rapid development of tourism. The resort of Ayia Napa on the south coast has sold itself as a party destination. Local people have been horrified by the bad behaviour of tourists on the beaches and in the bars and nightclubs (Photo **D**) and many have moved away from the noisy coastal area to nearby villages inland.

Across the island massive building projects have changed the environment and put pressure on services such as electricity and water supplies. Building developments have destroyed beach turtle breeding grounds in some areas, resulting in a decline in their numbers.

Activities

1. a   Draw a pie chart to show the information in Table **A**.

    b   Describe and suggest reasons for the pattern shown in your pie chart.

2. Use examples to explain the benefits of tourism to more developed countries.

3. Suggest how the growth of tourism can create conflict in some areas.

extension   Investigate and write a report on the importance of tourism to the coastal areas of Spain.

links

Learn about the top attractions the UK offers to visitors at
www.beabritdifferent.com

Did you know ??????

Travel and tourism is a US $1.3 trillion industry in the USA.

Why are some countries more developed than others?

There are many, often quite complicated, reasons why one country is more developed than another. Some countries have abundant natural resources. Kuwait, for instance, has gained a lot of money from oil and has used this to provide services such as education and health to improve the quality of life for its population. Development in other countries has been restricted because of natural disasters such as floods and droughts or by civil wars and conflict. Lack of technology, education and poor health can also have negative effects on a country's development.

How is development measured?

For many years the United Nations considered the amount of money a country earned the best way to judge the level of development. This was done using **gross national income** per person (GNI per capita). To calculate the GNI all the income generated from the **economic activity** in a country is added together and then divided by the total number of people living in the country. Sometimes the final figure is adjusted to take into account the purchasing power in each country – rice, for instance, is much cheaper in India than in the UK.

Moving away from money – other development indicators

Judging levels of development by simply using GNI does not always give an accurate picture of the living conditions in a country. Just because a country has a high GNI does not make it a comfortable place to live. Equatorial Guinea (in West Africa) has a relatively high GNIs but the money is in the hands of a few, very wealthy, people. The majority of the population may exist in poverty with poor housing, limited food and the constant threat of disease. In order to get a more accurate picture of development a broader range of statistics, known as **development indicators**, is now used. These include:

- Social indicators such as health, education and population – examples include life expectancy (the average age people live to), adult literacy, infant mortality and access to health care.
- Economic indicators such as average income, number of mobile phones per 1,000 population and access to the internet. The potential to make money is also important and can be measured by looking at how many people have skills that will get them a job.
- Environmental indicators such as access to clean water and sanitation systems and levels of air pollution.

More recently, the United Nations has used the Human Development Index (HDI) as an indicator of development. The HDI combines social and economic factors – life expectancy, educational attainment and GNI. Each of these variables is ranked, with 0 as the poorest and 1 as the best. The HDI is the average of the three scores and, using the final figure, it is possible to rank countries according to their level of development. Table **A** shows the HDI rank and selected indicators for a number of different countries.

In this section you will learn:

why some countries are more developed than others

how development is measured.

Key terms

Gross national income (GNI): a way of measuring the wealth of a country.

Economic activity: all the businesses and activities that create wealth for a country.

Development indicators: health, wealth and social statistics that show the level of development of a country.

Did you know ??????

Botswana has a high GNI thanks to tourism and abundant natural resources, including diamonds. However, it has one of the highest rates of HIV/Aids in the world so its HDI rank is much lower than would be expected. Costa Rica, meanwhile, has a lower GNI but has better health and education so its HDI rank is higher.

AQA **Examiner's tip**

Know some of the indicators used to measure the development of countries and learn the advantages and disadvantages of using each of these indicators.

A *Development indicators for selected countries*

Country	HDI rank	GNI per capita (US$)	School enrolment (%)	Life expectancy (years)	Adult literacy (%)	Mobile phones (per 1,000 people)	Internet users (per 1,000 people)
Iceland	1	36,510	95.4	81.5	100	1,024	869
Australia	4	33,035	100	81.0	100	90.6	698
United States	15	43,968	92.4	78.0	100	680	630
Spain	16	29,208	96.5	80.7	97.4	952	348
United Kingdom	21	32,654	89.2	79.2	100	1088	473
Cyprus	30	25,837	77.6	79	97.6	949	430
Costa Rica	50	9,889	73.0	78.6	95.8	254	254
Maldives	99	5,008	71.3	67.6	97.0	466	59
Kenya	133	1,436	59.6	52.6	73.6	135	32
Sierra Leone	179	630	44.6	40.2	22.9	22	2

Source: United Nations Development Programme (2008)

The Millennium Development Goals

An investigation carried out by the United Nations showed that living conditions for millions of people were unacceptably low. As a consequence the UN decided on eight areas that had to be improved for the world's poorest people by 2015. These are called the Millennium Development Goals. These goals will be judged using specific development indicators, such as reducing child poverty and the number of children who die young.

Tourism growth and development indicators

Many less developed countries have used tourism as a vehicle for development. Belize in Central America, for instance, has developed as a long-haul destination because of its natural rainforest and coral reef which attract nature lovers and divers (Photo **B**). Tourism now makes up almost 30 per cent of the country's GNI and is the number one foreign exchange earner. Belize has used this money to improve education and health facilities, which has increased literacy rates and life expectancy.

⚭**links**

Learn about the Millennium Development Goals programme at **www.un.org/millenniumgoals** and **www.endpoverty2015.org**

B *Belize has sold itself to divers as a long-haul holiday destination*

Activities

1 Suggest reasons why some countries are more developed than others.

2 a Draw a scattergraph using the figures for GNI and life expectancy in Table **A**.
   b Describe and explain the relationship shown by your graph.

3 Suggest how tourism can improve living conditions in a less developed country.

extension The UN's Millennium Development Goals are:
■ Goal 1: Eradicate extreme hunger and poverty
■ Goal 2: Primary education for all
■ Goal 3: Equal treatment for women and men
■ Goal 4: Reduce infant mortality
■ Goal 5: Improve health of pregnant women and new mothers
■ Goal 6: Fight HIV/Aids, malaria and other diseases
■ Goal 7: Environmental sustainability
■ Goal 8: Global partnership to help development

Find out more about the development goals from the website listed above. Do you think they will be achieved by 2015?

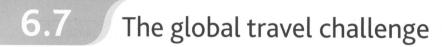

■ The problems of developing a tourism industry

Tourism can bring significant economic advantages to both local areas and national economies. There are, however, social and cultural challenges that affect people working in the tourism industry and living in communities that are dominated by tourism.

Rich or poor – common problems

Many of the issues associated with increased tourism are common to all countries, irrespective of their level of development. The following list outlines some of these issues:

- Tourist industry incomes are low and jobs often seasonal and insecure.
- Working conditions may be poor, with long and unsociable hours for restaurant and hotel staff.
- Tourist developments often use former farmland meaning that less food is produced locally and people have to buy more expensive, imported food.
- Less land is available for building houses so local people are forced to live elsewhere and have to commute to work. Second-home seekers buy houses in the areas they visit and prices rise beyond what local people can afford.
- Young people – tourism's main employees –move away from their communities to work in the tourism industry leaving an ageing population behind.
- In some areas electricity and water are limited and are supplied to holiday resorts first. Local people have to cope with an irregular or rationed supply.
- Other infrastructure cannot keep up with the demand from increasing tourist numbers so roads fall into disrepair, congestion increases and there are problems with waste disposal.
- Tourists can be insensitive to local people, intruding on their privacy by taking pictures of them without asking permission.
- Lack of respect for religious beliefs and customs means that some tourists dress inappropriately, for instance appearing semi-naked in mosques and temples.

The way these problems affect different tourist destinations can be seen in the following articles.

Gambling Problems Hit Home

Las Vegas, the gambling capital of the USA, received over 39 million visitors in 2007. The vast majority spend some time at the roulette tables and slot machines – 84% of visitors spent more than three hours a day trying to win their fortune.

But while many will spend money without getting hooked, some local people are suffering from the free and easy availability of gambling. Across Las Vegas's home state of Nevada, 6% of all adults are now addicted to gambling while 10% of young people are at risk of developing gambling problems.

The Strip runs Dry

Each day countless tourists wander up and down the desert-based Las Vegas strip (Photo **A**), in awe of dancing fountains, sinking pirate ships, tropical landscaping, pools and water features. Even now, with the region in the grip of the worst drought on record, Las Vegas consumes around 870 litres of water per person per day. Environmentalists are warning that water supplies could run dry within the next 50 years.

A   Las Vegas attracts almost 40 million visitors a year

Moonlighting Cabbies Opt for Dollars over Diseases

Getting into a taxi in Cuba's capital, Havana, my driver is as likely to give me advice on my painful knee as he is to know where he's taking me.

With jobs in tourism one of the few ways of getting hold of US dollars – needed to buy luxury goods in the state-owned shops – many professionals such as doctors are turning their hand to looking after the country's visitors. This often takes their much-needed skills away from the local population.

Your hotel receptionist could be a dentist enjoying time off, your bartender a cocktail-mixing university professor and your bellboy an English teacher in search of a big dollar tip.

B   *Working in tourism is the main source of income for many people in Cuba*

Tourism – an industry of exploitation?

Many of the companies that own hotels and tourist services are transnational corporations (TNCs) from more developed countries, so much of the money generated (up to 80 per cent) is earned by the TNC rather than the country. This frustrates governments in less developed countries, which see tourism as a big potential earner but have limited resources to set up competitive businesses.

Local people in less developed countries see tourists spend huge sums of money, compared with what they can earn. This may result in increased crime rates. Thefts from holidaymakers can occur and in extreme cases can lead to violence and even murder. In some countries, prostitution and drug trafficking have grown as a response to tourist demand.

Many see this increase in developing world tourism as a form of **exploitation** where the industry is controlled by the rich countries at the expense of the poorer people in the host countries.

Activities

1. Look at the problems tourism can cause. Make a list of those that affect more developed countries, those that affect less developed countries, and those that are common to both.

2. Use the articles to highlight the advantages and disadvantages of tourism in Cuba.

3. Explain how increased tourism may lead to an increase in crime.

extension   Using the Tourism Concern website, outline some of the other social and cultural problems associated with an increase in tourism.

AQA   Examiner's tip

Tourism brings problems as well as benefits. Be able to explain some of these problems with reference to examples in more and less developed countries.

Key terms

Exploitation: the misuse of people or resources.

Did you know ??????

Jamaica had 1,500 murders in 2007 but this had little effect on the tourist industry, which remains its highest foreign money earner. Across the whole of the Caribbean, tourists are far less likely to be the victims of violent crimes than local people.

links

More details of exploitation and social and cultural problems associated with tourism can be found on the Tourism Concern website **www.tourismconcern.org.uk**

Can tourism reduce the development gap?

All countries are developing at different rates, so the gap between rich and poor countries widens. This is called the **development gap**. In order to reduce this, countries need to improve social and economic conditions and many less developed countries have tried to do this by developing their tourism industry. While this can create economic benefits it can cost a lot of money to put in place adequate tourist facilities (Figure **A**).

* Want to sell your country and gain some tourist cash? This is going to cost but it could be worth billions!

* Firstly, is your country up to it? What are the airports like? Are they efficient and clean enough for soft, foreign visitors? Get that luggage delivery sorted or they won't come back.

* What about the roads? Potholed streets will jar their bones and send them straight back home. Lay down the tarmac now and let them arrive in style!

* What kind of hotels will they find? Get rid of that rat-infested, cockroach-ridden hovel with the 70-year-old toothless night watchman and build BIG! We're talking 30 storeys of mirror-reflecting glamour with bars, clubs and a swimming pool on the roof.

* Now sort out the attractions. Get Disney into town or at least build some roller-coasters. Got any historic monuments? Cover them in bling – MAKE YOUR CASTLE ROCK!

* So all that's cost you a few dollars. Got any money left? Bring in the advertisers and let's get down to USPs (Unique Selling Points). What have you got that nobody else has? Are you the hottest or friendliest? Do you have the best beaches this side of Benidorm? Flaunt it! Get on the internet, get in the papers and sell yourself!

* Remember: the millions you spend now will all be worth it when those rich visitors flood in.

A *Selling your country to the world!*

The downside of closing the gap through tourism

The **volatility** of tourism means that countries have to be very careful when developing the industry. Despite the economic advantages (Table **C**), some countries have an over-reliance on tourist incomes. Holidaymakers are easily persuaded by the 'next big thing' and once-popular destinations, such as the The Bahamas, can quickly go out of fashion, leaving debt and rising unemployment.

In some cases, governments and local people have been too greedy. Tourists have been put off by the environmental damage caused by too many hotels and overcrowding on beaches. There are other reasons why people may stop visiting. In St Lucia in 2007 tourist arrivals dropped 7 per cent after an international **boycott** when the island said it supported the whaling industry.

Key terms

Development gap: the difference between the rich and poor.

Volatility: when something is apt to change, often very quickly.

Boycott: showing your disapproval by refusing to go somewhere.

Multiplier effect: increased spending in one part of the economy generating spending in another.

Tsunami: a large wave caused by an undersea earthquake.

B *The 2004 tsunami had an immediate impact on tourism in many South-east Asian countries*

C *Economic advantages of increasing tourism for less developed countries*

Increased tourism means:

- increased taxes for governments to spend on improving social and economic conditions
- a better educated population who will set up industries and have a wider range of job opportunities
- more money to spend on infrastructure such as roads, ports and airports in order to increase trade
- increased trade attracts more industry and foreign investment
- increased business opportunities through the multiplier effect.

As money flows into the country from tourism:

- more people working in tourism spend more money in their local communities
- more money is spent in local businesses – this is known as the **multiplier effect**
- people can afford to improve their living conditions.

Other advantages of increased wealth include:

- less tension between rich and poor, and increasing government stability
- greater mixing of different cultures
- greater awareness of the importance of the environment and investment in environmental protection.

Natural disasters also have an effect on tourist numbers. Many tourist destinations in South-east Asia were hit by the **tsunami** wave in December 2004 (Photo **B**) that killed nearly 300,000 people. After the tsunami, tourist numbers dropped in the area and many local people lost their main source of income. On the Maldive Islands in the Indian Ocean, almost 40 per cent of the workforce relies on tourism. In the months following the tsunami, visitor numbers dropped 70 per cent. As the industry supplies three-quarters of the GNI, this had obvious negative impacts.

Recently, an increase in the fear of terrorism has seen tourist numbers decrease in some countries and outbreaks of violence have also affected countries like Kenya as described in the following case study.

⬤⬤ links

Read about tourism in Kenya at www.magicalkenya.com

The decline of Kenya's tourism industry

Case study

Kenya was one of the first African countries to develop a tourist industry, attracting big game hunters and developing safari holidays from the 1930s.

Following independence in 1963, the government saw tourism as a way to improve the economy. National parks were set up to protect the country's wildlife and there was investment in beach resorts such as Mombasa. For many years, Kenya was the number one African country for foreign visitors.

Since 2000, Kenya's tourist industry has declined. Terrorist attacks in the capital Nairobi led to Western governments advising their citizens not to travel there, and people started to go to nearby Tanzania and other destinations such as South Africa for wildlife and beach holidays.

Things became worse following disputed presidential elections in December 2007 when more than 1,000 people died in rioting and violence. Tourists stayed away – a 36 per cent fall in numbers in the first half of 2008 meant that the country lost an estimated £500 million.

There has been a growth in local tourism but this does not generate much income. It will now be very difficult for Kenya to fight off competition and reclaim its place as a major tourist destination.

Activities

1. a Why is tourism a 'volatile' industry?
   b What problems can this volatility cause?

2. Suggest how tourism can reduce the development gap.

3. Using Figure **A**, explain how a less developed country can develop its tourist industry.

extension Watch the promotional videos for some of the tsunami-affected countries at www.world-tourism.org/tsunami/eng.html

What is being done to help the tourism industry recover from the effects of the tsunami?

The development of tourism can create social and environmental **conflict** when people want or expect different things (Figure **A**). Conflict happens most in places where the largest numbers of tourists gather – sites known as **honeypots** such as the major towns in the UK's **national parks**. Here, tourists come to browse in small local shops selling traditional goods. Residents, meanwhile, may want a new supermarket built to make their own lives easier.

The following example describes some of the conflicts created by tourism in the Maldives.

> The Maldives are a collection of 1,200 mainly uninhabited islands in the Indian Ocean. Thousands of people flock to this tropical paradise each year and tourism makes up almost three-quarters of the country's income. Outside of the resorts, visitors are only allowed brief trips to the inhabited islands, to cut down on contact with the strictly Muslim population.
>
> Tourism still creates conflict. Local Maldivians are very poor and often resent the richer tourists who come to visit. Most of the money spent by visitors goes to package holiday companies with little benefit to local communities. There is pressure on food as farmers and fishermen may sell to the tourist hotels before local people. Conflict also results between fishermen (Photo **B**) and tourists who all want to use coral reef areas. Finally, tourists produce a lot of waste which is difficult to get rid of on a tropical island and can be dumped in areas out of the sight of tourists, but close to the homes of local people.

A   *Conflict in paradise*

B   *For these Maldivian fishermen who fish the coral reefs, tourism can affect their livelihood*

In this section you will learn:

- why tourism may cause problems in some communities
- how conflict created by tourism can be reduced.

Tourism conflicts in the Lake District National Park

The Lake District National Park (LDNP) in north-west England (Map **C**) has a **resident population** of 42,000 but receives 12 million visitors each year. Of these, 10 million are day trippers and, on a summer bank holiday, it can feel as if they have all come on the same day (Photo **D**)! Conflicts can occur between visitors and local residents (including farmers) and also between different groups of visitors who may want to use the area for different activities.

Conflict between visitors and local residents

- Roads can become congested with slow-moving cars and caravans. This makes it difficult for local people to go about their daily business, causes air pollution, makes parking difficult and can even delay emergency services.

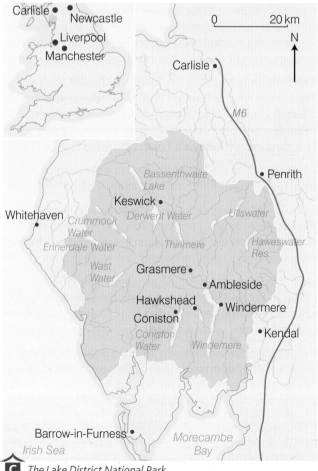

C   *The Lake District National Park*

- Some towns have their character almost completely changed by tourist shops. Residents in the honeypot town of Grasmere have no problem buying hiking boots but may find it hard to find bread and milk – and when they do, they often have to pay higher prices.

- Visitors buy second homes, increasing house prices so that local people are pushed out of the area. This affects the local community, with services such as schools closing down as demand decreases.

- Tourists may walk over farmers' land damaging crops and may leave gates open causing animals to escape.

Conflicts between visitors

- Many people visit the Lake District for peace and quiet. Some want to fish on the lakes. Others want more active pursuits, using jet-skis and motor boats. Different activities are not always compatible.

- People go walking in the hills to 'get away from it all' but the millions of footsteps can increase the rate of footpath erosion. Mountain biking can cause even more damage to sensitive environments.

- On popular days, there will be thousands of people in small towns like Ambleside. Competition for parking spaces and places in restaurants is often fierce and overcrowding causes stress – sometimes even fights break out!

Cutting down on the damage

There are many organisations working in the Lake District National Park to look after the interests of local people and to protect the environment. As well as the government-funded National Park Authority there are a number of voluntary organisations paid for by public donations.

The National Trust buys land in order to preserve it, often by keeping it as farmland which local farmers manage. The British Trust for Conservation Volunteers carries out practical work by repairing footpaths and building drystone walls. Meanwhile, the Friends of the Lake District campaign on a range of issues including water quality, public transport and the building of wind farms.

D *Many Lake District honeypots get very busy*

Activities

1. Describe the basic economic, cultural and environmental conflicts between tourists and local people in the Maldives.

2. Look at the map showing the location of the Lake District. Why do you think the area gets so many visitors? It may be helpful to use an atlas.

3. a Suggest why conflicts may develop between different user groups in the Lake District.

   b What could be done to minimise these conflicts?

extension Download the factsheet on traffic problems in the Lake District National Park from **www.townleygrammar.co.uk/departments/library/lake district/traffic.pdf**. Write a short report describing the problems caused by traffic in the park and the solutions being put forward to solve them.

Did you know ??????

Almost 90% of people visiting the Lake District get there by car. However, 50% of the total complaints received by the park authority are about traffic congestion and overcrowding.

∞links

Learn about the work of the British Trust for Conservation Volunteers at **www2.btcv.org.uk** and what the Friends of the Lake District do at **www.fld.org.uk**

Tourism is rarely an environmentally-friendly industry. There is often too much money to be made too quickly to worry about the effects on nature. Even though many people, especially in more developed countries, say they want to protect the environment, this is often forgotten when they go on holiday. While many effects of the growth in global tourism are local, some could have serious environmental impacts for us all.

In this section you will learn:

about the effects of tourism on different environments

how increased air travel may be contributing to climate change.

The environmental impacts of coastal resorts

Coastal areas often have very sensitive environments and can be easily damaged. In the Caribbean, large areas of coastal forest have been cleared to make way for hotels and tourist facilities. Inland, deforestation has provided land and wood for the houses of tourism workers. When the forest cover is removed, habitats are lost and the land is left bare. During heavy downpours, topsoil is washed into rivers. Eventually it settles on the sea floor, killing coral reefs, as seen in Jamaica, Puerto Rico and Dominican Republic.

Human waste from coastal resorts can be dumped into the oceans. In many less developed countries there is little money to dispose of it properly. If it is washed back onto the beach it causes visual **pollution** and health risks for the tourists. If washed out to sea, it can destroy sensitive marine habitats.

Tourism on the dry Spanish coasts is using up the once-huge underground water stores. In Benidorm, water is pumped from these stores to supply 30,000 swimming pools as well as golf courses, hotels and other tourist facilities. This has resulted in a fall in the **water table** and shortages of water for agriculture and local people.

Away from coastal resorts, the environment is always at risk in areas where large numbers of tourists gather. This is illustrated in the two articles.

Environmental Impacts in Honeypots

Yosemite National Park in the USA receives over 3 million visitors a year – almost all arriving by car and visiting the same areas. The building and widening of roads and car parks means less space for wildlife. There are also problems with air pollution from car exhausts. Sometimes the resulting smog is so thick Yosemite valley is hidden from sight and this has impacts on plants and animals. Noise pollution from both vehicles and humans is also a serious worry as it scares animals away and 'detracts from the pristine nature' of the park.

Trouble in Aguas Calientes

One of the most important archaeological sites in South America, Peru's Machu Picchu, is visited by almost 500,000 people each year. Thousands clamber over the ruins while guards run regular patrols to try to control them. The real problem lies in the tourist town of Aguas Calientes in the valley below the site. Here, unrestricted development in a confined area has led to landslides as hotels replace forests on steep hillsides. Large amounts of litter can be seen blowing around the surrounding mountains, while sewage and rubbish is dumped in the nearby Urubamba river – a major source of water for people downstream.

A Aguas Calientes suffers from the thousands of visitors to Machu Picchu

Long-haul travel and climate change

Although the impacts of tourism on the environment can be severe, most are fairly local. The increase in air travel fuelled by the global tourism boom, however, could have serious consequences worldwide.

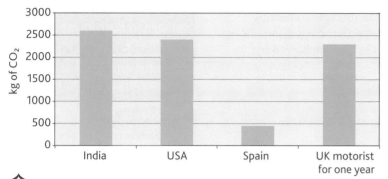

B   *Carbon dioxide emissions per passenger (return flight)*

Source: Centre for Energy Conservation and Environmental Technology, Netherlands

Air travel is the world's fastest growing source of **greenhouse gases**, such as carbon dioxide (CO_2), which add to the problem of global warming. The world's 16,000 commercial aircraft generate more than 600 million tonnes of CO_2 a year – the same as that produced by the whole population of Africa. One flight can produce more CO_2 than an average UK motorist does in a year (Graph **B**). A recent report by the world's top climate scientists has highlighted the problems caused by air travel (Table **C**). Further increases in flights over the coming decades may add to the problem and increase the risk of flooding and extreme climatic events.

C   *The damage caused by aircraft pollution*

A report by the Intergovernmental Panel on Climate Change suggests that:

- aircraft produce around 3.5% of greenhouse gases and by 2040, this figure could rise to 15%
- pollutants released at altitude have a greater effect than those released at ground level
- aircraft vapour trails – seen from the ground – form cirrus clouds which increase the global warming effect
- the impacts of climate change from aircraft will be greater over Europe and the USA
- improvements in aircraft technology will not stop the increase in airplane pollution.

Source: IPCC

While people will not stop flying, environmental campaigners Friends of the Earth have outlined steps that can be taken to reduce the damage. These include greater use of high-speed trains, the development of more efficient engines for larger aircraft and increased tax on aeroplane fuel to make flying more expensive and possibly reduce demand.

AQA   *Examiner's tip*

Learn at least two case studies, one in a more, and one in a less developed country, where tourism has had a negative impact on the environment.

⚭ links

Learn more about tourism and climate change from the WWF at assets.wwf.org.uk/downloads/tourism_and_cc_brochure.pdf

Activities

1 a Describe the tourism development shown in Photo **A**.

   b Suggest how the growth of tourism has created environmental pressures in this area.

2 Using an example, explain what environmental problems may result from the development of honeypot sites.

3 Explain why air travel will have an increasing effect on climate change over the next few decades.

extension   Look at the brochure on tourism and climate change from the WWF website. Pick any of the countries or regions studied. Describe the effects climate change will have on tourism in your chosen area.

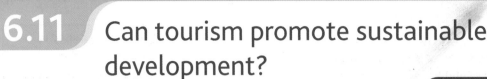

6.11 Can tourism promote sustainable development?

Growing concern for the environment is forcing many countries and companies to move towards more **sustainable** tourism – allowing development to continue today without damaging the environment and the cultural heritage for the future. This is being achieved by:

- encouraging tourists to act responsibly
- the sustainable management of tourist areas
- increasing interest in **ecotourism**.

Responsible tourism

Companies are trying to increase 'tourism responsibility' by:

- making sure tourists know about the culture, politics and economy of the places they visit
- respecting local customs
- using local businesses which keep traditional values and preserve traditional culture
- buying goods from small businesses so money goes directly to the local economy
- using companies that minimise pollution, waste, energy consumption and water use.

Responsible tourism can help a country to develop by making sure more of the money spent by tourists goes directly to local people. Jobs are created and facilities such as roads and health centres are often improved. The multiplier effect also spreads the benefits across the community. Holidays of this kind, however, cost a lot more than a package tour and many people cannot two them.

Sustainability hits the mainstream

As more and more people have become concerned about the environment, so have big tour companies. Many have **corporate responsibility** programmes to appeal to their customers. Virgin Holidays now checks all the hotels it uses to make sure they are managed in an environmentally responsible way. The company looks at energy, water and waste management as well as how hotels treat their staff, suppliers and local communities. Many airlines now offer customers ways to offset (or compensate) for the greenhouse gases their flights produce. Offsetting ideas include planting trees and providing low-energy lighting for schools in Africa.

Sustainable tourism is also increasing in the business tourism sector, which sees millions of people travelling the world each year to attend international conferences. San Francisco's Moscone Convention Center has a strong environmental programme. It includes using solar power, recycling and composting waste food.

Becoming sustainable is increasingly becoming good business. A strong environmental profile is seen as a good selling point for customers.

In this section you will learn:

about strategies used to manage tourism increasingly sustainably

about the growth of ecotourism.

Key terms

Sustainable: meeting the needs of the present population without damaging the environment and local community for future generations.

Ecotourism: holidays that do little or no damage to the natural environment and local community.

Corporate responsibility: how a company manages its impact on local communities and the environment.

Indigenous: naturally occuring in a particular place.

AQA Examiner's tip

Ensure that you can define the term *ecotourism* and be able to give detailed case study evidence of an ecotourism development.

Did you know ??????

Ornithologists flock to the Madidi National Park in Bolivia – it has 11% of the world's 9,000 different species of birds.

Costa Rica is aiming to become the world's first carbon neutral country by 2021.

The growth of ecotourism

The past decade has seen a huge increase in the demand for ecotourism – responsible travel to areas that conserve the natural environment while providing income for local communities.

Ecotourism is often centred around unique natural environments or wildlife habitats. Ecotourists often travel in small groups and like to visit national parks, game reserves and coral reefs that are carefully protected and managed.

There has been a big growth in eco-lodges (small, environmentally-friendly hotels) in rainforest areas such as Chalalan in the Madidi National Park in Bolivia. Here, the local **indigenous** community runs the lodge, teaches tourists local crafts and customs and takes them on guided wildlife walks in the forest.

The following case study describes how one country has promoted itself as the ultimate ecotourist destination – Costa Rica in Central America.

Activities

1 Explain the main features of sustainable tourism.

2 Suggest reasons why tourist companies are becoming more environmentally friendly.

3 Look at Map **A** and Photos **B** and **C**. Describe how Costa Rica appeals to ecotourists.

extension Compare the facilities at Lapa Rios and Chalalan. What are the main similarities and differences between the two eco-lodges?

The ecotourism capital of the world

More than 10 per cent of the land in Costa Rica is protected – most of it under the national parks system (Map **A**). A futher 17 per cent is set aside as forest reserves, 'buffer zones', wildlife refuges and Indian reserves. The country contains 5 per cent of the world's total species of plants and animals but is only one-fifth the size of the UK. Nature-lovers come to visit from across the globe and the well-educated and industrious local people have taken full advantage of tourism opportunities. Tourism now contributes 17 per cent of the country's income and the industry is growing at 5 per cent each year.

Staying in Costa Rica is not necessarily cheap. The award-winning Lapa Rios eco-lodge (Photo **B**), found in its own private nature reserve, costs hundreds of dollars a night but promises waterfall and bird-watching walks as well as gourmet meals – all with almost zero impact on the rainforest itself.

As other countries have begun to compete with Costa Rica, the local people have found imaginative ways to attract ecotourists. You can now canoe or raft through the rainforest on some of the world's most exciting white-water rivers. If that is too tame, you can listen to the sounds of the jungle as you bungee jump or use zip-wires through the forest canopy (Photo **C**).

∞ links

Learn more about Lapa Rios at **www.laparios.com** and Chalalan at **www.chalalan.com**

Other examples of ecotourism in areas of rainforest can be seen at **www.rainforestconcern.org**

Case study

A *National parks and protected areas of Costa Rica*

B *The Lapa Rios eco-lodge*

C *Costa Rica is now appealing to more adventurous ecotourists*

Can local people learn to love tourists?

Trying to reduce the potential conflicts between tourists and local people is a difficult task. In more developed countries it is often done through planning. For example, traffic management to reduce congestion around tourist hotspots or introducing laws which protect people and environments. It is more difficult in less developed countries where conflict is often the result of the differences in wealth between tourists and local people. Efforts are being made in some countries to make sure there is greater contact between the two groups to help them understand each other.

Managing the conflict

In the UK, the government has set up organisations to manage the most popular tourist destinations. The Lake District National Park Authority (LDNPA) works closely with the local tourist board, local councils, other government agencies and voluntary organisations to make sure everyone can enjoy the park. The LDNPA works within national parks planning guidelines in order to ensure that development in the Lake District is sympathetic to the area and the environment is preserved (Figure **A**).

Despite the work of the LDNPA it is very difficult to maintain a balance between the needs of the visitors, the needs of local people and of the environment. In some villages where car parking has been restricted to reduce congestion, shopkeepers have complained that visitors can no longer stop and buy goods. Getting the balance right is not always easy.

In some less developed countries there may be much less regulation and the development of tourism continues with little thought of sustainability. As foreign companies set up hotels and resorts, governments may abandon restrictions designed to protect the environment. The government of the Maldives, for instance, has announced plans for resort hotels on 31 new islands. This has brought criticism from environmental campaigners but economic pressures mean such concerns have been ignored. In the Himalayan country of Nepal, unplanned development of hotels has also brought conflict with local people (Diagram **B**).

In this section you will learn:

about the strategies used to minimise conflict at popular tourist destinations

about the growth of community tourism.

The LDNPA tries to balance the needs of residents with those of visitors by:

- refusing planning permission for activities it thinks will damage the environment and cause conflict

- improving traffic management, introducing one-way systems and traffic calming in the busiest towns, restricting car parking, making some roads 'locals-only' and improving public transport

- employing park rangers to advise the public about conserving the environment in the LDNP

- employing workers and encouraging voluntary groups to repair footpaths and walls and plant trees to screen quarries and car parks from public view

- insisting that homes are built for local people

- listening to local people about ideas they have for improving their towns and villages.

A *The work of the Lake District National Park Authority*

There is no water – it's been diverted for use by the hotels.

No one from here is benefiting from tourism.

Bright lights on the hilltop – but what about us? A woman has to wait 25 minutes in a queue for a bucket of water. We use the same tap for washing clothes, bathing water and drinking.

If we look for employment in hotels, nobody gets it. We only get low-paid work such as cleaning in poor-quality hotels close to our villages.

B *Effects of tourism on the Nepalese village of Naldum*

Concern about the impacts of tourism on local people has led to the growth of a new sector in the global tourism industry – community tourism.

◼ Getting close to communities

Many tourists no longer want to stay in large hotels but would prefer to get to know the people of the countries they are visiting. Cuba, a popular tourist destination in the Caribbean, was one of the first countries to start this trend. As tourism in the country increased, the few hotels quickly became full so the government encouraged local people to charge tourists to stay in their homes.

The idea has been very popular and **grassroots** organisations in other countries are now following Cuba's example. South Africa has become one of the leaders in this kind of tourism (Photo **C**). In rural areas tourists can stay with local tribes on game reserves or they can share a drink with local people in the big cities. **Community tourism** can also have a big effect in reducing tension between local people and visitors, as shown in the following article about Jamaica.

Staying at Home with the Locals in Jamaica

Community tourism businesses are becoming increasingly popular on the Caribbean island of Jamaica.

Guests stay in bed and breakfast accommodation in rural areas or in private homes to get to know the family way of life. In the wider local community they spend money in businesses such as arts and crafts shops and local restaurants and bars.

Community tourists benefit from:

- much more interaction with the local people and their culture
- a closer connection with the natural environment than found in the main tourist resorts
- a feeling that their money is going to local people.

The local community also benefits by:

- sharing culture and increasing understanding with people from overseas
- bypassing big tourism businesses and receiving more money directly in communities and rural villages.

Community tourism could be a big feature in the future of Jamaican tourism and organisations promoting this type of tourism are increasing.

Key terms

Grassroots: run by local people to benefit local communities.

Community tourism: tourism that has close contact with, and mainly benefits, local communities.

C   *Township tours are an example of community tourism in South Africa*

AQA *Examiner's tip*

Be able to give examples of how conflicts between local people and tourists can be managed.

Did you know ??????

Jamaica receives more than a million visitors from cruise ships every year but the majority stay less than a day and spend little money.

Activities

1. Describe how management and planning help to reduce tourism pressures in the Lake District National Park.

2. Suggest reasons for the growth in popularity of community tourism.

3. Explain how community tourism helps local people.

extension   What could be done to increase the benefits of tourism for the villagers of Naldum in Nepal? You should think of strategies that could be introduced both by the government and the local businesses involved.

CO links

Find out more about community tourism in Jamaica at **www.mona. uwi.edu/jct** and in Southern Africa at **www.community-tourism-africa. com**

A tourism success story

The Great Barrier Reef, located off Australia's eastern coast, is one of the world's natural wonders (Map **A**). It is the largest coral reef system on Earth, measuring more than 2,575 km in length. The 2 million visitors it receives each year come to dive (Photo **B**) or stay on island resorts, cruise the area on ships or fly over in helicopters and planes. Tourism brings in a lot of money for both the local and national economy. The huge numbers of tourists, however, put a lot of pressure on the reef environment. Threats include overfishing and pollution from industry and agriculture which can damage the marine environment and kill the coral.

Managing the reef is a huge task but the Great Barrier Reef Marine Park Authority (GBRMPA) has won national and international awards for the excellent job it is doing protecting the environment while also managing the large numbers of visitors.

The goal of the Great Barrier Reef Marine Park Authority is:

To provide for the long-term protection, ecologically sustainable use, understanding and enjoyment of the Great Barrier Reef through the care and development of the Great Barrier Reef Marine Park.

Management of the Great Barrier Reef Marine Park

The GBRMPA aims to protect the 'natural qualities' of the reef while making sure it is still available for people to use. It is committed to sustainable tourism. To do this the Authority has to work to reduce conflict between many different user groups. Apart from the tourists, there are fishermen to consider from the major towns along the coast and also aboriginal communities and people living on the islands of the Torres Strait who have used the reef for centuries.

The GBRMPA uses a number of different strategies to manage the area:

- Any organisation or project wanting to use the reef has to prepare a full report on how the environment will be affected.
- Tourists and tourism companies must obtain permits before diving, camping or fishing in the area.
- Staff at visitor education centres make sure people know how their trips will affect the reef.
- Ten patrol boats check for illegal activity in the park and there are very heavy fines for criminal activity – polluting the reef, for instance, can result in a fine of up to £500,000.

Reef zoning

Parts of the reef have very important collections of plants and animals and need more protection, in some cases even isolating them from tourists. The GBRMPA has surveyed the whole reef to map its **biodiversity**. After talking to all reef users the authority produced zoning maps showing where different activities can be carried out. In some zones, certain types of fishing are allowed while others need a permit. There are areas set aside for fishing by tourists and for traditional fishing methods

A *The Great Barrier Reef lies off the eastern coast of Australia*

B *Diving is one of the most popular tourist activities on the reef*

used by the **indigenous** communities (Photo **C**). There are also a number of 'green zones' which are completely protected from human interference.

The reef and climate change

Worldwide climate change is a particular threat to the Great Barrier Reef because of the negative effects that increased sea temperatures and rising sea levels have on coral reefs. As one of Australia's greatest attractions, this is of major concern because of how it might affect local communities and the national economy. There is little that the GBRMPA can do on its own to stop climate change but it has completed studies into the impacts of climate change on the reef and the vulnerable wildlife. The authority is working with the Australian government to educate the public about the effects of climate change. It is also helping local communities who depend on the reef to prepare for the worst if it is damaged by the effects of climate change.

Lessons from the GBRMPA

The management of the Great Barrier Reef has been hailed as a world-leading example of how sustainable tourism can be carried out. The GBRMPA has won international recognition and awards for the way it communicates with local people, listens to tourists and tries to make sure the users of the reef are involved in planning for the future. Plans for the reef and the need for environmental protection are both part of the education programme carried out by the GBRMPA. The authority also has law enforcement options through its patrol boats and park officers. It is this multi-layered approach that has made the sustainable management of the park so successful and provides a model that can be copied by other, similar areas throughout the world.

C   *Local communities still carry out traditional fishing on the reef*

Activities

1   Explain how tourists may damage the Great Barrier Reef.

2   Describe the actions taken by the Great Barrier Reef Marine Park Authority to manage the reef.

3   What lessons from the GBRMPA's management could be applied to other sensitive tourism environments?

extension   Go the website for the Iwokrama forest reserve in Guyana at **www.iwokrama.org** → eco-tourism
Prepare a report on ecotourism in the reserve, looking at:

- the characteristics of the reserve

- the activities available for ecotourists and those carried out by the local people

- why different activities may conflict with each other

- how management reduces potential conflict between different user groups.

Key terms

Biodiversity: the number and variety of plant and animal species that live in a particular area.

∞links

Learn more about the management of the Great Barrier Reef on the Marine Protection Authority's website at **www.gbrmpa.gov.au/corp_site**

7.1   Energy use and development

How are energy use and development linked?

The following paragraph briefly describes the daily life of a teenager in Mali (West Africa), one of the poorest countries in the world.

> 66 Most people in Mali live in small villages and rely on farming and gathering to survive, selling one or two animals a year to earn a little money. Our village is made up of about 50 huts. It is a small community where daily tasks such as collecting water and firewood are shared. None of the villages in this area has electricity; open fires are used to cook and boil water. The main sources of fuel are wood and dried animal manure. There is a small school and clinic about 2 hours' walk away, but even they don't have electricity. 99

Measuring development and energy use

Economic development is often measured by using a figure of gross national income (GNI) per capita (each person). This is the total value of goods and services produced by a country divided by its population. It gives an average measure of wealth per year in US dollars.

Energy use is measured by calculating the equivalent amount of oil used per person each year in kilogrammes (kg). Table **A** shows data for a number of countries in 2008.

A   *GNI and energy use data for a number of countries in 2008*

Country	GNI/capita (US$)	Energy use (oil equiv./person/year)
High income countries		
Iceland	26,940	12,420
UK	27,200	4,260
USA	34,420	8,640
Middle income countries		
Brazil	4,760	1,690
Mexico	6,270	1,980
South Africa	7,200	2,620
Low income countries		
Bangladesh	420	160
India	890	460
Mali	290	48

In this section you will learn:

why development and energy use are linked

to understand why renewable energy will become increasingly important in the future.

Activities

1. a   Produce a simple 'energy diary' for yourself by writing down every way your daily life uses electricity.

    b   Compare your 'energy diary' with the teenager's life in Mali.

2.   How different would your life be without reliable and affordable access to electricity?

∞ links

Learn more about energy resources at www.un.org
www.shell.com
www.siemens.com
www.energysavingtrust.org.uk

Why do countries use more energy as they become more developed?

As countries develop and become wealthier there is an increasing demand for energy. There are a number of reasons for this, including:

- the growth of industry
- the increased use of machinery in agriculture and industry
- a growing need to transport raw materials and finished products
- the development of energy infrastructure (power stations, transmission lines, cabling)
- improved housing and an increasing number of houses with electricity
- increases in individual wealth that leads to greater demand for consumer goods such as cars and electrical goods
- increased leisure facilities and opportunities for travel.

Managing increasing energy demands

Fossil fuels (coal, oil, gas) are the most important global energy **resources** and make up the largest proportion of the world's energy mix (Diagram **B**).

They are used in two different ways:

directly:
- by burning coal to produce heat.

indirectly:
- as a primary fuel in power stations to generate electricity
- as a refined fuel to power vehicles and machinery.

Fossil fuels, however, are **non-renewable** and **finite** (they will eventually run out). See Graph **C**.

As fossil fuels become increasingly scarce they will become more expensive, and this may mean higher fuel and electricity prices.

The energy challenge for the 21st century will be to move to an increasingly sustainable global energy mix. In order to do this there will be a need to:

- produce increasing amounts of energy using **renewable** methods
- find more efficient ways of producing energy from fossil fuels
- find more efficient ways of using and conserving energy.

Key terms

Resources: anything that can be used to meet human needs.

Non-renewable: can only be used once.

Finite: limited in quantity.

Renewable: can be used again.

Reserves: estimated amount of a resource that is available for use.

Did you know ??????

Global energy demand is expected to increase by 50% in the next 25 years. The fastest rates of increase will be in rapidly developing countries such as China and India.

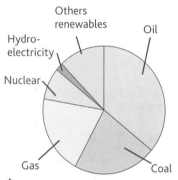

B The global energy mix

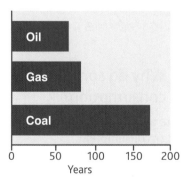

0   50   100   150   200
Years

These estimates are based on:
- known **reserves**
- present demand
- current levels of technology.

C Global fossil fuel reserves

Activities

3 a Draw a scattergraph to show the relationship between GNI and energy use.

b Describe and suggest reasons for the relationship shown on your scattergraph.

4 Explain the energy challenge for the 21st century expressed on this page.

What is the energy gap?

In this section you will learn:

the importance of energy to the development process

how the use of fuelwood is a threat to people and environments.

The energy gap is a term that describes the gap in energy use between rich and poor countries. This can be clearly seen by looking at a world map showing energy consumption (Map **A**).

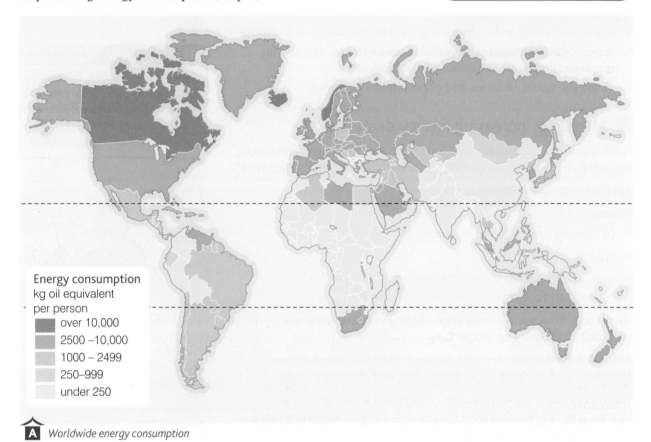

Energy consumption
kg oil equivalent
per person

- over 10,000
- 2500 –10,000
- 1000 – 2499
- 250–999
- under 250

A *Worldwide energy consumption*

Why do some countries have low levels of energy consumption?

There are a number of reasons why some countries have low levels of energy consumption.

- A lack of natural resources – some countries have limited reserves of fossil fuels and cannot afford to import them.
- In some countries the natural environment provides limited opportunity for the development of renewable energy.
- Lack of economic development, and poverty, mean that countries cannot afford to import energy resources or develop an energy infrastructure (power stations and transmission lines) to produce and distribute electricity.

Did you know ??????

The richest 1 billion people in the world consume 50% of the world's energy. The poorest 1 billion people in the world consume only 4% of the world's energy.

Energy issues in Mali, north-west Africa

Mali faces a number of energy challenges:

- It has no fossil fuels.
- It is a landlocked country which makes it difficult to import coal and oil.
- It is one of the poorest countries in Africa.
- There is a lack of electricity infrastructure – only 10 per cent of the population has access to electricity.

What are the options for Mali?

- Increase the use of energy-efficient stoves rather than open fires.
- Develop the use of biofuel crops which can be used to produce vehicle fuel.
- Introduce small-scale solar energy collectors.

◼ The fuelwood crisis

In many of the poorest parts of the world, fuelwood (firewood) and animal manure are the major sources of energy (Table **B**). Using fuelwood is a major issue in some parts of the world because of the effect it can have on the local environment and the health of the people.

B *The energy mix in two African countries*

Mali	%	Kenya	%
Fuelwood	77	Fuelwood	82
Oil	8	Oil	13
Hydro	12	Coal	1
Other renewable	3	Other renewable	4

C *An open fire burning fuelwood*

The fuelwood crisis in Africa

Many African families have little option but to use locally cut wood, or dried animal manure, as sources of energy. In most sub-Saharan African countries the majority of the population live in remote villages which are not connected to an electricity supply. Most rural villagers cannot afford to buy cooking stoves or the coal or oil to fuel them, so they rely on open fires to heat water and to cook food (Photo **C**). The problem is that in many areas, trees are being cut down faster than they can grow. This can leave the soil open to the effects of wind and rainstorms, leading to soil erosion and the increasing threat of desertification. Burning animal dung instead of returning it to the soil reduces the fertility of the soil and makes farming increasingly difficult. The problem is that many people have no choice but to continue with the practice of using fuelwood and animal manure – without it they could not cook food properly or boil water, thus adding to the threat of disease.

Very few people in rural villages in Kenya have electricity in their homes. They rely on wood-burning stoves, which often produce high levels of smoke and lead to a range of health problems. Individual families cannot afford to buy or run generators so they find themselves in a vicious circle: having to cut down trees to use for fuel, which damages the very land they depend on for farming.

What can be done?

A number of non-governmental organisations (NGOs) are helping countries to develop and produce of basic stoves which use less fuelwood and create less smoke.

Did you know ??????

According to the World Health Organization (WHO):

- in developing countries more people die from smoke-related illness than from malaria
- smoke from cooking fires causes up to 2 million deaths per year.

∞links

Learn more about reducing the threat of smoke in houses in developing countries at www. practicalaction.org.uk/smoke

Activities

1 Describe the global pattern of energy consumption shown in Map **A**.

2 Explain how the lack of a reliable and affordable energy source can hold back development.

3 'Using fuelwood is bad for both people and the environment.' Explain this statement.

7.3 Reducing the energy gap

There is a clear link between energy consumption and economic development. Many economists suggest that the lack of a reliable and cheap energy source is a major factor in holding back development.

The United Nations (UN) has identified Africa as the least developed continent. Many sub-Saharan countries have **Human Development Index (HDI)** figures significantly below the average for developing countries.

At a recent international conference an African government minister said:

> 66 *Imagine how different your life would be without electricity. That is the reality for most Africans. A reliable source of energy would give millions of people in Africa the opportunity to improve their living conditions and give governments the chance to develop modern industry and create job opportunities.* 99

The challenge for Africa is to provide sustainable energy to some of the poorest and most remote parts of the world. The examples on these two pages describe a number of smaller-scale energy projects that are either being planned or are currently operating.

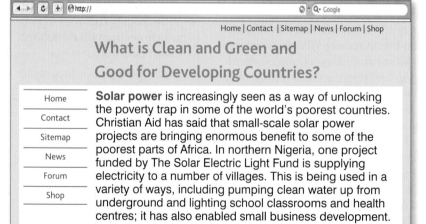

◀ ▶ C + 🌐 http://   ◎ ▾ Q▾ Google

Home | Contact | Sitemap | News | Forum | Shop

What is Clean and Green and Good for Developing Countries?

Home
Contact
Sitemap
News
Forum
Shop

Solar power is increasingly seen as a way of unlocking the poverty trap in some of the world's poorest countries. Christian Aid has said that small-scale solar power projects are bringing enormous benefit to some of the poorest parts of Africa. In northern Nigeria, one project funded by The Solar Electric Light Fund is supplying electricity to a number of villages. This is being used in a variety of ways, including pumping clean water up from underground and lighting school classrooms and health centres; it has also enabled small business development.

In one village a sewing workshop has started and in another a number of workshops offering a range of services have opened. The Shell Foundation, which supports energy projects in developing countries, has helped a number of villagers buy solar panels. With a high number of 'sunshine days', solar energy offers a cheap, reliable form of electricity. It is especially useful in rural areas that are not connected to an energy supply system.

Adapted from the Shell Foundation website
www.shellfoundation.org

In this section you will learn:

to understand the need to reduce the energy gap

about the importance of small-scale sustainable energy projects in developing countries.

Key terms

Human Development Index (HDI): a way of measuring development using information about income, education and life expectancy.

Solar power: producing electricity using the Sun's rays/light.

Hydroelectricity: producing electricity using flowing water.

Did you know ??????

- Nearly 2 billion people worldwide do not have access to electricity.
- Over 2.5 billion people use wood or charcoal for heating and cooking on a regular basis.

⬭ links

Using the internet, research renewable energy at
www.solar-aid.org
www.renewableenergyworld.com
www.climateactionprogramme.org
→ energy

Energy projects in Africa

Mali

A company has set up a business supplying basic photovoltaic solar cells and battery systems to rural communities. The cheapest system provides enough electricity for two light bulbs. This can be upgraded to include an electrical socket outlet. It is proving popular in small villages and is increasingly being used in schools and health clinics.

Cameroon

Micro wind turbines are being built, each capable of supplying electricity to five households. Each turbine costs about £100 and they are easy to maintain (Photo **B**).

Rwanda

Rwanda has the largest solar electricity plant in Africa, developed as part of the 'Energy for Africa' foundation. It produces enough electricity for a small town.

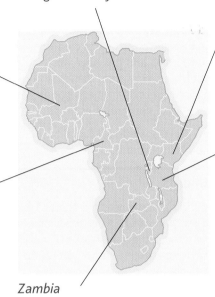

A　*Africa*

Zambia

A number of 'micro-hydro' schemes use normal river flow to generate electricity and do not harm the environment (Photo **C**).

Kenya

Kabri Pico is a small hydroelectricity plant supplying over 200 homes.

Portable solar collectors which can be moved around in rural communities are being used. They supply enough electricity for individual houses, schools and health centres.

Tanzania

Micro solar schemes for over 100 schools provide lighting and electricity. The schemes also provide training about the use and maintenance of solar energy collectors.

Solar hybrid systems combine the use of solar energy with traditional generators that run on oil. The oil is made from local crops, producing biofuel. Each system provides sufficient energy for a community of around 1,000 people.

Activities

1　Consider the difference that having a regular energy supply has made in the areas described on these two pages.

2　Explain why the examples described are:
- sustainable
- appropriate for developing countries.

B　*Micro wind turbines*

C　*A micro-hydro scheme*

The impact of exploiting fossil fuels

Fossil fuels provide the resources for most of the world's energy generation and virtually all the fuel for modern transportation systems.

The exploitation of fossil fuel resources creates both economic opportunities and challenges for local communities. In many parts of the world the development of coal, oil and gas resources has created jobs, brought large amounts of money into areas and has been an important factor in improving living conditions. However, the removal and transportation of vast quantities of fossil fuels can put environments under pressure and create conflicts among local communities.

The following case studies consider how large-scale fossil fuel exploitation can affect communities and environments.

In this section you will learn:

how the exploitation of fossil fuels can cause conflict in local areas

how the exploitation of fossil fuels can harm the environment.

Case study

Removing oil from fragile environments

The USA is the world's largest user of oil and has a growing need to import oil as its own reserves run dry. Currently about 20 per cent of all USA's oil production comes from northern Alaska. It is transported through the trans-Alaskan Pipeline to the southern port of Valdez for shipment in supertankers to other parts of the USA (Map **A**). Alaska has been called the 'last great American wilderness'. Over 20 million hectares of the northern part of Alaska are environmentally protected areas. The Arctic National Wildlife Refuge (ANWR) is the largest protected wildlife area in the USA. This area is home to polar bears, grizzly bears, caribou, musk oxen, and many rare birds and marine animals. It is recognised as one of the world's most fragile and sensitive ecosystems.

Did you know ?????

There have been a number of oil spills in Alaska, both on land and at sea. In March 1989 the supertanker Exxon Valdez ran aground in the Gulf of Alaska, spilling about 40,000 tonnes of oil. It is estimated that the oil spill killed half a million sea birds, up to 3,000 seals and otters, 250 bald eagles, and 22 killer whales. A study carried out in 2004 found that many species had not yet recovered.

∞ links

Learn more about ANWR and the impact of oil development at www. **savearcticrefuge.org**

Use the internet to find out more about the Exxon Valdez disaster and other oil spills.

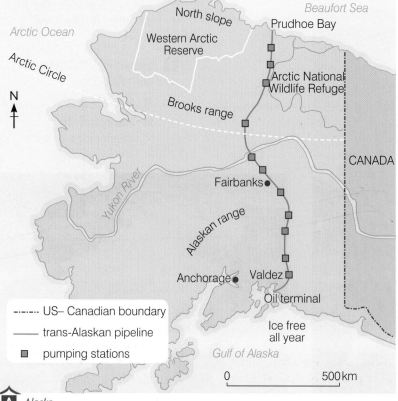

A *Alaska*

B *Oil developments at Prudhoe Bay*

Wilderness Threatened By Oil Developments

A growing conflict is developing in northern Alaska as oil companies push for further development of the coastal plain. The local area is home to the Inupiat – native Americans who rely on the area for fishing and whale hunting. They fear that oil development will scare away local marine life and disrupt breeding patterns. The area is home to a number of protected animals, and environmentalists fear that further development will damage the ecosystem.

One local person said: 'Who wants to live in a place with hundreds of oil wells all lit up with orange lights and connected up by massive overground pipelines? Gas flares also affect the atmosphere; you only have to look at the area around Prudhoe Bay to see the air pollution.'

The exploitation of oil in Alaska has meant developing large drilling sites, storage facilities and pipelines, as well as the massive oil terminal at Valdez.

Most of the oil produced in Alaska comes from Prudhoe Bay, on the north coast (Photo **B**). A plan has been proposed to develop further the northern coastal plain and shallow coastal waters in order to recover up to 10 billion barrels of oil. Most of the development will be within environmentally protected areas and many people are concerned about the effect on local communities and wildlife. The articles express views about the proposed development.

Oil Brings Wealth to Alaska

Development of the north Alaskan oilfields could bring millions of dollars to the area and help to improve living conditions in one of the harshest parts of the USA. As one local said:

'Before oil this was the poorest state in America. Only 50 years ago people lived in houses without electricity, inside toilets or telephones. Today, every home has these facilities and incomes are 50 per cent higher than the national average. Locals are concerned about the environmental effects of oil developments and the threat of accidents, but they are also concerned about their living standards.'

Opencast coal mining – Merthyr Tydfil in South Wales

In 2006 British planners considered 12 applications for the future development of opencast mines (Photo **C**). Ten were approved, including a site of 400 hectares at Ffos-y-fran near Merthyr Tydfil which could be excavated to a depth of nearly 200 metres in order to reach 10 million tonnes of coal.

Over 10,000 local people signed a petition against the mine, largely because of the effect on the environment and the health of the local people. One local resident said: 'The mine will be only 50 metres from the nearest houses. It will be open for 20 years, with heavy machinery and explosives being used from 7am to 11pm five days a week. The noise, smoke and dust will totally change the lives of local people.' The companies involved claim that the scheme is in an area of derelict, poor-quality land and will create a large number of jobs.

Key terms

Opencast mining: mining resources by firstly removing the material that covers them.

C   *An opencast mine*

Activities

1   Explain how the exploitation of energy resources can damage environments.

2   Explain how the exploitation of energy resources can bring benefits to local communities.

extension   The development of Alaskan oil resources has been called 'a battle between oil companies and the environment'. Discuss.

Find out ...

Use the internet to find out more about the impact of opencast mining on the environment.

The environmental cost of burning fossil fuels

Fossil fuels are burnt in power stations to generate electricity or burnt directly to produce heat. The majority of the world's vehicles operate by burning refined oil (petrol/diesel fuel) and aircraft burn aviation fuel, also refined from oil.

Burning fossil fuels releases a range of gases into the atmosphere (Photo **A**) including sulphur dioxide, nitrogen oxide and carbon dioxide. The release of these gases into the atmosphere can cause acid rain and add to the problems of global warming.

■ What is acid rain?

Acid rain is caused when gases released by power stations and vehicles mix in the atmosphere with water vapour to form weak solutions of sulphuric and nitric acid. This is moved by the wind, eventually returning to Earth as rainfall. Because the rain is slightly acidic it can harm plant and animal life, increase the rate of weathering on buildings and damage materials such as plastic and paint.

■ What is global warming?

The Earth's atmosphere contains a number of 'greenhouse gases', including carbon dioxide. Greenhouse gases allow radiation from the sun to filter through to the Earth but act like an insulation blanket, slowing down heat loss from the Earth. Without greenhouse gases in the atmosphere the Earth's temperature would be 25–40 °C lower. In the last 100 years the amount of greenhouse gases in the atmosphere has increased so less heat is escaping, resulting in global increases in temperature.

The effects of global warming

Global warming is increasing the rate at which the ice caps are melting, causing sea levels to rise. This will increase the risk of coastal flooding in the future. Other possible effects of global warming are (Map **B**):

- changes to weather patterns and increasing frequency of storms
- changes to habitats as a result of climate change
- shifts in farming patterns and food production
- more extreme climate events such as droughts in tropical areas, leading to an increased risk of famine
- the spread of climate-related disease – it is estimated that by 2100 up to 200 million people in Africa could die from diseases caused by the effects of climate change.

■ Using clean coal technology to reduce carbon emissions

Fossil fuels provide most of the fuel for electricity generation and this is unlikely to change in the near future. However, burning fossil fuels creates carbon dioxide, the major influence on climate change. This means that reducing carbon emissions from fossil fuel power stations is a major challenge.

In this section you will learn:

about the causes and effects of acid rain and global warming

how technology can reduce carbon emissions.

A *Air pollution from factories*

∞ links

Learn more about the effects of global warming at **www. christianaid.org.uk/whatwedo/ issues/climate_change.aspx**

Learn about clean coal technology at **www.shell.com**

Did you know ??????

- As ice sheets melt, increasing amounts of oil and gas will become accessible – further adding to the pressures to use fossil fuels.

Did you know ??????

- A scientist said recently: 'If coal cleans up its act it could become the fuel of the future.'
- Over 70% of all coal in the UK still lies underground. This is enough to last hundreds of years!

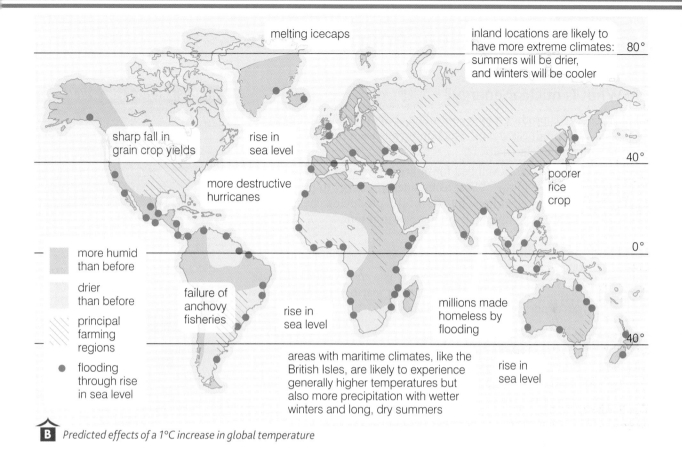

melting icecaps

inland locations are likely to have more extreme climates: 80° summers will be drier, and winters will be cooler

sharp fall in grain crop yields

rise in sea level

40°

more destructive hurricanes

poorer rice crop

more humid than before

drier than before

principal farming regions

flooding through rise in sea level

failure of anchovy fisheries

rise in sea level

millions made homeless by flooding

0°

40°

areas with maritime climates, like the British Isles, are likely to experience generally higher temperatures but also more precipitation with wetter winters and long, dry summers

rise in sea level

B *Predicted effects of a 1°C increase in global temperature*

How can it be achieved?

- Technology has made fossil fuel power stations increasingly efficient and more environmentally sensitive. Modern power stations have acid gas and particulate control systems to reduce pollution levels.

- Carbon capture and storage (CCS) – the basic idea behind CCS is that carbon dioxide is collected from power stations and oil refineries and pumped into safe underground storage areas such as old oil and gas fields. At the same time the carbon dioxide can be used to force out any remaining oil or gas.

- Coal gasification is a technique in which gas is pumped through underground coal seams to produce coal gas. This gas is then cleaned of pollutants and used in a power station to generate electricity. All the waste materials and pollutants remain underground.

ZeroGen, Australia

A demonstration power plant is being built in Queensland using both carbon capture and storage (CCS) and coal gasification technology. If it is successful it will be the world's first low-emission coal-based power station.

Case study

Activities

1. Use the internet to help you draw annotated diagrams to explain the causes and effects of:
   - acid rain
   - global warming.

2. Describe how global warming will increasingly affect people.

3. How may clean coal technology reduce carbon emissions?

extension   Why may coal become the 'fuel of the future'?

⊙⊙ links

Learn more about technology in the energy industry at **www. powergeneration.siemens.com**

What is nuclear energy?

Nuclear energy is produced by a controlled chain reaction that creates heat. This heat produces steam, which in turn is used to drive a turbine, generating electricity.

Nuclear technology was developed for military purposes during World War Two (1939–45). In the 1950s, using nuclear energy to produce energy was seen as a great hope for the future, producing cheap electricity whilst using only small amounts of uranium.

Is nuclear a renewable energy source?

Nuclear energy is often considered a non-renewable energy source because it requires uranium, a finite resource. Fast breeder reactors convert uranium into other types of nuclear fuel to produce energy.

Nuclear energy in the UK

The world's first nuclear power station was opened in 1956 in Cumbria. By 1990 there were 38 nuclear reactors in the UK producing over 20 per cent of the UK's electricity (Map **A**).

The original predicted lifespan of most of the reactors was approximately 40 years, although a number have run for longer than expected. The first reactors were shut down in 1989 and it is expected that 30 of the original reactors will be shut down by 2010. Another 7 are due to close by 2025, leaving just 1 plant at Sizewell (Suffolk) operating until 2035. Unless new reactors are built, it is expected that nuclear electricity generation will fall from a peak of over 30 per cent of UK needs to less than 10 per cent by 2020.

No new nuclear power stations have been built in the UK since the 1980s. Growing concerns about the cost of construction and the problems associated with radioactive waste, and two major accidents in other parts of the world, have seen the popularity of nuclear energy decline in the UK.

Major nuclear accidents

- In 1979 a major accident at the Three Mile Island nuclear plant in Pennsylvania (USA) resulted in mass evacuation and panic. The plant was brought back under control but the incident resulted in the American government restricting further nuclear energy developments.

- In 1986 the nuclear reactor in Chernobyl (Ukraine) exploded, creating a radioactive cloud that drifted across Europe (Photo **B**). The immediate area was evacuated and vegetation was contaminated as far away as Scandinavia. The impact of the accident is still not fully known, although there has been a significant increase in certain cancers in the local area.

⬭⬭ links

Learn more about nuclear power in the UK at
www.bbc.co.uk/topics/nuclear_power

In this section you will learn:

why nuclear energy may play an increasing role in the future

why there are differences of opinion about the increased use of nuclear energy.

Closures/proposed closures
- ● Shut down
- ● 2005 - 2008
- ● 2008 - 2015
- ○ 2015 - 2025
- ● 2025 - 2040

A Nuclear power stations in the UK

Did you know ??????

In 1960 Pennsylvania (USA) became the world's first nuclear-powered city.

B The exploded reactor at Chernobyl

Is nuclear energy the fuel of the future?

People are divided about the use of nuclear energy. Companies such as British Nuclear Fuels (BNFL) and energy companies such as EDF (French) are keen to see nuclear energy development; the Confederation of British Industry (CBI) stated in 2008 that 'the government has reached the right conclusion about nuclear's role in meeting the challenge of climate change and energy security'. Environmental groups such as Greenpeace oppose nuclear energy development (Illustration **C**) and renewable energy groups feel that the development of nuclear energy may take investment away from renewable energy developments.

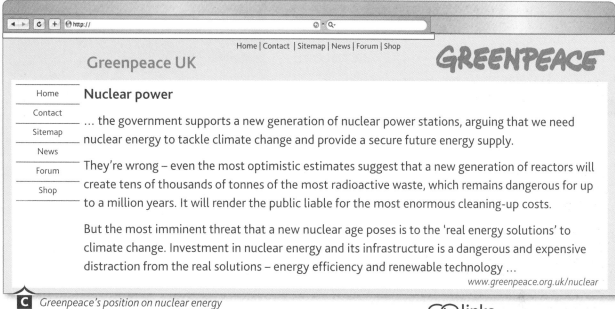

◄ ► C + http://   ☉ Q

Home | Contact | Sitemap | News | Forum | Shop

Greenpeace UK   **GREENPEACE**

Home
Contact
Sitemap
News
Forum
Shop

Nuclear power

… the government supports a new generation of nuclear power stations, arguing that we need nuclear energy to tackle climate change and provide a secure future energy supply.

They're wrong – even the most optimistic estimates suggest that a new generation of reactors will create tens of thousands of tonnes of the most radioactive waste, which remains dangerous for up to a million years. It will render the public liable for the most enormous cleaning-up costs.

But the most imminent threat that a new nuclear age poses is to the 'real energy solutions' to climate change. Investment in nuclear energy and its infrastructure is a dangerous and expensive distraction from the real solutions – energy efficiency and renewable technology …

www.greenpeace.org.uk/nuclear

C *Greenpeace's position on nuclear energy*

The nuclear debate

'This is the right time for nuclear energy development. The new reactors being developed in the USA and Europe will':

- last at least 60 years
- use less fuel, and so provide less waste
- have advanced safety features
- produce cheaper electricity (approx. 2.5 pence per kW hour compared with 6 pence per kW hour from a current nuclear power station).

'Nuclear energy is not a sustainable option because':

- nuclear power stations have a limited life
- low-cost uranium will be exhausted in 50 years
- nuclear power stations are expensive to build
- there is absolutely no safe way of dealing with nuclear waste.

What about the global situation?

In 2008 there were nearly 450 nuclear reactors operating in 30 countries, and 35 new reactors were under construction in 11 countries. Twenty of these were in Russia, China and India. These 3 countries also have over 100 proposed nuclear energy plants.

∞ **links**

Learn more about global nuclear energy at **www.world-nuclear.org**

Activities

1. Explain why fossil fuel shortages and environmental concerns may encourage the global expansion of nuclear energy.

2. Suggest reasons why some countries have a greater reliance on nuclear energy than others.

3. a Write a paragraph in support of the increased use of nuclear energy in the UK.

   b What are the arguments against the increased use of nuclear energy in the UK?

Renewable energy is often called 'green energy' because it does not add to the problem of carbon emissions. It uses the natural environment to generate electricity and is considered sustainable because it does not use finite resources.

Hydroelectricity is the most important source of renewable energy. Its greatest use is in South America where it accounts for over 25 per cent of electricity generation (Photo **A**).

Other renewable energy sources include:

- wind energy
- solar energy
- tidal energy
- wave energy
- geothermal energy
- biomass.

Renewable energy in the UK

The UK government has a target of 10 per cent of electricity production from renewable sources by 2010. By 2007 the actual figure was approximately 5 per cent, showing a gradual increase over the previous 10 years. In the UK renewable energy comes from a variety of sources (Diagram **B**), including;

- Hydroelectricity has been used for many years in the UK, but only accounts for about 1 per cent of electricity demand.
- Biofuels – using fast-growing trees as a source of fuel or producing biofuel from crops is seen as a potential area for development and may become more significant in the future.
- Landfill gas – collecting gas given off from landfill sites accounts for about a quarter of the UK's renewable energy supply.
- Wind energy – there has been a steady increase in the development of wind farms in the last 20 years. It is estimated that wind turbines could produce up to 20 per cent of total electricity needs.
- Others – the use of solar, tidal and geothermal energy have not been widely exploited in the UK. Tidal energy is considered to have the greatest potential and could produce 25 per cent of total energy needs.

Renewable futures – tidal power

For many years there has been an ongoing debate about building a tidal barrage across the River Severn between England and Wales. Supporters of the idea say that if it were built it could provide 5 per cent of the whole of the UK's electricity needs for the next 100 years, and reduce carbon emissions because fewer fossil fuel power stations would need to be built. One engineer stated that:

'It would be a giant step forward for green energy production in the UK.'

However, at a cost of £20 billion it would not be cheap and it would totally change the natural environment of the Severn estuary, much of which is a protected environment because of its rare plant and animal life. Whilst the barrage was under construction it would be 'one of the biggest building sites in the world.'

A *A hydroelectric power station*

B *UK renewable energy mix, 2006*

(Pie chart labelled: Others, Hydro-electricity, Biofuel, Wind energy, Land fill gas)

Renewable energy – issues and conflicts

Although renewable energy is seen as 'clean and green', the development of areas for renewable energy generation can be controversial. The following examples consider the issues associated with renewable energy developments.

Case study

The Three Gorges Dam scheme, China

The Three Gorges Dam scheme is one of the largest and most controversial multi-use river schemes ever built (Photo **C**).

C Construction of the Three Gorges Dam

Advantages of the scheme

- It will produce up to 10 per cent of China's energy needs and reduce the need to burn fossil fuels.
- It will supply towns and cities with electricity and encourage economic development.
- It will create thousands of jobs in a poor area of China.
- It can be used to protect areas from flooding.

Disadvantages of the scheme

- A lake 600 km long will be created, flooding nearly 5,000 settlements.
- Nearly 1.5 million people will be forced to leave their homes.
- The landscape will be totally changed.
- Historical and tourist sites will be lost.

Case study

Cefn Croes wind farm, mid Wales

In June 2005 the most powerful onshore wind farm opened at Cefn Croes in mid Wales. A total of 39 wind turbines, some as tall as 100 metres, were built in a rural area considered to have a high level of environmental and scenic value (Photo **D**).

The wind farm produces electricity for up to 40,000 homes and has a lifespan of 25 years.

D The wind farm at Cefn Croes

The wind farm development caused considerable conflict in the local area. Some people saw it as a great opportunity to create clean energy, whilst others were concerned it would harm the environment and damage the local tourist industry.

Biomass – a climate-friendly fuel?

- Biomass in the form of wood or charcoal is mankind's oldest source of energy.
- Today biomass is used to produce alcohol fuels and biodiesel to power vehicles.
- It is climate friendly because it is carbon neutral. This is because it releases the same amount of carbon when burnt as is used up whilst growing as a crop.
- However, it does use up valuable land that could be used for food crops.

⬭ links

Learn more about renewable energy at www.energysavingtrust.org.uk

Find out ... 🔍

Use the internet to find out more about the Three Gorges Dam scheme. Think about:

- the scale of the project
- the advantages and the disadvantages of the scheme.

Find out ... 🔍

Use the internet to find out more about the Cefn Croes development and the conflicts it created.

Find out ... 🔍

Use the internet to find out more about the 'biomass debate'.

Activities

1 a Draw a bar chart to show the UK renewable energy mix in 2006.

   b Which types of renewable energy are likely to be developed in future in the UK? Explain your answer.

2 'Renewable energy is clean but not always green'. Discuss.

3 What are the advantages and disadvantages of small-scale and large-scale renewable energy projects?

One of the major uses of energy is heating, lighting and powering residential and commercial buildings.

As countries become increasingly developed and people strive to improve their living conditions, the demand for energy in residential buildings is likely to increase. The challenge for the 21st century is to produce increasingly energy-efficient carbon neutral buildings (Diagrams **A** and **B**).

Reducing energy use in industry

Industry uses a large amount of energy and is a major part of the carbon footprint in urban areas. Companies are increasingly realising that energy-efficient buildings save them money and are good for their reputation. At a recent business conference one company director said:

Energy accounts for nearly 15 per cent of our costs. Even reducing this by 2–3 per cent would save nearly half a million pounds a year. Also, being seen as an environmentally friendly company is good for our image.

In this section you will learn:

how building technology can reduce energy consumption

how buildings can become increasingly carbon neutral.

Did you know ???????

A 'carbon footprint' is the carbon impact individuals or communities have on the environment.

If a development is 'carbon neutral' it does not add to the amount of carbon dioxide in the atmosphere.

Case study

The Energy+ building in Paris

An example of an energy-efficient office block is being built in Paris. The Energy+ building is designed to create space for over 4,000 employees and will produce more energy than it uses. The major features of the building are shown in Diagram **A**.

∞ links

Learn more about energy-efficient buildings at www.zedfactory.com
www.energysavingtrust.org.uk
www.bedzedhouse.co.uk
www.zerocarbonhouse.com

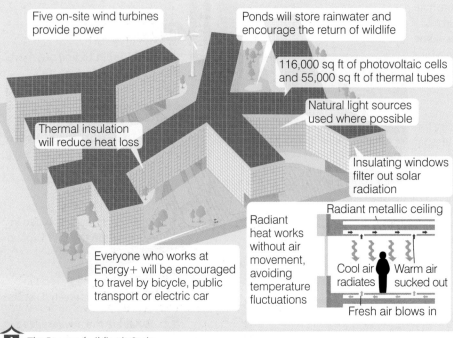

Five on-site wind turbines provide power

Ponds will store rainwater and encourage the return of wildlife

116,000 sq ft of photovoltaic cells and 55,000 sq ft of thermal tubes

Natural light sources used where possible

Thermal insulation will reduce heat loss

Insulating windows filter out solar radiation

Radiant metallic ceiling

Radiant heat works without air movement, avoiding temperature fluctuations

Cool air radiates

Warm air sucked out

Fresh air blows in

Everyone who works at Energy+ will be encouraged to travel by bicycle, public transport or electric car

It will have a credit of 48 tonnes of CO_2 a year – a typical office building emits 3,240 tonnes of CO_2 a year

Renewable energy technologies minimise maintenance and extend the life of the building

Solar air conditioning provides 75% of cooling requirements; the remaining 25% provided by geothermal heat pump

Sustainable energy production combined with reduction of the building's energy needs through efficient design and technology means Energy+ will produce a 20% energy surplus

A   *The Energy+ building in Paris*   ©SOM

extension   How do companies promote their environmental reputation in their television and newspaper advertising?

The Energy Saving Trust: Making homes more energy efficient

Did you know ? ? ? ? ? ?

The UK's 20 million homes pump nearly 40 million tonnes of carbon into the atmosphere each year.

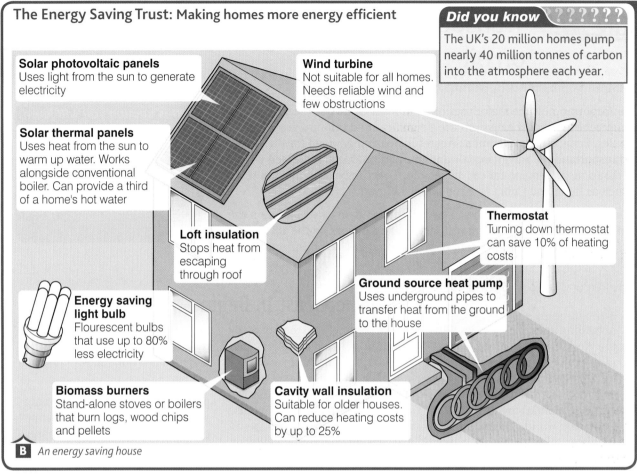

Solar photovoltaic panels
Uses light from the sun to generate electricity

Solar thermal panels
Uses heat from the sun to warm up water. Works alongside conventional boiler. Can provide a third of a home's hot water

Wind turbine
Not suitable for all homes. Needs reliable wind and few obstructions

Thermostat
Turning down thermostat can save 10% of heating costs

Loft insulation
Stops heat from escaping through roof

Energy saving light bulb
Flourescent bulbs that use up to 80% less electricity

Ground source heat pump
Uses underground pipes to transfer heat from the ground to the house

Biomass burners
Stand-alone stoves or boilers that burn logs, wood chips and pellets

Cavity wall insulation
Suitable for older houses. Can reduce heating costs by up to 25%

B *An energy saving house*

Supermarkets Join the Carbon Revolution

All major supermarkets have set ambitious environmental targets including:

- reducing carbon emissions from shops and distribution centres
- reducing vehicle emissions
- reducing the amount of waste created
- increasing the amount of recycling
- reducing energy consumption.

A number of measures have already been introduced in some supermarkets. These include:

- the use of geothermal heating
- the use of solar/wind energy
- putting doors on cold storage units
- using increasing amounts of natural light in buildings.

Activities

1. Why is reducing energy use good for business and the environment?

2. Describe five ways in which homes can be made more energy efficient.

3. Should all new homes be built:
   - using energy-efficient techniques?
   - with their own micro-generation facilities?

   Explain your answers.

Micro-generation Can Make a Difference

A recent report on domestic energy supply concluded that if more homes had their own micro-energy sources such as wind turbines or solar panels, they could produce as much energy as five large power stations. The use of micro-generation could also reduce carbon emissions by 30 million tonnes a year.

Transportation is the major user of oil in most countries (Diagram **A**) and vehicle exhaust emissions are a significant addition to greenhouse gases. Economic development creates increasing demand for the transportation of raw materials and finished products. Increased wealth creates more demand for car ownership. This can be seen in countries such as India and China (see the article below).

In highly developed countries the whole economy is often based on the efficient transportation of goods, services and people. In the UK, it is estimated that over 80 per cent of all personal and business journeys over 3 km are made by car (2008).

In this section you will learn:

how new technology can reduce the use of oil in motor vehicles

how improvements in public transport could reduce the use of cars.

Going Nowhere Fast In Beijing

According to a recent report by the World Bank, 16 of the world's most polluted cities are in China. In 2006 Beijing was voted the air pollution capital of the world. Rapid economic growth has made China the world's second largest producer of greenhouse gases.

In Beijing the growth in traffic has been partly responsible for the pollution problem. It is estimated that in 2000 there were about 1 million vehicles on the road. By the time of the Olympic Games in 2008 this number was over 3 million and it is expected to reach 6 million by 2015! The situation is made worse because many people use cheap petrol that has high levels of sulphur, a major source of pollution.

At a recent conference a local environmentalist said: 'Pollution levels will triple in the next 12 years unless the growth in the use of energy and vehicle use does not slow down.'

The costs of increases in pollution are not only environmental; doctors blame poor air quality for increases in the numbers of respiratory illnesses and lung cancer.

The impact of growing vehicle numbers

The growth of vehicle use has a number of effects, including:

- increasing demand for oil
- increasing congestion in towns and cities, which adds to business costs and personal stress levels
- increasing air pollution, especially when vehicles sit in traffic jams
- increase in respiratory illnesses as people breathe polluted air
- increased pressure for the continuing building of roads and car parks.

How can the dependence on oil be reduced?

1 More environmentally friendly vehicles

Reliance on motor vehicles is not likely to decrease in the near future. Consequently in order to reduce the dependence on oil:

- motor vehicles will need to become increasingly oil efficient
- motor vehicles that use alternative sources of power will need to be used more widely.

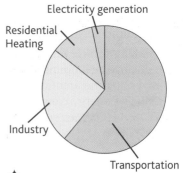

A *Oil use by sector in the USA, 2008*

Did you know ??????

In a recent conference discussing urban problems it was said that 'the management of movement is the major challenge in most urban areas today'.

The following examples (Adverts **B** and **C**) look at different ways in which car manufacturers are moving towards less oil-dependent vehicles.

HONDA
The Power of Dreams

The latest petrol/electric hybrid is 20 per cent more powerful and 5 per cent more efficient than the old model. The petrol engine is used for accelerating and the electric motor takes over once cruising speed has been reached.

- Incredibly low CO_2 emissions
- Combined fuel economy of 61.4 mpg (compared with 44 mpg for a petrol-only car)

 The 1.4i-DSIplus IMA

www.honda.co.uk

BMW – the Mini E

The Mini E will be powered by an electric motor fed by a rechargeable battery. It will create no sound or emissions and the battery will have a range of 250 km.

 The Mini E

Did you know ??????

Honda has developed the world's first flexible fuel vehicle. It can run on oil-based fuel or bioethanol, or a mixture of both. Bioethanol is made from plants and is in widespread use in Brazil, where it is made from sugar cane. Because plants absorb carbon dioxide (CO_2) when they grow, the amount of CO_2 released when they are burnt does not add to the carbon balance.

Honda has also begun production of a zero-emission hydrogen fuel-cell propelled car. It runs on electricity that is produced by combining hydrogen with oxygen and emitting only water vapour.

'This is a step closer to the day when fuel-cell cars will be part of the mainstream.' – The executive vice-president of American Honda

2 Public transport

The majority of car journeys are taken by people going to work. Encouraging more people to use public transport would reduce oil consumption and also reduce traffic congestion and air pollution in town centres. The following are some examples of traffic reduction strategies.

Integrated bus systems

Integrated or 'joined-up' bus systems are being developed increasingly in urban areas across the world. One of the most successful is in Curitiba (Brazil). It is estimated that the introduction of the Curitiba Integrated Bus System has reduced car journeys by nearly 30 million a year, and that 28 per cent of bus users previously used their cars.

Light railway/metro systems

One of the first metro systems was the Bay Area Rapid Transport System (BART) which opened in San Francisco (USA) in 1972. Many cities in the UK also have rapid transport systems, for example the London Docklands Light Railway and Metrolink Manchester.

Park and ride

Park-and-ride schemes reduce the number of vehicles entering town and city centres and are increasingly popular across the world.

∞ links

Learn more about Honda's latest developments at **www.world.honda.com**

Learn more about integrated public transport systems at **www.urbanhabitat.org** → transportation

Learn more about light railway and tram systems at **www.thetrams.co.uk** **www.bart.gov**

Learn more about park-and-ride schemes in the UK at **www.parkandride.net**

Find out ... 🔍

Use the internet to investigate the latest innovations from the major car producers.

Activities

1. Explain the link between vehicle use and economic development.

2. How may advances in vehicle technology reduce the need for oil in the future?

3. Why is public transport 'good for both people and the environment'?

4. Suggest why it may be difficult to encourage people to use public transport.

8 Water: a precious resource

8.1 The water cycle

The water, or **hydrological**, cycle is the circulation of water between stores (oceans and lakes), the atmosphere and the land (Diagram **A**). It is called a cycle because it is a natural system that recycles water.

There are four main components to the water cycle:

1 Inputs – water entering the system through precipitation
2 Stores – water held in oceans, lakes, ice, rocks, vegetation and the atmosphere
3 Transfers – processes that move water through the system such as surface run-off and underground flow
4 Outputs – where water is returned to the stores.

Heat from the sun evaporates over 100 cm of water from the surface of all oceans and lakes each year. A third of this water vapour falls on the Earth from clouds, mostly soaking into the ground. The majority of rainfall is returned to the oceans within two weeks.

■ Groundwater aquifers

An aquifer is an underground layer of rock that holds water. The top level of the underground water is called the water table. This can rise or fall according to the amount of rainfall and how much water has been removed for human use.

Aquifers hold over 95 per cent of the world's fresh water supply and are used to supply the world's population with drinking water. In some parts of the world aquifers have been polluted by agricultural and industrial chemical discharges seeping into rocks. This has had disastrous consequences for people who rely on the water for drinking.

Did you know ??????

Water is used at a rapid rate. If it was not recycled the world would run out of water in less than a month!

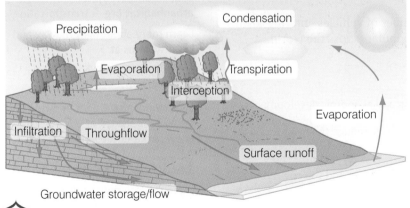

A *The natural water cycle*

Key terms

Hydrological: relating to the study of water.

River basin: area drained by a complete river system.

■ Interrupting water flow

There are a number of ways that the natural water cycle is adapted for human use. This is done by changing storage patterns, altering flows and withdrawing water for domestic and industrial use. In many places **river basins** have been totally changed to meet human needs (Diagram **B**). The following examples look at how two of the world's largest rivers have been adapted for human use.

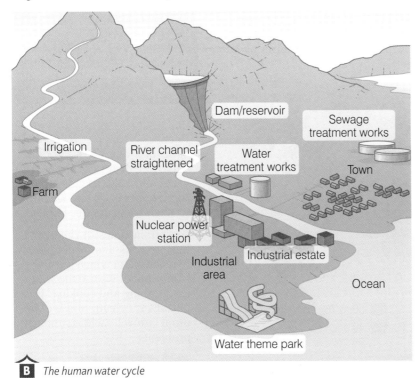

B *The human water cycle*

The Colorado River – USA

The Colorado River and its tributaries flow through seven American states before reaching the Mexican border. Since 1935 a number of dams and canals have been built on the river, making it one of the most 'managed' rivers in the world. It is used as a source of water for farming and to provide drinking water for the growing cities of western USA. The development of tourism around the desert city of Las Vegas has created an added demand for water. With 8 million visitors a year, water demand from hotels, theme parks and golf courses is huge. So much water is removed from the river that at some times in the year it reaches Mexico as a mere trickle!

The Mighty Yangtze – China

Nearly a thousand billion tonnes of water flow down the Yangtze River each year. The river is used to produce hydroelectricity (Photo **C**), irrigation for farming and drinking water for 500 million people. It is also a rubbish dump for human, agricultural and industrial waste.

In the coastal city of Shanghai a quarter of the city's sewage is dumped in the river. As one resident said:

❝ *The tap water is often a yellow-brown colour and always has a strange smell. Most people boil it before use.* ❞

The river starts over 6,000 km away in the Himalayas, fed by glaciers in the mountains of Tibet. Few people live in this area and the river is largely unchanged for the first 2,500 km. After that the river becomes an increasingly human feature, with over 20 cities using it as both a water source and a dump.

C *The Three Gorges Dam is an example of how the Yangtze River has been adapted for human use*

Activities

1 Explain how the natural water cycle in an area may be affected by:

■ heavy rainfall   ■ drought.

2 Describe and explain the ways that the water cycle is adapted for human use.

3 Suggest how the use of rivers may cause problems for people and the environment.

extension Use the internet to investigate the use of the River Ganges in India.

Water is one of the most important natural resources and is essential for all living things. People can survive for long periods with limited food, but only for a few days without water. Over 50 per cent of the world's population lack access to safe water (Map **A**). In many parts of the world getting sufficient water for drinking, washing and cooking is a constant challenge, and finding water for farming an additional burden. Even when water is available it may be many kilometres away, or contaminated (Photo **B**).

> ### In this section you will learn:
>
> that there are variations in the levels of access to clean water and sanitation
>
> that rapid urbanisation creates challenges for the management of water supply and sanitation systems.

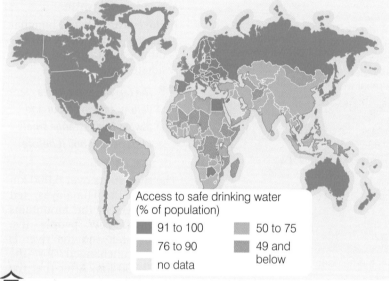

Access to safe drinking water (% of population)

- 91 to 100
- 76 to 90
- no data
- 50 to 75
- 49 and below

A   *Global access to safe water*

■ The use of water

There are three main uses for fresh water – agriculture, industry and domestic use. Agriculture is the major user, especially in the drier parts of the world. In some sub-Saharan African countries up to 90 per cent of all water is used for agriculture. Water is not only used for growing food – it is also used in the food processing industry. As the global population increases, the demand for both food and water will also increase.

Industry is also a major user of water. It takes more than 10,000 litres of water to produce a pair of jeans and nearly half a million litres to produce a car!

Rural–urban differences in less developed countries

In rural areas lakes and rivers are often the only source of drinking water, and these are also used for washing and by animals. In urban areas, because a lot of people often live close together, it is possible to build clean water pipelines and sanitation networks, resulting in higher proportions of urban dwellers having access to safe water and sanitation systems (Table **C**).

However, the rapid growth of urban areas in less developed countries is putting increasing pressure on water supply and sanitation systems (see the article on the next page).

Rachel Sebula lives in Tanzania, one of the poorest countries in Africa; she is 12 years old and spends up to three hours each day walking to fetch water for her family.

'At certain times of the year I have to walk many kilometres to reach water which is usually from a pond. We use the water for drinking and cooking. It is not always clean, and we are often unwell with stomach problems ...'

B   *Women in Africa collecting water from a river*

∞ links

Learn more about access to safe water and sanitation at

www.water.org

www.wateraid.org

www.who.int/water_sanitation_health

C   *Access to safe water and sanitation in some less developed countries*

Country	Safe water		Sanitation	
	urban %	rural %	urban %	rural %
Bangladesh	78	36	46	24
Ethiopia	44	18	31	8
Mozambique	58	23	68	18
Pakistan	98	36	52	14

(Figures are approximate)

Water Shortages in Chinese Cities

The population of many cities in China is increasing so rapidly that there is a growing problem of water shortages. It is not just population increases that are causing the problem – it is also agricultural and industrial development that uses millions of litres of water every day. Water shortages are so serious that some cities have to reduce water supply at certain times of the day. Between 1994 and 2004 it is estimated that the number of Chinese cities with water shortage problems doubled. On the North China Plain, which includes the cities of Beijing and Tianjin, water supply is an increasing challenge. Rainfall is unreliable and the level of underground water is falling. A government spokesperson said:

'It is not just a problem of growing demand for water – in some areas rainfall patterns have changed …'

▇ Sanitation

Lack of effective sanitation systems is a major cause of disease in less developed countries. About 40 per cent of the world's population do not have access to sanitation systems (Map **D**). Rapid urbanisation is increasing the number by millions each year as people occupy slum areas with no effective safe water or sanitation facilities.

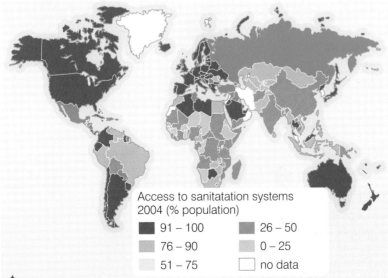

Access to sanitatation systems
2004 (% population)

▇ 91 – 100	▇ 26 – 50
▇ 76 – 90	▇ 0 – 25
▇ 51 – 75	☐ no data

D   *Global access to sanitation systems*

Activities

1   What are the three main uses of fresh water?

2   a   Draw a bar chart to show the differences in access to safe water and sanitation between urban and rural areas for the countries shown in Table **C**.

  b   Explain the differences.

3   Why are urban areas in less developed countries facing increasing water supply problems?

4   Explain each of the 'international year of sanitation' messages.

extension   Find out the GNI (US $), access to safe water (%) and access to sanitation (%) for a range of countries, from the least to most developed countries. What does your data suggest?

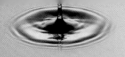

Scientists predict a number of possible effects of climate change, including:

■ *Rising sea levels and flooding*
This could lead to increasing rates of contaminated water in less developed countries, such as Bangladesh.

■ *Changing temperature patterns*
Hot areas may become even hotter, increasing evaporation rates and the risk of drought.

■ *Increasing climate extremes*
Some areas may become wetter while others become drier. In parts of the world where rainfall is already unreliable the situation may become even worse.

All of these effects will add to the risk of 'water stress', as described in the article on the right.

■ Water stress

It is clear that when looking at a map of the world, those areas with the lowest precipitation are often the areas that suffer from water shortages, especially when population numbers are increasing.

The term 'water stress' is used to describe countries that need to use high proportions of available fresh water to satisfy basic demands. Up to 50 per cent of fresh water is lost due to natural drainage, pollution and inefficient water distribution systems. Consequently, if a country is already using over 40 per cent of its available fresh water, sudden changes in rainfall patterns may push it into a water crisis.

The United Nations (UN) predicts that by 2025 large parts of the world will be in a 'water stress' situation partly as a result of changing patterns of rainfall brought about by climate change (Map **A**). It is also suggested that as water supplies become increasingly scarce, conflicts between countries may develop.

■ Climate change and water supply

A recent report by the international Tearfund agency said that climate change will threaten the lives of millions of people as rising temperatures reduce water supplies. The report, called 'Adapting water resource management to climate change', states that the number of people living in water-stressed areas is set to rise to 5 billion by 2050. Studies in north-east Brazil and Niger (Africa) found that farmers are already

In this section you will learn:

how climate change may affect water supply

how climate change may increase the risk of water-related diseases.

Increasing Threat of Water Wars

Changes in rainfall patterns and increasing demand in areas of water shortage may lead to humanitarian disasters and conflicts in the next 50 years.

Parts of the world already prone to drought may find the situation getting worse, resulting in food shortages and, in extreme cases, famine. This has already been seen in East Africa where extreme droughts in 2004 left nearly 3 million people in need of food aid.

Water shortages in areas where there are **international river basins** may lead to potential disputes or even war. The African countries of Sudan and Ethiopia want increasing amounts of water from the River Nile, which may lead to a reduction in the amount of water flowing downstream into Egypt, where the Nile is a major source of water. This type of conflict may become increasingly common in the future.

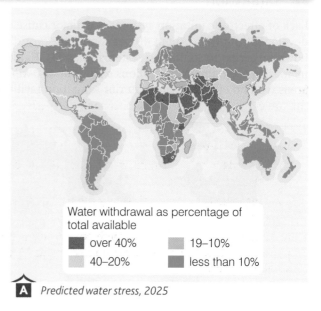

Water withdrawal as percentage of total available

■ over 40%   ■ 19–10%
■ 40–20%   ■ less than 10%

A *Predicted water stress, 2025*

having to share dwindling water supplies with their animals, putting them at increasing risk of illness and disease.

It has been suggested that the greatest impact of climate change will be found in the poorest countries. The following statements describe how four less developed countries may be affected.

Bangladesh (Asia)

With most of the country at sea level, any rise in sea level will increase the threat of flooding. Increasingly extreme climatic events may bring both flood and drought periods at different times of the year. Much of the country relies on tube wells for drinking water. Increases in flooding will mean wells will be contaminated with polluted water (Photo **B**).

Botswana (Africa)

With three-quarters of the land classified as semi-desert, rainfall is a precious resource. Climate change will increase the length of dry periods and be a threat to both food production and fresh water supply. Already in the last five years crop yields have fallen as a result of unreliable rainfall.

Egypt (Africa)

As Egypt relies on the River Nile for over 90 per cent of its fresh water, any change to the pattern of rainfall that reduces the flow of the Nile may cause severe water shortages (Photo **C**).

Burkina Faso (Africa)

Located on the edge of the Sahara Desert, Burkina Faso is one of the world's poorest countries. Rates of **desertification** have increased as climate patterns have become more extreme. As temperatures rise, rates of evaporation will increase, leaving less fresh water for farming and domestic use.

Will climate change affect water-based diseases?

Climate change may mean that the physical conditions needed for the development and spread of water-based diseases will be extended. Scientists are warning that some diseases may spread as a result of climate change. Those identified as particular risks are:

- malaria – mosquitoes that carry malaria are expected to spread as rainfall patterns change
- cholera – develops in warm, contaminated water which may become more widespread
- sleeping sickness – transmitted by the tsetse fly whose distribution is increasing
- tuberculosis – transmitted through contaminated milk because cattle are forced to drink contaminated water. The disease is then spread to people.

Activities

1 What is meant by 'water stress'?

2 Briefly explain how climate change may affect fresh water supply and levels of water contamination.

extension Use the internet to find out how climate change may affect rainfall patterns and water supply.

Did you know ??????

97.5% of the Earth's water is salt water. If the whole of the world's water fitted into a bucket, only 1 teaspoonful would be drinkable. (WaterAid)

Key terms

International river basin: river basin that crosses country borders.

Desertification: land that increasingly shows desert-like characteristics.

B *Increased flooding will contaminate wells in Bangladesh*

C *Egypt relies on the River Nile for its supply of fresh water*

∞links

Learn more about the effects of climate change on less developed countries at **www.oneworld.net**

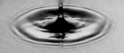

8.4 Problems of contaminated water and poor sanitation

The following statements were made by an aid worker in north-west Africa:

In this section you will learn:

about the link between contaminated water, poor sanitation and disease.

> " *For many people in less developed countries, going to the toilet means squatting by the side of a road, river or on the beach.* "

> " *Lots of aid agencies are supplying money to buy food or dig wells and yet the management of faeces could save millions of lives.* "

Nearly half of all global disease is linked to contaminated water supplies or poor sanitation systems. Today, water-related diseases are confined largely to the poorer parts of the world, many of which do not have adequate sanitation systems (Table **A**).

Clean water supply and good sanitation systems in more developed countries have largely eradicated water-related illnesses, giving them a much healthier lifestyle. In many less developed countries, untreated water is used for drinking whilst sewage is left on the streets or emptied into streams and rivers.

The following articles show how contaminated water and inadequate sanitation are a threat to people's lives.

A *Proportion of population with sanitation systems (2006)*

Region	Rural %	Urban %
North Africa	62	91
Sub-Saharan Africa	29	58
South America	51	86
Asia	38	72

A Day in the Life! Living in a slum in Bangladesh

Hasing lives in a slum in Dhaka, the capital city of Bangladesh. Her house overlooks a lake where local people wash and children fish. Her home is a wooden shack 3 metres square built on boggy land at the edge of the lake (Photo **B**). There is no clean water in the area and a part of the shore of the lake is used as a toilet. When it rains the level of the lake rises and raw sewage swirls beneath the shack.

The problem here is not a lack of water – there is too much! During the monsoon the nearby toilets flood, bringing sewage to the surface and any drinking water wells are contaminated.

In this part of Dhaka, diarrhoea is endemic and outbreaks of dysentery and cholera are common. Lack of clean water and sanitation are major killers in the area, where infant mortality rates are over 100 per 1,000 births.

Across the city nearly 4 million people live without sanitation and a million do not have any access to clean water. These numbers continue to grow as more people move into the city.

B *Slum dwelling in Bangladesh*

Kibera – the Largest Slum in Africa

The Kenyan slum of Kibera, part of the capital city of Nairobi, is one of the poorest parts of Africa. With nearly a million people living on 200 hectares of mud and rubbish, the most overwhelming feature is the smell, a mixture of smoke, rotting rubbish and excrement. There is limited running water in the slum – hosepipes bring water in from outside – but it is too expensive for most of the residents.

There are a small number of earth toilets. When they are full boys empty them into the nearby rivers. Everywhere you look there are plastic bags full of excrement – with no toilets residents use the bags and throw them out of their windows. Local people call the bags 'flying toilets'! There are regular outbreaks of typhoid and cholera – serious water-borne illnesses that can kill.

How are water-related diseases transmitted?

Water-related diseases are usually classified by the way in which they are passed on:

- Water-borne diseases – caused by drinking water contaminated by human or animal faeces or urine. Illnesses linked to this include dysentery, cholera and typhoid.

- Water-washed diseases – caused by a lack of hand washing and skin and/or eye contact with contaminated water. This can cause diarrhoea, skin and eye infections and in some cases blindness.

- Water-based diseases – caused when parasites found in water are eaten or burrow into the skin. Examples include bilharzia and guinea worm.

- Water-related diseases – caused by insects that breed in water (especially mosquitoes) and transmitted when they bite. Examples include malaria, dengue fever and yellow fever.

WaterAid

The following articles from the WaterAid website describe problems of a lack of water and sanitation systems and how water supply is being improved in one part of Bangladesh.

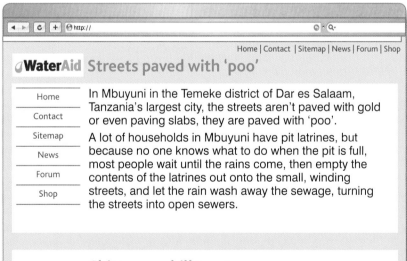

Did you know ??????

- Every year over 5 million people die from water-related disease.
- A third of all deaths are due to diarrhoea.
- Over 80% of all water-related deaths are among babies and children.
- One gram of human faeces contains 10 million viruses and 1 million bacteria. (UNICEF)
- Every year 60 million babies are born into homes without sanitation systems. (UN Water)

∞ links

Learn more about WaterAid schemes and more water facts at **www.wateraid.org**

Activities

1 Explain the ways in which water-related diseases may be transmitted.

2 Describe the problems caused by a lack of sanitation systems in the urban slums of Dhaka and Kibera.

3 Explain why clean water is good for both health and wealth in less developed countries.

■ Why do water shortages occur?

Water shortages may occur for a number of reasons.

Changing rainfall patterns

Short-term and long-term changes to rainfall patterns may create water shortages. In more developed countries, temporary water shortages are managed by measures such as hosepipe bans or other water restrictions. Long-term changes to rainfall patterns require water management schemes to be developed in order to ensure a reliable water supply. In the poorest parts of the world, where water storage facilities are limited, any change to expected rainfall can have serious consequences.

Interference with natural systems

Water shortages may result from human interference with the landscape. Removing trees or increasing the amounts of hard surface will mean that rainfall reaches rivers faster and is therefore lost to the area. Changing the flow of water by diverting rivers or building **reservoirs** in one place may cause water shortages elsewhere.

Irrigation schemes

Farming uses vast quantities of water. Large-scale irrigation schemes may remove millions of litres of water from rivers and underground water sources (Photo **A**).

Industrial and domestic demand

Industrial development and urbanisation increase the demand for water. Where the local area cannot supply the water needed it has to be pumped in from other places, creating possible shortages elsewhere.

■ Drought in North Africa

Drought is defined as 'a lack of rainfall over a prolonged period of time'. In areas such as the Sahel (sub-Saharan Africa), people are so poor that they are not able to cope with long periods of drought. An aid worker said:

> 66 *When the rains fail famine is not far behind* 99

The following extract is taken from a UN report into drought in North Africa.

A report produced by the United Nations Environment Programme (UNEP) in 2007 about the drought in North Africa concluded that:

- rainfall was down by over 25 per cent in the last 40 years
- the Sahara Desert is advancing 20 km every 10 years
- yields of basic food crops have fallen by 50 per cent in the last 20 years
- because of desertification, farmers are being forced to move onto neighbouring lands, causing local conflicts.

In this section you will learn:

that different factors influence water supply

that water shortages may affect both less and more developed countries.

A   *A large-scale irrigation scheme*

Did you know ??????

In order to supply Beijing with water during the Olympic Games in China in 2008, 300 km of pipelines were built, bringing in water from distant farmland. In some farming areas this resulted in water shortages as groundwater levels fell. Many farmers lost their crops and had to abandon their homes and move elsewhere.

Key terms

Reservoirs: artificial stores of water.

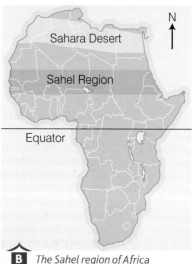

B   *The Sahel region of Africa*

Water shortages in Las Vegas (USA)

Las Vegas is one of the fastest-growing cities in the USA. Increasing numbers of people are moving to the area because of job opportunities and the sunny climate (Photo **D**). The last 40 years has seen a massive growth in tourism and the development of many resort hotels. The problem is that the area only receives a few centimetres of rain each year.

In recent years there have been a series of droughts in the USA, with 2007 the driest year on record for many parts of the country (Map **C**).

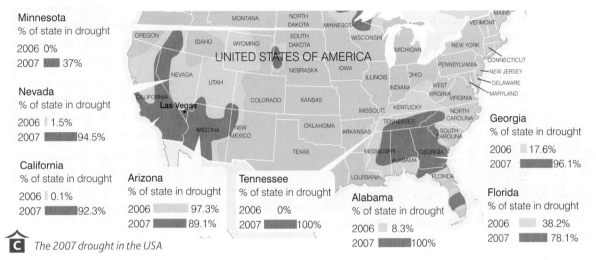

Minnesota
% of state in drought
2006 0%
2007 37%

Nevada
% of state in drought
2006 1.5%
2007 94.5%

California
% of state in drought
2006 0.1%
2007 92.3%

Arizona
% of state in drought
2006 97.3%
2007 89.1%

Tennessee
% of state in drought
2006 0%
2007 100%

Alabama
% of state in drought
2006 8.3%
2007 100%

Georgia
% of state in drought
2006 17.6%
2007 96.1%

Florida
% of state in drought
2006 38.2%
2007 78.1%

C *The 2007 drought in the USA*

There are different views about how water shortages should be managed in Las Vegas.

❝ *Building new pipelines and transporting water from wetter areas is the best option. Some people say that this would create water shortages elsewhere, harming farming and the environment. But that is not our problem.* ❞

❝ *Restricting business development would slow down the increase in water demand and fewer people would move into the area. The problem is that business and tourism create billions of dollars for the USA.* ❞

❝ *What is required is a more sustainable approach to water use. Building swimming pools and golf courses in a semi-desert environment is madness! We need to make the water we have go further. Water conservation is happening in some places – one of the major hotel casinos has its own water recycling plant. It cleans half a million litres of water a day and reuses it to water the grounds.* ❞

D *Las Vegas, a desert city*

Activities

1 Explain how natural and human factors may cause water shortages.

2 a Explain the aid worker's quote (page 192).

   b Suggest why the effects of water shortages may be different in countries at different stages of development.

3 What do you think is the best water management solution for Las Vegas?

extension Use the internet to investigate drought and the management of drought in the UK.

⦾ **links**

Learn more about the UN policies on water at **www.un.org**

What are water transfer schemes?

Water transfer schemes are engineering projects that collect and store water in areas where rainfall or river volumes are higher, and transfer it to areas where demand is greater than local supply. The water is stored in reservoirs and lakes and usually transferred by artificial channels or underground pipes. In some cases rivers are joined so that water can be transferred directly from one river to another.

Water transfer schemes are used to match up supply and demand for water. In an increasingly urban world, large numbers of people live in small areas. In order to ensure these areas have enough water for domestic and industrial use it may be necessary to transfer water from other areas, sometimes hundreds of kilometres away. Virtually every country uses water transfer schemes of some scale. The following case studies look at two of the largest schemes in the world.

In this section you will learn:

why water transfer schemes are required

that large-scale water transfer schemes may be controversial.

Case study

The Central Valley Project, California (USA)

California has seasonal patterns of rainfall with a dry period in the summer.

Rainfall is higher in the north whilst the best farming land is in the south.

There has been a growing demand for water since the 1970s because of:

- the growth of coastal cities
- the expansion of farming in the central valley
- the growth of tourism.

The Central Valley Project (Map **A**) is a series of dams, reservoirs, canals and aqueducts which collect and store water from the wetter areas and transport it to the drier farming regions in the south, and the coastal cities (Photo **B**). The project has changed a semi-desert area into highly productive farmland, where fruit, vegetables and cotton are grown.

However, there have been concerns about the project, including:

- the financial cost, which makes the real cost of water very expensive
- increasing salinity as water is evaporated, leaving behind high salt levels in the soil
- the cost of removing salt deposits from the land
- damage to the original semi-desert environment.

Find out ... 🔍

Use the internet to find out more about the Central Valley Project.

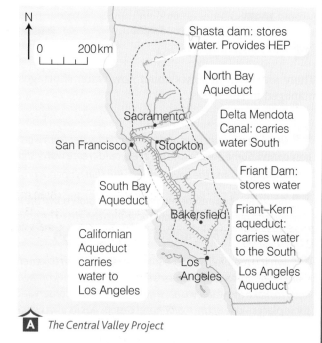

A   *The Central Valley Project*

B   *The All-American Canal and intensive farmland in the Central Valley*

The South–North Water Transfer Project, China

The North China Plain is the most rapidly developing part of China. A population of over 350 million and high rates of urban and industrial growth are increasing the threat of water shortages in the area. The problems of managing water supply are made more difficult by the pattern of rainfall, with a wet period between June and September followed by a longer dry period. Also, in recent years the annual pattern and amount of rainfall has become increasingly unreliable.

The Chinese government has decided that the way to resolve the water shortages on the North China Plain is to transfer water from further south. The South–North Water Transfer Project (SNWTP) will transfer 50 billion cubic metres of water a year from the Yangtze River in the south to the Yellow River which flows through the North China Plain. This will be used to supply the major industrial cities of Beijing and Tianjin.

C *The South–North Water Transfer Project*

The transfer of water will be achieved by building three major routeways and a number of storage reservoirs, created by building dams. In total the three routeways will involve building over 4,000 km of canals at a cost of over US $60 billion. The plan is to complete the central and eastern routeways by 2010 and the western by 2050. `The scheme is very controversial – some views about it are expressed below.

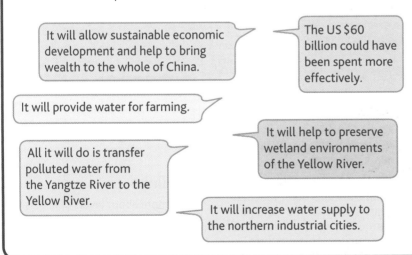

Did you know ??????

The Middle East and North Africa (MENA) is the largest area of water shortage in the world. The area has not been self-sufficient in water for the last 30 years.

Water demand is being met in a number of ways, including:

- using dams and transfer schemes
- exploiting groundwater sources
- recycling waste water
- desalination of sea water.

∞ links

Visit **www.internationalrivers.org** to find out more about the water transfer project.

Did you know ??????

In China, water efficiency rates are as low as 40% compared with an average of 80% in Western countries.

Activities

1 Why are water transfer schemes needed in most countries?

2 **a** Create a table to summarise the advantages and disadvantages of the South–North Water Transfer Project in China.

   b Do you think that going ahead with this project was the right decision? Explain your answer.

8.7 Improving access to water systems in less developed countries

In the United Nations (UN) Millennium Report (2000), Kofi Annan, the UN Secretary General said:

> 66 *No single measure would do more to reduce disease and save lives in the developing world than bringing safe water and adequate sanitation to all.* 99

There are significant effects when clean water and adequate sanitation are scarce:

- Health – rates of disease are higher.
- Wealth – the ability to work and earn money is reduced.
- Food – the ability to grow food and produce healthy meals is reduced.
- Education – fewer children go to school because they spend hours collecting water each day, or are unwell.

How may access to clean water and sanitation be improved?

The following examples show how water and sanitation systems are being improved in some of the poorest parts of the world.

In this section you will learn:

how improved water supply and sanitation may increase levels of health and wealth

how water supply and access to sanitation are being improved in less developed countries.

Did you know ??????

Article 24 of the United Nations Convention on the Rights of the Child states that every child should have the right to clean drinking water.

Key terms

Pasteurisation: the process of sterilisation by heating.

Water Filters

In Kuru, Nigeria, the streams are contaminated by salmonella, worms and bacteria. The people regularly suffered from severe stomach pains and diarrhoea. The danger to children was the worst of all. For them these terrible diseases could be fatal.

CAFOD's (Catholic aid agency) local partner helped the villagers of Kuru build a water filter in their village. They provided the sand, gravel and charcoal and did all the work ... then the wonderful moment came when the first bucket of water was poured through the filter.

One villager said:

'We drink the filtered water, our bodies feel fine. The water went in dark green, smelling foul, and just 10 minutes later clean pure water poured out from the bottom.'

To the people of Kuru, constant diseases and sickness seem like a thing of the past. No more stomach pains, no more water-borne worms, and most importantly, far fewer babies dying from preventable disease.

Diagram labels: plastic lid, plastic barrel, storage drum, sand 3 buckets, charcoal 2 buckets, gravel 3 buckets, drinking water

A *A simple water filter saves lives every day*

Aquapak – using the sun to purify water

Aquapak is a new invention designed to heat water to over 65°C using only sunlight. At this temperature water-borne bacteria and parasites will be killed, making the water safe to drink.

The Aquapak is made of plastic and air-filled bubblewrap and has an indicator to show when the required temperature has been reached to start the **pasteurisation** process. It is estimated that the Aquapak could be made for less than US $1 and produce up to 20 litres of drinking water a day. Find out more at **www.watersolutions.info**.

Did you know ??????

Access to clean water may reduce infant mortality rates by up to 50%.

⚭ **links**

Learn more about levels of access to safe water and sanitation at **www.wateraid.org**

◑WaterAid

WaterAid is a specialist development charity based in the UK. It works with people and governments in less developed countries to improve water supply and sanitation systems. Examples of WaterAid projects can be seen below.

Ethiopia – the Hitosa water supply scheme

In parts of rural Ethiopia people rely on contaminated pond water for drinking, washing and cooking.

Hitosa is a mainly rural area of approximately 200,000 people where most people live in small farming settlements. Traditionally women and children spent many hours a day collecting water from ponds and rivers.

The Hitosa water scheme collects clean water from mountain springs and uses gravity (slope) to transport it through over 100 km of pipeline to 120 distribution points.

The scheme serves over 70,000 people and has made a significant difference to the health of the population.

Burkina Faso – the importance of new wells and toilets

Marie Edith Kinda says:

'Before, we had to go to the toilet in the bushes. When women had diarrhoea they couldn't get far from home and had to go to the toilet in front of everyone else. Having latrines has not only helped our health, it has restored our dignity and pride'.

Laurentine Yameogo says:

'Before WaterAid rehabilitated our well we were afraid to collect water from the pond because of crocodiles. Before we had the safe water we had lots of illness, especially stomach problems. When the children were ill we went to the clinic. It is very expensive. Since the well has been rehabilitated we haven't had these illnesses.'

B   *A water sanitation block built by WaterAid*

Bangladesh – a new sanitation block

Hasina says:

*'Before getting this sanitation block (Photo **B**) I used to be lucky to wash once every three days. Now I bathe every day and feel so much more clean and comfortable. I would say that sanitation was the biggest problem for people in this area before this block was built. Now the popularity of good hygiene and sanitation has spread. Everyone wants clean lavatories and a clean and private place to wash – children are so much cleaner and healthier now.'*

www.wateraid.org

The Thames Water Marunda project in Jakarta

Jakarta is the capital city of Indonesia, in Asia. The population of the city has grown from 8 million in 1990 to over 15 million today. Local authorities cannot keep up with the demand for clean water and sanitation systems, resulting in high rates of water-related disease. The situation is particularly bad in slum areas (Photo **C**) such as Marunda.

Thames Water, working with the Jakarta authorities and local people, has built a project that supplies fresh piped water to over 12,000 people in Marunda. The project was built and is maintained by local people. The cost of the water is significantly less than bottled water. As one local resident said:

'Not only are we much healthier, we can also spend more money on basic needs such as food and clothes.'

C   *A slum area in Jakarta*

Find out more at
www.globaleye.org.uk

Activities

1   Explain why the CAFOD water filter and Aquapak are appropriate for less developed countries.

2   Explain how improving water systems in less developed countries is good for people's health and wealth.

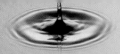

8.8 Using water more efficiently

How we use water

People often see water as a free resource because it falls from the sky and is recycled by the natural environment. Because of this water is often wasted. Think about the following questions:

- Do you leave the tap running when cleaning your teeth?
- Do you run the cold tap for a few seconds before you take drinking water?
- How much water do you use when washing the family car?
- Do you water the garden more than is absolutely necessary?
- Do you need to use drinking water to flush the toilet?

How efficiently is water used?

A recent study suggested that there are wide variations in the efficiency of water use. In more developed countries, water efficiency is usually between 60 and 80 per cent whereas in less developed countries water efficiency is usually between 25 and 40 per cent.

What do these figures mean?

The lower the water efficiency rate, the higher the general level of water wastage. There are number of reasons why water efficiency rates are low, including:

- leakages in pipes and water supply systems (Photo **A**)
- spillage in water collection systems
- using too much water for particular tasks
- discharging water to drains that could be reused for other activities
- using machines that are not water efficient.

Improving water efficiency

The following **conservation** methods can be used to improve water efficiency.

Rainwater harvesting

Rainwater can be collected from roofs via normal guttering systems and stored in tanks. The water can then be used in a number of ways (Diagram **B**).

Greywater recycling

Greywater is usually defined as wastewater from all sources other than toilets.

Building water-efficient homes and industrial buildings

Water collection systems can be installed in new buildings along with water-efficient appliances.

In this section you will learn:

how recycling may reduce water use

how building technology may reduce the demand for water.

Key terms

Conservation: protecting resources (using resources more efficiently).

A   *A leaking standpipe*

Did you know ???????

- Predictions of climate change suggest that large parts of Europe will see increased periods of drought and flooding.
- Improved drainage may provide the answer to flooding.
- Water conservation methods will be needed to cope with drought.

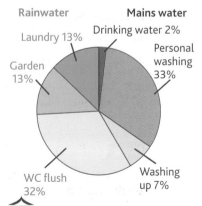

Rainwater   **Mains water**

Laundry 13%   Drinking water 2%

Garden 13%   Personal washing 33%

WC flush 32%

Washing up 7%

B   *Mains and rainwater uses*

Rainwater harvesting

Rainwater harvesting is simply collecting rainwater from a roof, storing it and then filtering and reusing it (Diagram **C**). Systems can be developed for both domestic and business premises.

Rainwater harvesting has two major advantages:

- It may reduce water costs by up to 50 per cent (Table **D**)
- It may reduce the risk of local flooding because less rainwater is getting into streams and rivers.

Greywater recycling

Greywater recycling systems collect all wastewater except where it has been used to flush toilets or is contaminated with chemicals. The water is then treated biologically to stop bacterial growth. It can then be used for toilet flushing and watering gardens. Water savings can range from 5 to 30 per cent. An average-sized house with a garden will typically save 15 per cent of its water costs.

Water-efficient buildings

The following example looks at ZEDHomes' plan for producing water-efficient homes (Article **E**).

C Rainwater harvesting

D How much water can be collected m³/year

Rainfall (mm/year)	Roof area (m²)		
	50	100	150
500	15	30	45
1,000	30	60	90
1,500	45	90	135

Conservation

ZEDHomes – aims to cut household mains water consumption by a third by:

- installing water-efficient domestic appliances
- using lower-volume baths and fitting taps with water-saving flow restrictors
- installing dual-flush toilets
- storing rainwater and recycled water in large tanks built into the foundations.

Water treatment

ZEDHomes treat the wastewater by a small-scale sewage treatment system located on site. It is a biologically based system; it extracts the nutrients for food for plants and treats the water to a standard that allows it to be recycled back to the underground water tanks to supplement rainwater for flushing the toilet, watering the garden and even washing cars.

E Water conservation

Activities

1. Describe five ways in which you waste water.

2. What is meant by:
   - rainwater harvesting
   - greywater recycling?

3. The 'pay-back time' for rainwater harvesting systems is approximately three years. What does this mean?

4. Describe and explain the water-saving measures that could be incorporated into new housing.

5. 'Water recycling is good for both the environment and the economy'. Explain this statement.

∞ links

Learn more about Zedhomes at www.zedhomes.com

Learn more about water conservation at

www.stormsaver.com

www.freerain.co.uk

www.freewateruk.co.uk

www.environment-agency.gov.uk

www.therenewableenergycentre. co.uk

The development of towns and cities puts pressure on river environments because:

- rivers are often used as a dumping ground for rubbish
- in some places residential and industrial areas discharge waste into rivers
- pollution from boats and ships finds its way into rivers, harming plant and animal life
- land alongside rivers is sometimes used for industrial development
- rivers are often artificially changed by building concrete riverbanks and removing vegetation in order to make water flow faster.

■ Why are river environments a valuable resource?

River environments are a valuable economic and social resource. They provide water supply and transport links and may be important green spaces in urban environments. Rivers and riversides are also increasingly seen as valuable areas for recreation and leisure activities.

The following case studies look at how river management schemes are improving water quality and river environments in different parts of the world:

In this section you will learn:

how urban and industrial development puts pressure on river environments

how river quality and river environments may be improved.

Find out ...

Use the internet to find out more about how the Olympic development will improve the Lea Valley.

Find out ...

Use the internet to find out more about the Ganga action plan and how successful it has been.

Case study

The London Olympics will improve the river environment

The Olympic Games is being used as an opportunity to improve the environment of the Lea Valley in east London. Industry is being removed from the riverside and pollution control measures put in place to improve the water quality of the River Lea. The riverside areas are being landscaped and parks and walkways developed, along with woodland and wetland areas. Community play areas for children and cafés will be built alongside the river.

A   *An artist's impression of the Lea Valley*

Case study

Managing the River Ganga (India)

Over 60 per cent of available water in India is polluted, resulting in high rates of water-related disease. The River Ganga basin drains nearly a quarter of the country and is home to 20 per cent of India's population. By the late 1980s rapid urban and industrial growth had turned the Ganga into one of the most polluted rivers in Asia. In 1988 a visitor to the riverside city of Varanasi wrote:

'A boat trip along the river shows just how bad conditions are. Every few hundred metres there are pipes discharging raw sewage and industrial chemicals into the river, often near where water is being removed for drinking! The river is a community facility – people bring their cows to the river to drink and people wash themselves in the shallow water, which is considered sacred. The riverbanks are used for cremations; bodies are placed on wooden platforms and set alight before being pushed into the water.'

In the late 1980s the Indian government introduced the River Ganga Action Plan in an attempt to clean up the river. There has been a lot of debate about the ongoing success of the plan. Some people say that it has improved the quality of the river environment while others feel it has made little difference.

Restoring the River Skerne in north-east England

The River Skerne flows through an area surrounded by housing and industry. Over the years the river has been straightened and the shape of the river banks changed because of building and dumping of waste material. The river has also been used as a drain for local roads and a sewer outfall.

How has the River Skerne been restored?

B *New meanders on the River Skerne*

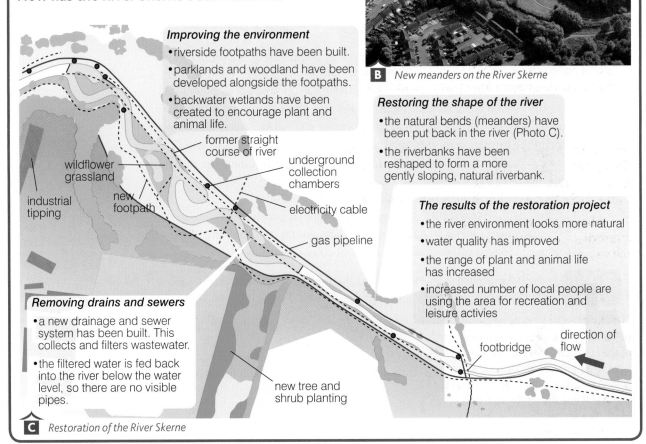

Improving the environment
- riverside footpaths have been built.
- parklands and woodland have been developed alongside the footpaths.
- backwater wetlands have been created to encourage plant and animal life.

former straight course of river

underground collection chambers

wildflower grassland

industrial tipping

new footpath

electricity cable

gas pipeline

Restoring the shape of the river
- the natural bends (meanders) have been put back in the river (Photo C).
- the riverbanks have been reshaped to form a more gently sloping, natural riverbank.

The results of the restoration project
- the river environment looks more natural
- water quality has improved
- the range of plant and animal life has increased
- increased number of local people are using the area for recreation and leisure activies

Removing drains and sewers
- a new drainage and sewer system has been built. This collects and filters wastewater.
- the filtered water is fed back into the river below the water level, so there are no visible pipes.

new tree and shrub planting

footbridge

direction of flow

C *Restoration of the River Skerne*

Activities

1 Why is the quality of river environments often poor in urban areas?

2 Explain how large-scale developments such as the Olympic Games may be used to improve our environments.

3 a Describe the methods used to improve the River Skerne.

b How has the River Skerne restoration scheme improved both environmental and social conditions?

extension Investigate the plan to clean up the Singapore River and Kallang Basin in Singapore. Find out what the problems were and what is being done to improve the area.

A useful starting point may be www.unescap.org → Singapore

⬭links

Learn more about this and other restoration projects at www.theRRC.co.uk or www. environment-agency.gov.uk

AQA Examination-style questions

It is important to note that the examination-style questions in the following section are practice questions in the style you might expect to find in the paper but are not representative of the full range of questions you will find in the examination.

Unit 1

1 The coastal environment

1   Using examples you have studied, explain why coastal areas are often called 'multi-use areas'.

2   How can coastal areas provide opportunities for economic development?

3   How can coastal environments be protected from over development?

4   Explain how weathering and erosion can create distinctive coastal landforms.

5   Explain the formation of spits and bars.

6   How can hard and soft engineering techniques be used to reduce the threat of coastal erosion and flooding?

7   Using an example you have studied, describe:

   (a) how overdevelopment is putting the coast under pressure

   (b) the measures being taken to ensure the long term sustainability of the area.

8   How can managed retreat reduce the risk of coastal flooding?

 The use of annotated diagrams often helps when explaining physical processes and features. Use well located examples to help you show your understanding.

2 The urban environment

1   Using examples you have studied, describe the environmental hazards found in urban areas.

2   Using an example you have studied:

   (a) explain why some urban areas are at risk of natural hazards

   (b) describe how the threat of a natural hazard can be reduced.

3   Explain how urban redevelopment strategies are being used to improved economic and environmental conditions in developed countries.

4   Using examples you have studied, describe the methods being used to reduce traffic congestion in urban areas.

5   Why are urban areas in developing countries growing rapidly?

6   Describe the challenges and opportunities created by urban growth in developing countries.

7   Explain how conditions for the urban poor are being improved in developing cities.

8   Describe the methods that can be used to:

   (a) Make urban areas increasingly carbon neutral

   (b) Increase the amount of green space in urban areas.

9   What factors need to be considered if a planned settlement is going to be sustainable?

 Use well located examples to help you show your understanding.

Unit 2

3 Living with natural hazards

1   Describe the effects of either an earthquake or a volcanic eruption. Use examples from an area that you have studied.

2   Explain how either an earthquake or a volcanic eruption occurs. Use a labelled diagram to support your answer.

3   Describe ways in which the damaging effects of either an earthquake or a volcanic eruption might be reduced.

4   Explain why the damaging effects of a tropical storm might be greater in a less developed country.

5   Describe ways in which the damaging effects of a tropical storm might be reduced.

6   Suggest how climate change might affect the frequency and strength of tropical storms.

7   Explain the natural and human causes of wildfires.

8   Describe ways in which the damaging effects of a wildfire might be reduced.

4 The challenge of extreme environments

1   Explain why some areas are hot deserts. Use a labelled diagram to support your answer.

2   Explain the causes of desertification. Use examples from an area that you have studied.

3   Describe ways in which the fringes of hot deserts can be managed sustainably.

4   Explain why some areas have tropical rainforests. Use a labelled diagram to support your answer.

5   Explain why some areas of tropical rainforest are being removed. Use examples from an area that you have studied.

6   Describe ways in which damage to tropical rainforest environments might be reduced.

7   "Antarctica must be protected against development." Do you agree with this statement? Give reasons for your decision.

8   Describe ways in which cold environments can be protected. Use examples from an area that you have studied.

Unit 3

5 The globalisation of industry

Extended questions

1   (a) Describe the operations of one Transnational Corporation you have studied .

    (b) Explain how Transnational Corporations can bring advantages and disadvantages to local communities.

2   Why has industry become increasingly globalised?

3   Using an example from a more developed country you have studied, explain how industrial investment can create benefit for local communities.

4   (a) Describe the main features of Science Parks.

    (b) Explain why the number of Science Parks has increased.

5   Describe and explain the methods used to compare levels of development.

6   Explain how industrial growth can improve living conditions in a less developed country.

7   Using an example you have studied, describe the effect of industrial decline.

8   Explain the use of appropriate technology in creating economic opportunities.

9   Explain how industrial development can be managed sustainably.

6 Global tourism

Extended questions

1   (a) Describe the global spread of tourism in the last 50 years.

       (b) Suggest reasons for the growth of tourism in the last 50 years.

2   How does the physical environment provide opportunities for different types of tourist activities?

3   Explain how tourism has brought benefits to a more developed country you have studied.

4   Describe and explain the methods used to compare levels of development.

5   Explain how the development of tourism can be used to improve living conditions in a less developed country.

6   Explain how tourism development can create social conflicts.

7   Using an example you have studied, describe the effects of tourism decline.

8   Explain how tourism development can damage local environments.

9   Using an example you have studied, explain how ecotourism is good for people and the environment.

 Examiner's tip Try to use geographical language in your answers – it is a useful way of showing understanding.

Unit 4

Geographical issue investigation

This unit of study will be assessed by investigating a question set by the examination board. The questions will ask you to investigate a particular issue linked to the unit of study. You will need to produce a brief report based on the question. This will involve:

- collecting appropriate information about the question
- presenting your information
- explaining what your information shows
- answering the question by writing a brief conclusion.

 Examiner's tip **What is an issue?**

An issue is something over which there is a difference of opinion. It could be:

- a basic discussion about whether something should be built or not
- about making a decision from a number of options.

There is not always a right or wrong answer – it is often a matter of opinion. That is why it is an issue.

How will your Unit 4 report be marked?

The following marking criteria will be used to mark your report.

The full mark scheme can be seen on the AQA website at www.aqa.org.uk

Marking criteria	Guidance	What you need to do to achieve the highest mark
Research evidence (6 marks)	Research can take many forms, including: • books, atlases, newspapers, photographs • television, DVD, radio • interviews, questionnaires • primary research – counting/ measuring.	• make sure you have a wide range of evidence – at least three or four sources • make sure the evidence you collect is closely linked to the question • make a note of where your evidence came from – you could include a bibliography at the end of your report. This is helpful in showing the range of research.
Geographical understanding (3 marks)	While carrying out the research make sure you make a note of the key words that are important.	• write a brief introduction to the topic. This will help you to set the scene and say what it is about • the use of geographical terminology (key words) is very important. You need to use them in your report • putting the key words and definitions in a 'definition box' on the opening page of your report might be helpful.
Presentation skills (6 marks)	This is not just about particular skills (graphs etc). It is also about general presentation and organisation. Good use of basic skills (headings, underlining, titles etc) can make a big difference to the look of your finished work.	• you must include the use of ICT in your final report • a range of presentation skills, including some more complex skills will help you achieve higher marks. Complex skills might include, proportional symbol maps, annotated maps, diagrams, photographs or the use of statistical correlation techniques • your final report needs to be well organised with clear sections and headings
Values and attitudes (6 marks)	The investigation will always be about a topic where there might be: • differences of opinion • different ways of doing things. Make sure you identify any of these factors in your research.	• in order to achieve the highest mark you need to identify different views or opinions about the topic • you need to explain three different views/opinions (could be government, local people, pressure groups etc) • don't forget that you could use your own opinion or carry out local interviews to see what people think about a particular issue (as long as it is appropriate to the topic).
Conclusion (3 marks)	The conclusion is where you return to the original question and make a final judgement.	• you must use your evidence to reach a valid conclusion and not simply make general statements The highest mark will be achieved when you: • reach a clear decision/judgement • say clearly why you have come to that judgement • select detailed evidence from your research to back up your judgement.

Glossary

A

Acid rain: rainwater that contains chemicals which come from the burning of fossil fuels.

Aftershocks: smaller tremors occurring after an earthquake.

Appropriate technology: a technology that is suitable and sustainable for the place where it is to be used.

Arid: dry.

B

Backwash: movement of water down the beach.

Beach: an accumulation of sand and shingle.

Beach profile: the shape of the beach.

Biodegradable: able to decay naturally and harmlessly.

Biodiversity: the number and variety of plant and animal species that live in a particular area.

Biofuel: fuel derived from plants as an alternative to fossil fuels.

Biotechnology: using living things like cells and bacteria in industrial processes.

Boycott: showing your disapproval by refusing to go somewhere.

Brand: a symbol or name that distinguishes a company from its competitors.

Bronchitis: inflammation of the tubes (bronchioles) leading into the lungs.

Brownfield: old industrial or housing area that has become derelict.

Building code: set of regulations about the required ability of a building to withstand an earthquake.

C

Call centres: place where the employees answer customer telephone calls.

Carbon-zero: does not use resources that create carbon dioxide.

Community tourism: tourism that has close contact with, and mainly benefits, local communities.

Commuters: people who moves daily between place of work and home.

Conflict: contrasting demands between people with different desires and opinions.

Conservation: the protection and management of natural resources.

Consumer goods: products like televisions, dishwashers etc. that people want to buy.

Cooperative: a company owned and managed by the people who work in it.

Coppicing: method of encouraging re-growth of trees by cutting them back to near ground level.

Corporate responsibility: how a company manages its impact on society and the environment.

Crest: the top of a wave.

D

Demography: the study of population.

Deprivation: where a person's quality of life falls below a level that is regarded as the acceptable minimum by the government of the country. This usually means that such a person does not have access to enough resources for a healthy life.

Deprived areas: places where economic/social and environmental conditions are very poor.

Dereliction: previously used land/buildings fallen into disuse and decay.

Desalinisation: removal of salts from seawater.

Desertification: the spread of a desert – the process in which land slowly dries out until little or no vegetation can survive.

Development gap: the difference between the economic development of the world's richest and poorest countries.

Development indicators: health, wealth and social statistics that show how developed a country is.

Distribution centre: huge warehouses where companies such as supermarket chains get their products from.

Drought: a long period of low rainfall.

E

Earth bund: constructed mound of earth.

Earth's crust: the solid, outer layer of the Earth.

Eco-homes: homes that have a minimum impact on the environment.

Ecological footprint: the impact of an individual on the Earth (measured in hectares per person).

Economic activity: all the businesses and activities that make money for a country.

Economic effects: those affecting money and business.

Eco-settlements: settlements that do not harm the environment because they meet the needs of people without damaging the environment or exploiting resources.

Ecosystems: communities of plants and animals within a particular physical environment.

Ecotourism: the responsible development and management of tourism, which helps to preserve the environment.

El Niño: a warming of the ocean surface off the western coast of South America.

Entrepreneur: someone who starts their own business.

Epicentre: the point on the Earth's surface directly above the focus of an earthquake.

Equatorial: existing at or near the equator.

Estuary: the tidal part of a river.

European City of Culture: a city designated by the European Union for a year to show off its cultural life.

Evacuation: movement of people away from a place of danger to a place of safety.

Event tourism: travel based around specific events whether they are sporting, cultural or historical.

Exploitation: taking advantage of resources or people.

Export revenues: money a country gains by selling products to other countries.

Extraction: removal of oil from below the ground.

Eye: the calm, clear area at the centre of the tropical storm.

F

Fair Trade tourism: makes sure the benefits go directly to those whose land, natural resources, work, knowledge and culture are being used.

Fair Trade: a type of trade that guarantees reasonable wages and long-term stability for farmers and businesses.

Finite: limited in quantity.

Floodplain: a low-lying area next to a river that is vulnerable to flooding.

Food chain: the feeding relationships between species in an ecosystem.

G

Genetically modified (GM): crops that have had their DNA changed through genetic engineering.

Geographical Information System (GIS): electronic system used for storing, analysing, managing and presenting data, which is linked to a location.

Globalisation: the increasing international interaction in trade, politics, society and culture.

Grassroots: run by local people to benefit local communities.

Green space: parkland, vegetated walkways in urban areas.

Greenbelt: countryside around urban areas that should be kept natural and exempt from building.

Greenhouse gas emissions: gases from industry that pollute the air and cause global warming.

Gross national income (GNI): a commonly used way of measuring how rich a country is (also known as GDP).

Growth poles: areas used for business development.

Groyne: wooden or concrete barrier built across a beach.

H

Headlands: where land juts out into the sea.

Heritage tourism: travelling to see historical aspects of a country that still exist.

High pressure: cold air is slowly sinking, pressing down on the Earth.

Honeypot: a place of attractive scenery or historic interest that attracts large numbers of visitors.

Human Development Index (HDI): a way of measuring development using information about income, education and life expectancy.

Hydroelectricity: producing electricity using flowing water.

Hydrological: relating to the study of water.

I

Ice sheet: thick layer of ice covering a large area of land.

Impact: the effect of an action on an area.

Incentives: something that encourages a company to do something.

Indigenous people: people native to an area.

Indigenous: naturally existing in a place or country rather than coming from somewhere else.

Industrial estate: an area of land developed for industrial buildings.

Industrialisation (industrial development): increasing the amount of industry in a country.

Infrastructure: basic networks such as transport, power supplies and telecommunications.

Integrated management: management of the whole of an area/system rather than parts of it.

Integrated transport system: all parts of the system fit together to make it efficient.

Interdependent: people, countries and businesses depending on, and helping, one another.

International river basin: river basin that crosses country borders.

Investment: money spent on buildings and equipment to make a business more effective.

Irrigation: the artificial watering of the land.

K

Katabatic wind: a strong, cold wind flowing downhill.

L

Land degradation: a reduction in the ability of the soil to support life.

Landform: a physical feature that has been shaped by erosion/weathering.

Laser ranging: using laser beams and mirrors to detect minute changes in the shape of the land.

Latitude: a location north or south of the equator.

Levels: areas of flat land, often with many rivers/streams.

Life expectancy: average number of years a person may expect to live.

Liquefaction: the loss of strength that can occur in soil during earthquake shaking.

Long-haul: travelling a long distance.

M

Magma: liquid rock below the Earth's surface.

Mandatory evacuation: an evacuation that is commanded by the authorities.

Mantle: the layer of the Earth between the crust and the core.

Manufactured goods: products made in large numbers, usually in a factory.

Marine erosion: the wearing away of rocks by the action of the sea.

Markets: the people and businesses that may want to buy something.

Mass tourism: large numbers of people heading to the same area.

Megacity: a city of 10 million people.

Mixed use: has a mixture of uses – commercial, leisure, residential etc.

Mortality: death, usually expressed as deaths per 1000 of the population.

Multiplier effect: increased spending in one part of the economy positively affecting another.

N

NASA: National Aeronautics and Space Administration – the US space agency.

National parks: areas set aside to protect the landscape so that it can be enjoyed by visitors now and in the future.

Natural cycle: series of events in nature that are repeated over and over again.

Newly industrialised countries (NICs): countries, mostly in Asia, that underwent rapid and successful industrialisation in the 1980s.

Non-governmental organisation (NGO): organisation that is independent of government control, usually charitable organisations such as WaterAid, Oxfam, Save the Children.

Non-renewable: can only be used only once.

O

Opencast mining: mining resources by firstly removing the material that covers them.

Overcultivation: growing too many crops, year after year on the same piece of land, without allowing the soil to regain its fertility.

Ozone hole: the depletion of ozone in the Earth's atmosphere.

P

Package holiday: a tour where transport, accommodation and food are all included in one price.

Pasteurisation: the process of sterilisation by heating.

Permafrost: permanently frozen ground.

Photochemical smog: where smog combines with sunlight to form ozone, causing serious health problems such as breathing problems, eye irritations, vomiting.

Physical effects: those affecting natural and built materials.

Pollution: damage caused by harmful substances and waste.

Pressure groups: special interest groups that try to influence the views of others.

Prevailing winds: the winds blowing most frequently from one particular direction.

Primary effects: those resulting directly from the event itself.

Primary products: food, crops, minerals and other raw materials usually used to make something else.

Pulaski: a tool that is a cross between an axe and a hoe.

R

Raw materials: materials used to make another product, e.g. iron is a raw material in making a car.

Reafforestation: the replanting of trees.

Redevelopment: renovation and improvement of areas that were previously run-down.

Redundant: being made unemployed

Reefs: ridges of rock near the surface of the sea.

Renewable: can be used again.

Research and development: activities to improve old products and make new ones.

Reserves: estimates amount of a resource that is available for use.

Reservoirs: artificial stores of water.

Resident population: the permanent population living in a certain area.

Resources: anything that can be used to meet human needs.

Retrofitting: the addition of new technology to older buildings.

Richter scale: a measure of earthquake strength.

River basin: area drained by a complete river system.

Rock bund: mound of rocks built for protection.

S

Science parks: industrial estates set up near a university or research centre to attract and develop high-tech industries.

Secondary effects: those that result from the primary effects.

Sediment: material that is eroded and deposited by the action of water or the wind.

Sedimentation: deposition of fine sand.

Seismic activity: movements in the Earth's crust.

Self-help schemes: people take responsibility for improving their own living conditions.

Short-haul: a short-distance flight of three hours or less.

Slash and burn: chopping down and setting alight an area of forest.

Slipping plane: line of weakness, often where a previous landslide has occurred.

Slums: often called 'shanty towns' in developing countries. There are different names for shanty towns around the world including favelas in Brazil, barriades in Peru and bustees in India.

Smog: mixture of smoke and fog.

Social effects: those affecting people.

Soil conservation: protecting the soil for future use.

Soil erosion: the wearing away of soil by water and wind.

Solar power: producing electricity using the sun's rays/light.

Specialist holidays: holidays for a particular group of people, based on a particular area, interest or activity.

Squatter settlements: where people have no legal rights over the land on which they live.

Storm surges: abnormal rise of the sea along a shore as the result of a storm; sometimes called a tidal surge.

Subaerial processes: processes that attack the face and top of a cliff.

Subsistence agriculture: growing food to feed the family.

Suburbs: outlying districts of a town or city often dominated by housing.

Surface run-off: the overland flow of water.

Sustainable management: management that meets the needs of the present while preserving an area for future generations.

Sustainable: meeting the needs of people without damaging the environment or exploiting resources.

Swash: movement of waves up a beach.

Tectonic plates: large segments of the Earth's crust that move in relation to other plates.

Timber revetments: open structures of planks which act as breakwaters but allow sand to be carried through the gaps so that a beach develops.

Tourism: the short-term movement of people to places outside where they live and work, normally for pleasure but also for business.

Track: the path taken by a tropical storm.

Trade: buying, selling and exchanging goods and services between countries and people.

Transnational corporations: companies with branches and operations in several different countries.

Tropical: situated in the area between the tropics of Cancer and Capricorn.

Tsunami: a large wave caused by an undersea earthquake.

Turbine: a type of machine that uses the flow of water or air to produce electricity.

Urban heat island: where a built-up area has a higher temperature than its surroundings.

Urban regeneration: improving social and/or economic conditions in run-down urban areas.

Urban sprawl: the outward growth of urban areas.

Urbanisation: the process of urban growth.

V

Vandalism: intentional damage of property.

Volatility: when something is apt to change, often very quickly

W

Water table: the upper level of water held under the soil and rock.

Watershed development: the management of the whole catchment area.

Weathering: the breaking down of rocks by the action of the weather, plants or chemical action.

Wilderness: an area of land not farmed or built on or lived on.

Wildfire intensity: the severity of burning.

Wildfire season: the period of the year during which wildfires occur.

Wildland-urban interface: area where houses and other human development meet or intermingle with undeveloped land.

Wildlife refuge: an area in which wildlife is protected.

Index

Acknowledgements

The authors and publisher would like to thank the following for permission to reproduce copyright material:

Text and artwork: p20 text adapted from Defra's SMP. Crown copyright © material is reproduced under Class Licence No. CO1 W 0000195 with the permission of the Controller of HMSO and the Queen's Printer for Scotland; p46B adapted with permission from Cambridgeshire County Council www.cambridge.gov.uk; p54B and p55D © citu 2008 www.greenhouseleeds.co.uk; p57C © Friends of the High Line www.thehighline/org. Design by Field Operations and Diller Scofidio + Renfro. Courtesy of the City of New York; p59B adapted with permission from www.hanhamhall.co.uk and HTA; p61B and C © Arup; p76A NOAA Research www.noaa.gov; p112A and p177C Greenpeace for material from its website www.greenpeace.org.uk; p117 Table C and p121 Table B © Profile Books Ltd for material from The Economist: Pocket World in Figures (2008); p119 Table C © UNCTAD for material from UNCTAD Investment Brief, Number 5, 2006; p123 Table B and p151 Table A © Palgrave Macmillan for material from Human Development Report 2007/08, United Nations Development Programme (2007); p140A, p144 Table B and p148 Table A material from Tourism Highlights 2008. Copyright © UNWTO 9284401509; p142A courtesy of the Jamaican Tourist Board www.visitjamaica.com; p170 adapted from the Shell Foundation website www.shellfoundation.org; p191 and p197 Wateraid for material from its website www.wateraid.org.

Ordnance Survey maps: 19C, 22B, 26A: Reproduced by permission of Ordnance Survey on behalf of HMSO. © Crown Copyright 2009. All rights reserved. Ordnance Survey Licence Number 100017284.

Photographs:

Air Photos Ltd/Northumbrian Water 201B; **Alamy**/Atmosphere Picture Library/ Bob Croxford Aerials 173C, /John Arnold Images Ltd/Walter Bibikow 125B, /Adrian Page 189B, /aerialarchives 40A, /Alan Levenson 106B, /Alex Segre 132A, /allen russell 84B, /Ambient Images Inc./Peter Bennett 194B, /America 134A, /Available Light Photography CH1, /Bryan and Cherry Alexander 172B, /China Images/Liu Xiaoyang 131C, /Colin Underhill 140B, /Danita Delimont/Hugh Rose 112B, /Dave and Sigrun Tollerton 104C, /David Lyons 157D, /dbimages/Amanda Ahn 139D, / Gary Cook 169C, /Horizon International Images Limited 148C, /Howard Sayer 135B, /imagebroker 107E4, /imagebroker/Josef Beck 156B, imagebroker/Norbert Eisele-Hein 147D, /Interfoto 96B, /Jacques Jangoux 99C, /Jan Csernoch 161C, / Jeff Morgan alternative technology 179D, /Jenny Matthews 90D, /Jim Laws 22A, / John Birdsall 121C, /Jonathon Laming 18A, /Lee Foster 193D, /Lisa F. Young 76B, / MAISANT Ludovic/Hemis 122A, /Marcelo Rudini 47C, /Nancy G Fire Photography, Nancy Greifenhagen 81B, /Neil Cooper 77D, /Paul Thompson Images 45C, /Peter Widmann 141C, /Photoshot Holdings Ltd 101D, /Robert Harding Picture Library Ltd /Tony Waltham 17D, /Roger Parkes 51D, /Sean Sprague 186B, /Seescanner 10B, /Shangara Singh 43C, /Simon Price 20A, /Tony Cordoza 115B1, /Tony Watson 42A, /Wolfgang Kaehler 98B; **ardea.com**/David Hancock/Garma Festival 165C; **Associated Press**/Chile's Navy 109D; **BioRegional** 52A & 52B; **Corbis**/Albrecht G. Schaefer 62C, /Andrew K/EPA 179C, /Douglas Pearson 142B, /dpa 30A, /Du Huaju/ Xinhua Press 185C, /EDAW consortium/Handout/Reuters 200A, /Frans Lanting 80A, /Frans Lanting CH3, /Galen Rowell 158A2, /George Steinmetz 94A & 192A, /Gideon Mendel 163C, /Jason Hawkes 143C, /Reuters/ Antony Njuguna 48B, / Sergio Dorantes 197C, /Steve Starr 72A & 87C, /Sygma/Igor Kostin 176B, Sygma/ John van Hasselt 158A1, /Vittoriano Rastelli 70A; **Costadosaùipe** 13E; **David Payne** 24A, 24D, 24E & 24F; **Excellent Development Ltd**/www.excellentdevelopment.com 138A; **Fotolia** 104B &189C, /Eddie Cooper 152A; **Getty Images** 81D, /AFP 74B, 85C &154B, /AFP/Adek Berry 63E, /AFP/Antonio Scorza 99D, /AFP/Thony Belizaire 73E, /Deshakalyan Chowdhury/AFP 198A, /Gregoire Poutier/AFP 171B, /lalage Snow/AFP 190B, /Leila Gorchev/AFP 149D, /National Geographic Creative 107D, /Phillip/Fox Photos 146A, /Scott Olson 113E, /Stephen Shaver/AFP 115C, /Thonyt Belizaire/AFP 124A, /SEBASTIAN D'SOUZA/AFP 49C, /Tim Boyle 57B; **Honda (UK) Cars** 183B; **iStockphoto** CH2, 174A, 38A, 40B, 45D, 54C &174A, /Alison Cornford-

Matheson 33C, /Amy Dunn 107E3, /Andrea Gingerich 111C3, /Ann Taylor-Hughes 14A, /Anthony Brown 37D, /christinegonsalves 130B, /Daniel Rosenbaum 147C, /ddbell 67B, /Dennis Sabo 151B, /digitalskillet 107E5, /Douglas Stetner 164B, /Dr Flash 118A, /Gary Martin 16B, /George Clerk 103E, /Grant Dougall 108A2, /Haider Yousuf 12B, /Irina Irgumnova 107E1, /Jacynth Roode 109C1, /James Steidl 108A3, /Jennifer Trenchard 111C1, /Jonathan Heger 108A1, /Justin Horrocks 107E7, /LajosRepasi 107E6, /Lief Norman 178A, /Magdalena Duczkowska CH8, /Marc Dietrich CH6, /Mark Evans 6.13, /Mark Trost CH7, /Martin Pietak 82A, /Martin Strmko 28B, /NeelixVoyager 146B, /Oliver Childs 15E, /oversnap 109C2 & 109C3, /redmal 136B, /Robert Bremec 88B, /Shelly Perry 111C2, /Stanislav Fadyukhin 107E8, /Stefan Witas CH5, /Stephen Finn 84A, /Steve Estvanik 108A, /Thomas Gordon 107E2, /Tobias Helbig CH4; Kallang Basin. Taken by User:Sengkang of English.Wikipedia in Dec 2005 57A;

Lapa Rios Ecolodge 161B; **Malcolm Kerby** © 2007 23C; **Mike Page** © 2007 23D; courtesy of **MODIS Rapid Response Project at NASA**/GSFC 82B; **NASA** 13D & 87B; **Open Hands** 50B; **Panos**/Jeremy Hartley 92B; courtesy of **Pevensey Coastal Defence Ltd** 27B, 27C & 27D; **Photographers Direct**/Marcos Issa /Argosfoto/ 115B2, Stan Kujawa 19D; **Quintain Estates and Development PLC** 126A; Reuters/David Gray 133C; **Roundabout Outdoor (Pty) Ltd**/www.roundabout.co.za 139C; **Royal Bank of Scotland** 137C; **RSPB/Environment Agency** 31E; **Sam W. Stearman** 162B; **Science Photo Library**/Adam Hart Davis 171C, /British Antartic Survey 108B, /Planet Observer 91F, /Robert Brook 128B; © **Stanhope plc** by Hufton+Crowe 116A; **The Innovation Hub** 126B; used by permission of **Cambridge Science Park** 127C & 127D; **ViewPictures**/ESTO/Peter Aaron 68B; **WaterAid**/Juthika Howlader 197B.

Cover photograph: courtesy of Getty/Gazimal

Photo research: Charlotte Lipmann

Every effort has been made to trace the copyright holders but if any have been inadvertently overlooked the publishers will be pleased to make the necessary arrangement at the first opportunity.